Hospitality, Service, Proclamation

Hospitality, Service, Proclamation

*Interfaith Engagement as
Christian Discipleship*

Tom Wilson

scm press

Published in 2019 by SCM Press
Editorial office
3rd Floor, Invicta House,
108–114 Golden Lane,
London EC1Y 0TG, UK
www.scmpress.co.uk

SCM Press is an imprint of Hymns Ancient & Modern Ltd
(a registered charity)

Hymns Ancient & Modern® is a registered trademark of
Hymns Ancient & Modern Ltd
13A Hellesdon Park Road, Norwich,
Norfolk NR6 5DR, UK

British Library Cataloguing in Publication data

A catalogue record for this book is available
from the British Library

978 0 334 05799 4

Typeset by Regent Typesetting Ltd
Printed and bound by
CPI Group (UK) Ltd

Contents

Preface   vii

1 Why engage in interfaith relations?   1

2 Who engages in interfaith relations?   24

3 What does the Bible say?   55

4 When and where does interfaith engagement take place?   86

5 How can interfaith engagement take place?   115

6 Not just good, but Christian   141

Appendix: Engaging with particular faith communities   144
Bibliography   167
Index   175

Preface

Someone once described to me how a colleague of theirs writes books in order to work out exactly what he thinks about a particular topic. There is an element of that in this book. After a bit more than a decade of engaging in interfaith work as a Christian, I have a fair idea of why I do it, and what I think I am trying to achieve. But sometimes it is helpful to articulate a clear explanation. That is what this book attempts to do. I want to show you that there are Christian ways of doing interfaith work. Chapter 1 discusses why a Christian might engage in interfaith activities, and Chapter 2 introduces a range of different perspectives on the topic to help you make up your own mind about why and what you are looking to achieve. Chapter 3 presents ten short biblical reflections on how Christians might relate to those of other faiths. The following two chapters are practical in their focus: Chapter 4 discusses when and where, and Chapter 5 considers how to conduct interfaith activities. Chapter 6 draws the argument together. Finally, the Appendix suggests specific reading to guide Christians who want to engage with Jewish, Muslim, Hindu, Sikh, Buddhist, Confucian and Modern Pagan views of the world.

The people I most need to thank for help in writing this book will have to remain anonymous. They are my friends in different faith communities in different places in the UK who have graciously answered my questions, sharing of themselves as we have got to know each other better, discovering where we agree and where we disagree about a whole range of issues. I am also grateful to colleagues in the St Philip's Centre, Leicester, and across the Church of England's Presence and Engagement network for encouragement and advice over the years. Finally, I want to thank my family, for coping with me vanishing into my study to type when I could have been doing other things with them.

I

Why engage in interfaith relations?

The central argument of this book is that interfaith activity is not simply a good thing to do, but more importantly, a Christian course of action. To put it differently, I have found that <u>one sure method to grow as a faithful disciple of Jesus Christ</u> is to <u>spend time talking with and learning from people</u> who do not recognize him as their Lord and Saviour. That may seem a counter-intuitive point to make, but in my experience, both personally and also helping others to engage in interfaith activities, that is precisely the result. So why does interfaith remain a niche activity, regarded only as a specialism for a few brave (or foolish) enthusiasts who happen to find themselves surrounded by Sikh or Jewish people or are just particularly curious about the distinctions within different branches of Jainism? This opening chapter first sets out what I understand to be some of the main obstacles for Christians wanting to engage with people of other faiths. Second, it briefly outlines four of the questions I have been asked by people of other faiths, which have helped my faith to grow. Third, it offers a few brief thoughts about interfaith activity in twenty-first-century Britain, and last, it discusses intentional growth. The chapter ends with a short reflection on the writings of Lesslie Newbigin.

Three concepts guide the book: hospitality, service and proclamation. Hospitality is understood as welcoming in those of other faiths; service as taking active steps to meet their needs, even at personal cost; and proclamation as verbal explanation of the Christian hope in Jesus Christ. Hospitality is a common paradigm for interfaith engagement, and while I recognize its value, it is important to be clear that there are limits to hospitality. This is not simply to recognize that some behaviour is unacceptable, it is to believe that hosts are allowed to state that behaviour that is acceptable in one context is not acceptable in others. So, when I visit a mosque it is fine for someone there to give out tracts that explain Islam as the only true faith, but this behaviour is not acceptable when that person is the guest of a church community. Equally, if I invite a Hindu friend to a church meeting to share about her life and faith, there is no reason why that meeting cannot commence with prayer and worship as it normally does. A sensible host will choose a passage that will not cause unnecessary offence and will avoid directly challenging a guest to convert, but will carry out the act of worship nonetheless. In my experience, it is mainly Christians who think denying their own identity is a good way of practising hospitality; I have never met a Sikh or Hindu or Muslim (or indeed person of any other faith) who has said to me that because I'm visiting them they will not be praying today.

If we look at the life of Jesus we see that at times he plays the role of both host and guest. His pastoral ministry was entirely dependent on the generosity of others; the Gospels are full of stories of his being a guest at different people's homes and celebrations. But at other times Jesus is the host, most memorably and powerfully at the Last Supper (although, of course, that was in someone else's house), but also when he gathers audiences to teach them. Jesus defines the parameters of his hospitality, rebuking his overenthusiastic disciples that children are welcome (Mark 10.13–16), and that foreigners who proclaim the gospel are 'for us' (Mark 9.38–41). We can reflect on the hospitality of God, taking for example the picture of Psalm 23, of a gracious host welcoming the pilgrim home.

Hospitality is held in tension with proclamation; Christianity is a faith that has a message of good news to share, which includes speaking out the good news of Jesus Christ, sharing what he has done in our lives. In Mark, Jesus begins his public ministry with a call that announces the arrival of the kingdom of God (Mark 1.14–15), a message of repentance and radical transformation. The book of Acts and the various New Testament letters suggest that the first followers of Jesus were bold and uncompromising in their declarations of faith in Jesus the Messiah. This impulse to proclaim is balanced by the imperative to serve others. Christians are expected to love God and their neighbour, and as a parable of Jesus reminds us, 'neighbour' means everyone, friend and foe alike (Luke 10.25–37). Service of others can be a form of hospitality, but service may also include becoming a guest, making myself vulnerable and needy in order to allow others to serve me, a point illustrated by the interesting juxtaposition in John 12 and 13 of Jesus first having his feet washed by Mary before he in turn washes his disciples' feet. Throughout this book, I will return to these three concepts repeatedly, illustrating the tension that exists between them and demonstrating how they provide a framework for interfaith engagement as a form of Christian discipleship.

What gets in the way?

There are doubtless many reasons why Christians do not actively participate in what they explicitly term interfaith engagement. The overstated language is important here, as people who live and work in diverse areas may find themselves talking with their neighbours or colleagues about why they celebrate Diwali or the distinction between the two Eids or all manner of other points of connection and difference between their respective faiths. They might describe this as interfaith relations, but more likely they would just think of it as having a chat with Raj or Rabiha about what they are doing at the weekend. One of the Jewish rabbis who lives in Leicester is fond of talking about good interfaith relations being the fact that he can borrow his neighbour's hedge trimmer while he lends him his lawnmower. My point is that there are all kinds of day-to-day interactions between people of different faiths, or different perspectives on the same faith, and this is a vital form of interfaith relations, which helps keep the fabric of our society together.

But in an increasingly polarized world, where people are tempted to retreat to the comfort of their own homes, or their own self-constructed social media echo chamber, there is a need for people to make deliberate steps to meet up with those who are different from them, to ensure that there are places of interaction, where different truths can be told and different perspectives can sit in parallel. Sometimes it can be more comfortable to meet with people whose faith perspective is different from yours, but whose socio-economic and cultural expectations are remarkably similar. Intra-faith discussion can, at times, be more fraught with difficulty than interfaith discussion.

I find interfaith engagement an energizing and interesting place to be, but recognize that for some people, it is in fact a frightening place. There are different fears at play here. Some might be afraid of causing offence. They might think that asking the wrong question about Diwali or inadvertently doing the wrong thing while visiting someone else's place of worship would destroy a fragile relationship, or cause mass protests. An awareness of, for example, the controversy that surrounded the Danish newspaper *Jyllands-Posten* publishing cartoons of the Prophet Muhammad or the attacks on the French satirical magazine *Charlie Hebdo* after they republished them,[1] may lie, acknowledged or unrecognized, at the root of these fears. If this is the case, it is important to recognize the distinction between deliberate attempts to provoke and insult and accidental mistakes that happen because of ignorance, or simply because of real life. The former would produce a negative reaction. But mistakes are just mistakes, and most people are not upset if things go wrong through no fault of your own. Not long after I started my current role, my whole family visited Leicester's Progressive Jewish Synagogue for an open event one Sunday afternoon. My daughter had just turned three, and suddenly hearing a call of nature did not quite manage to make it to the toilet in time. Unfortunately, the place the accident happened was directly in front of the Ark, the place in the synagogue where the Torah Scroll is stored, and thus the most important, sacred space in the building. I thought there could not really have been a worse place for this particular mishap. But the response was entirely pragmatic: I was simply told where to find a mop and bucket, and met with the sympathetic response that such problems occur from time to time and all I needed to do was tidy up.

I have got many things wrong in my understandings of a particular faith or the place of a particular community within that faith. I visited a mosque recently and said to the committee member who was hosting us that I thought it was a predominantly Pakistani community who attended that mosque for prayers. He corrected me, stating that this was a common mistake made by outsiders. If I check my bookshelves, I can tell you the precise details of the five different branches of Jainism that are all represented in Leicester Jain Samaj (or you could just read Babb 2015 or Dundas 2002). But I would probably get some of the details a bit confused and my Jain friends would correct me. They would not do so in anger or upset, but in a desire to set the record straight, much as I would want to help them understand the difference between, say, being a Roman Catholic, Anglican or Pentecostal Christian. If you have an <u>attitude of humility</u> and <u>a willingness to learn</u>, then although you will get things wrong, either through misunderstanding or ignorance, you are unlikely to cause offence.

There are at least two other types of fear that some people face when thinking about interfaith engagement. Some are afraid that if they engage with people of other faiths their own faith in Jesus will suffer as a result. Once I was involved in organizing a visit for some Christian young adults to go to a mosque. They were interns in local churches, on a discipleship year out. Not everyone was comfortable with going into another place of worship, and indeed not all of them went, as they were concerned about the negative impact that entering a mosque might have on their relationship with Jesus. On a different occasion, when facilitating the interfaith engagement part of a Christian youthwork course, my staff and I had to be creative in designing an interfaith encounter that both met the course requirements and also did not push the students too far.

I always want to help Christians meet those of other faiths because in my experience this is always a beneficial encounter where mutual learning takes place, but I recognize that not everyone shares my enthusiasm. I also know that 'beneficial' is not the same as 'comfortable' or 'pleasant'. But then whoever said being a disciple of Jesus Christ was supposed to be either comfortable or pleasant? As Luther is reputed to have said, why, when Christ wore a crown of thorns, do his followers expect to wear a crown of roses?

The context of such encounters is, of course, crucial here. While conversations between Christians and those of other faiths in Britain are invariably civil (one notable exception being the debates at Speakers' Corner in Hyde Park), that is not the case across the world. I know that Christians in many countries suffer because of their faith, and are persecuted by people of other faiths, but that is not the focus of my argument here.[2] The point I wish to make is that Christians in the UK should not be afraid that meeting those of other faiths will destroy their faith in Jesus. You are likely to be challenged, perhaps in ways you did not expect, but this is not something to shy away from. It is something to rise to.

Apathy can be as great a problem as fear in preventing interfaith engagement. This issue is not peculiar to interfaith initiatives, but is a general feature of church life. Many areas of work are perceived as the preserve of a few specialists, who seem incredibly competent or knowledgeable about their particular field, and so others feel that there is no point or need for them to be involved. Work with children and young people is perhaps one of the more obvious examples. Interfaith engagement is likewise left to specialists, especially when community relations are peaceful.

However, it may not be apathy that prevents people from joining in with interfaith engagement; it may also be an issue of shortage, whether that is a shortage of time for engagement, of opportunities to meet in an atmosphere conducive to exchange of views, or of resources to enable meaningful interaction to take place. While all these are valid reasons, it is also true that we usually can make time for those activities we value the most. If we regard interfaith activity as important, then we allow it to take time, energy and resources that could otherwise be used elsewhere. So in the end, it probably comes down to deciding that there is sufficient value in meeting with people of other faiths for us to bother. For a Christian, one positive reason for any activity is that it helps you grow as a disciple of Jesus. In what follows I will give four examples of how interfaith engagement has helped me do just that.

Growing as a disciple of Jesus

The examples I have chosen here are from engagement with four of the world's major faith traditions. There are many others that I could have given, and indeed will give throughout this book, but these are sufficient to illustrate the point that interfaith engagement is a means to grow in relationship with Jesus Christ.

Why celebrate Christmas?

A Muslim friend once asked me why it was that Christians celebrate Christmas. 'After all,' he went on, 'Jesus did not tell you to. So why are you doing something that your teacher did not instruct you to do?'

I cannot remember the details of my answer. I probably talked about a number of different things. First, that there is a distinction between Christian celebrations of Christmas and Western cultural celebrations of Christmas. Having lived in Japan for a year during my university days, this difference was very clear to me, and I doubtless referenced this experience, probably including the surreal episode of me, over six foot tall and quite skinny, having to pretend to be Santa for a room full of bemused Japanese pre-schoolers. Second, since he was part of a Muslim group that was focused on outreach, I probably talked about the opportunities that Christmas provides for Christians to tell the story of the birth of Jesus, and invite people to engage with that story, and with the idea of following Jesus for themselves. Third, I hopefully mentioned the history of Christianity in the West, and how it had subsumed Pagan festivals, providing acceptable alternatives that enabled Christianity to flourish and other belief patterns to fade. Being asked about my faith by a Muslim made me think more seriously about my discipleship as I live in expectation that Jesus will return one day.

But the question remains, and it still nags me slightly, making me think about what I do to celebrate Christmas, and whether it is drawing me closer to Jesus. I am sure this question was the catalyst that made me take the season of Advent more seriously. For an Anglican Christian it is a penitential season, where we prepare our hearts and our lives for the coming of Christ, remembering his birth but looking also to his return. That must be part of my celebration of Christmas. If it is not, then am I celebrating as Jesus would want me to?

Thinking back now, I realize that there were all kinds of assumptions behind his question. I will outline two. First, he is a Salafi Muslim, a member of a reform movement established to bring Muslims back to the traditions of the *salaf*, the first three generations of scholars after the Prophet Muhammad. As such he is very concerned to follow only the precise instructions that Muhammad gave about every aspect of life. This includes the fact that the Prophet did not explicitly instruct his followers to celebrate his birthday (known as *Mawlid al Nabi*). Some Muslims do celebrate the festival, but Salafi Muslims do not, because they have received no explicit instruction to do so; and they argue vociferously that other Muslims are wrong in doing so. This is one of the assumptions he brought with him to the question he asked me about celebrating Christmas.

Second, there was the desire of the evangelist to catch me out; to show me that I was not following Jesus as I ought to. Christians do this all the time when trying to persuade others of the truth of the Christian faith. You try to show that your worldview is consistent, thought through and coherent, while other worldviews have inconsistencies, flaws and problems. The aim is to persuade others that you are right and they are wrong. Sometimes it can be very effective, but not always. As I reflected on what my friend was doing, it made me think about how I love everyone I talk to as a person made in the image of God. Verbal trickery is not the best way of persuading people of the truth of the Christian faith.

As is often the case in complicated conversations, my answer was probably less coherent and organized than my written reflection after the event. At the time, I simply carried on the conversation, doing my best to answer what I took to be an honest enquiry. That is, perhaps, the most important thing to remember about having conversations about faith: be honest, be real, and if you do not know the answer, say so. It is not really any different from having a conversation with anyone else about your faith.

Pause

How would you have answered this question?

Why eat meat?

A few years ago I went to the opening of the ISKCON (Hare Krishna) temple in Leicester. They had recently moved to a new building and had a formal opening ceremony that included lunch. Standing in line with a senior member of ISKCON in the UK, we were talking about the points of connection between our two faiths. He explained his Hindu perspective to me, which was something to the effect that everyone is on their way to heaven or enlightenment. The difference was that Christians were making a slow plod up lots of stairs while ISKCON devotees were in the express elevator. One of the reasons was this: 'How can you expect to make spiritual progress when you eat meat? How can anyone who benefits from killing draw closer to God?'

The lunch we were about to eat was, of course, vegetarian. More than that, it followed the strict diet of the ISKCON movement, avoiding certain vegetables as well. It was food aimed at facilitating maximum spiritual progress. Here was another question for a disciple of Jesus. I know that Jesus declared all foods clean (Mark 7.1–23). I know that Peter had a vision in which he was commanded to eat food he thought of as unclean as a means of encouraging him to preach the gospel to Cornelius (Acts 10) and that the Early Church greatly relaxed the stipulations of Jewish food laws as they included significant numbers of gentiles in their midst (Acts 15). Most Western Protestant Christians today have no concerns about what they eat from a purely religious point of view.

But that does not mean that a Christian should not think about what she or he eats. Reread the first three chapters of Genesis and ask yourself, was eating meat part of God's original plan for creation? Or is it a result of human sinfulness? Think also about the lessons of modern times, of salmonella outbreaks caused by human greed, feeding dead chickens to chickens in order to maximize profits regardless of animal welfare. Think about environmental arguments, for example about the destruction of rainforests or the amount of methane produced by the beef industry. There are many cogent reasons why Christians might want to take very seriously the questions asked by that Hare Krishna devotee, particularly to think again about what it means to 'be fruitful and increase in number; fill the earth and subdue it. Rule over the fish in the sea and the birds in the sky and over every living creature that moves on the ground' (Genesis 1.28). It made me realize that perhaps my Christian faith should make a difference to how and what I eat. Moving to a low or no meat diet, out of concern for creation, has become more common in Christian circles recently,[3] and in my case, I started thinking about this seriously because of conversations I had with Hindus who believed strongly that what they ate has a significant impact on their spirituality.

Pause

What difference does your faith make to what you eat?

Whom do you serve?

The question of whom we serve comes up pretty much every time I take a group of Christians to a gurdwara. One of the core principles of the Sikh faith is that of *langar*, the community kitchen in a gurdwara where a hot vegetarian meal is made freely available to anyone who comes regardless of their religion, caste, gender, economic status or ethnicity. In practice, there are a few restrictions, notably that anyone under the influence of alcohol or drugs is forbidden from entering a gurdwara, and that you must remove your shoes and cover your head before entering. But these are relatively minor compared with the fact that meals are served throughout the day to anyone who comes, no questions asked. The reality is that if a gurdwara is in a busy part of a town, many people will come there solely for a free lunch, and the Sikh community is happy to serve them. This makes Christians think in two different ways.

First, some churches or Christian groups run a community café or coffee morning. Normally there is a charge, to cover the cost of the food if nothing else. But the scale of the operation is invariably much smaller than that of even a small gurdwara, which would serve hundreds of meals a day. The idea of a community paying for food given freely to others is very much out of step with many churches, who expect people to put money on a plate even to have a slightly stale biscuit and a cup of luke-warm instant coffee after a service. I am not saying that Christians do not know how to be hospitable. There are countless examples of incredibly generous Christian hospitality, be that individuals or organized groups, running food banks, lunch clubs, providing meals for school children over the school holidays and much more. What I am saying is that visiting a gurdwara and experiencing *langar* can challenge Christians to think afresh about the hospitality they offer.

It has certainly caused me to reflect, and made me want to understand more clearly how the *langar* system operates. Some of the meals are funded by particular individuals to mark a special occasion. If, for example, you are marking your birthday, or celebrating the birth of a child, you might sponsor *langar* in the gurdwara on a particular day or weekend. At other times, individuals make donations of food or money to cover the costs. Ensuring that the hungry are fed is seen as a religious duty, one that equally applies to Christians, who are told by James that 'Religion that God our Father accepts as pure and faultless is this: to look after orphans and widows in their distress and to keep oneself from being polluted by the world' (James 1.27).

Second, experiencing *langar* is experiencing being the guest, not the host. There are quite a few cultural expectations that come with *langar*. The food is always vegetarian curry. It is normally eaten sitting on the floor. It is given to you, and although you have some chance to decide how much you want of any particular item, you may well not know what it is you are eating, which is a particular challenge for those who have allergies or strong likes or dislikes. Guests at *langar* invariably get what they are given and are expected to be grateful. My experiences as a guest make me reflect on my practice as a host. In what ways do I give people things they do not want, and am disappointed when they do not express gratitude? Learning how to be a guest is an important discipline for Christians, especially in a society that increasingly regards Christian faith with suspicion, if not active dislike.

Pause

What are your experiences of being both guest and host to people of other faiths?

What is your motivation?

My final question is one I ask myself as a result of conversations with a Jewish friend. She told me about an experience she had a few years ago. We live in the same area of Leicester, and every summer one of the streets is closed off on a Sunday as part of a community arts festival. The narrative she told me was of how she was walking through the different stalls when she noticed one run by a local evangelical church. They were, she said, running various activities for children, in order to draw families in and start talking to them, something Christians often do, she added. She stopped to say hello to one of those running the stall, and being a friendly person, soon got into conversation. As they were talking she explained that she was Jewish, and then, she said, 'His eyes lit up as if to say, "This is an interesting fish. How can I land this one?" and so I made my excuses and moved on.'

The question that story makes me ask is, what is my motivation? How transparent is that motivation? Jesus tells us to go and make disciples of all nations, and Christians have both the right and the duty to preach the good news of Jesus Christ. But we must also be wise as serpents and innocent as doves. If our outreach turns people into targets, scalps to be collected like trophies then, for me at least, it is slipping away from proclaiming the gospel into human pride and self-aggrandizement. The ethics of evangelism and outreach are complex, and interfaith engagement provides a good context in which to think them through. I will return to these issues a number of times in this book.

In the right time and the right place we should, of course, proclaim Jesus as Lord and Saviour and invite others to follow him. But if the good news is to be heard as good news then it must be a freely offered gift that people are under no obligation to accept. Therefore, when I engage in interfaith work my motivation is simply to build relationships, to love my friends as I love myself, to grow in my likeness of Jesus Christ and so to reflect him to everyone I spend time with, regardless of their interest in or reaction to him. There are contexts where it is appropriate to share faith with a view to conversion, and contexts where it would be wrong to do so.

When I run training sessions for Christians starting out in interfaith engagement, I often ask them to form a 'human rainbow' of their motivations for this type of work. The spectrum I offer them is from cohesion to conversion: that is, from just being friends to just wanting people to become Christians. It is a crude, artificial distinction that most groups initially comply with but soon reject as overly simplistic. Most Christians have a complex series of hopes and dreams when they talk with people of other faiths, which will be explored in more detail in the rest of this chapter.

Pause

Where would you put yourself on the human rainbow?

Interfaith in twenty-first-century Britain

These four questions highlight the tension that exists between the Christian desire to be hospitable, to serve others and to proclaim the gospel. Taking the last example, a desire to proclaim was so strong that one person felt unable to be a guest, even a temporary one, at a community event. The experience of being served in a gurdwara is uncomfortable for some Christians and the thought of having your dietary choices challenged may put others off ever entering a Hindu mandir. But I experienced both as examples of hospitality, where I was a welcome guest whose views were politely engaged with; it helped me learn how to be a gracious host who is nevertheless clear about what he believes.

Ours is an age of division, of social media echo chambers, of people feeling free to express opinions that just a few years ago would have been regarded as unacceptable, beyond the pale. It is an age of identity politics, of increasing connection, of freedom, used both for good and for ill. One of the reasons Christians are getting involved in interfaith work is to show solidarity and build relationships with those who are suffering because of who they are. While Christians may not want to become Muslims, they want to take a stand against anti-Muslim hatred. Far-right organizations such as Britain First have claimed a Christian identity, mounting 'Christian patrols' and storming mosques holding Bibles and crosses.[4] Their actions demonstrate that they are not followers of Jesus, who teaches us to love our enemies and pray for those who persecute us. Just as I would reject Britain First's claims to be representative Christians, so I understand why many Muslims find the claims of ISIS or Al-Qaeda to be abhorrent, and in no way representative of their Islamic faith. The complexities of this debate are outside the scope of this introductory chapter, but suffice to say the vast majority of Muslims in the UK are peace-loving, loyal to this country, and as concerned as most Christians are, if not more so, about radicalization and terrorism. We can build relationships of love and support for people of other faiths without having to reach complete agreement on all our doctrinal differences.

If we look across the globe, we see violence being done in the name of most of the major world faiths. There are far-right Jewish settlers in the West Bank, or Judea and Samaria as they would term it, who, claiming a biblical mandate, are violent in their actions against Palestinians as they seize land. There are Buddhist monks in Burma inciting hatred of and violence towards the Rohingya. There are Muslims in Syria, Nigeria and elsewhere in the world who do violence to their neighbours (including other Muslims) in the name of building an Islamic state. There are Christians in Uganda and the Sudan, calling themselves the Lord's Resistance Army, who have murdered and raped their way across vast areas. There are militant Hindus, especially in India in the far-right group the RSS, who persecute Sikhs, Christians and Muslims. There are Sikhs who, wanting to further their desire for a free Khalistan, have resorted to violence to advance their claims. I recognize that the real causes and nature of each situation are much more complex than the simple sentences above suggest. But there is sometimes a connection between violence and religion. I once organized a day seminar on the limits of religious freedom in the UK. One of our keynote speakers was Leicestershire Police's Chief Constable, who said in his opening remarks that he had arrested people of every faith, ethnicity and socio-economic background. People of faith do bad things, and in our era of identity politics and increasing intolerance of difference, religious identity becomes a badge to wear and a means of distinguishing the other and justifying violence against them.

That is why there is an increasingly urgent need for people of all faiths and no faith to come together. The strapline of the St Philip's Centre, the organization I work for, is that although the world is divided, we believe we can learn to live well together. Rooted in Christianity, especially in the Anglican tradition, we want to work with people of all faiths and no faith for the good of all, helping people to meet those who are different from them, developing greater understanding of worldviews other than their own. We do not expect people to agree with each other. In fact, I often joke at the start of a course that if the participants do agree on everything then I have failed; it means that the conversation has not gone deep enough. I have no interest in lowest common denominator state-ments. After all, if you include Pagans, Humanists and Buddhists in these discussions, you cannot even reference belief in one God. You have to say something like 'we support humanity' and 'please can people be nice to each other'. Both are true, but neither is enough to change the world. What we need are people who are so secure in their own identity that they are comfortable being friends with people who are completely different from them, who see the world in radically different ways. We need to build relationships of trust with people whose fundamental worldview is in opposition to ours. We have to cooperate with people whose moral and ethical frameworks are not the same as ours, who may share our goal but whose reasons, motivations and even methods are not the same as ours.

In his book *Christian Hospitality and Muslim Immigration in an Age of Fear*, Matthew Kaemingk explains that his fundamental commitments are 'an uncompromising commitment to the exclusive lordship of Jesus Christ' while simultaneously holding 'an uncompromising commitment to love those who reject that lordship' (2018, 16). He might be described as an exclusivist pluralist, that is, someone who is exclusivist in his understand-ing of salvation (on which more in Chapter 2) but at the same time pluralist in his vision for wider society. Kaemingk describes the type of pluralism he is aiming for as descriptive, juridical and normative. Descriptive pluralists take the deep differences in cultures, communities and religions seriously; rather than reduce things to the lowest common denomina-tor, they are willing to stand in the complexity, listening and learning about the differences. Juridical pluralism argues that the legal rights and freedoms of different communities, cultures, religions and associations must all be protected. Normative pluralism regards this variety as good, believing that God delights in the variety of human culture, advocating for structural and social diversity, which is seen in all aspects of life. But at the same time this recognition is not uncritical; faults are seen and named for what they are. Moreover, religious difference is neither praised nor celebrated (2018, 16–19). Kaemingk illustrates his point with a story he entitles 'the tolerance of the Fundamentalist'. It describes a conservative Christian pastor, the Reverend Kees Sybrandi, based in the Netherlands. He believes that Islam is a false religion and Allah a 'desert demon spirit'. Yet when mosques across the Netherlands came under attack in the wake of the murder of Theo van Gogh in 2004, he stood guard over his local mosque to protect it from attempted arson or violence against Muslims. He has never shown any interest or concern for Islam or friendship with Muslims. When Kaemingk was asked why he had stood up to defend the mosque, he simply replied, 'Jesus commanded me to love my neighbor – my enemy too' (2018, 25–6).

This is one example of a form of interfaith engagement as Christian discipleship. There are, of course, many examples of Christians building strong friendships of mutual trust and understanding with people of all faith backgrounds. Jesus told his followers that the greatest commandment is to love God with, as Eugene Peterson puts it in his *Message* translation, all our 'passion and prayer and intelligence and energy' and to 'love others as well as you love yourself' (Mark 12.29–31). One of the ways I do this is to work for the good of people of all faiths and no faith. As Andrew Smith points out, loving our neighbours means engaging with them, finding out their names, hopes, fears, dreams, standing alongside them when things are tough, celebrating when things are good, not simply tolerating or respecting at a distance, but being with and being for them (2018, 25). James Smith suggests that love of neighbour 'propels us to responsibility for the public life of the nations and communities in which we find ourselves as pilgrims and sojourners' (2017, 35), which surely includes interfaith engagement in a variety of forms.

What does it mean to love a Jain, say, as I love myself? I believe that three things are important. First, pray for God's blessing on them. As noted above, Jesus commands us to pray for our enemies as well as our neighbours (Matthew 5.43–48), and whichever you consider people of other faiths to be, you cannot duck Jesus' command that you pray for them. Second, seek good for them. If you love someone, you want them to flourish. So if I love my Pagan friend, I want her to flourish. That includes helping her develop, say, her leadership skills or understanding of how best to interact with local government. It might be being generous in sharing resources around safeguarding as a new Buddhist community gets to grips with the legal requirements in this area. Third, share Jesus in word and deed. In saying this I am mindful of my comments about motivation above. This action can only come out of a relationship built on the first two. It requires you to be sensitive to the promptings of the Holy Spirit, neither shying away from opportunities nor manipulating conversations to simply impose propositional truth. After all, we want the gospel to be heard as genuine good news. You may have to spend a decade building a relationship of trust before someone is actually able to hear you talk about Jesus as good news for them. This is, in fact, no different whether the person is a member of another faith community or has no faith at all. As Paul reminds us, whether we plant or water (or weed), we are simply called to be gardeners, as it is God who gives the growth (1 Corinthians 3.6).

A word about intentional growth

One of the many things I have learnt through interfaith engagement is that words matter. The language we use says a lot about our assumptions and presuppositions. This becomes very clear when you discuss exactly what it is people believe. The language we use to talk about faith and belief positions is often based on the presuppositions of Protestant Christianity: we talk about sacred scripture, about places of worship, about prayers, priests. And we talk about mission and evangelism. For many people of different faiths, especially those whose origins are in countries that used to be part of the British Empire, talk of Christian mission is inextricably intertwined with talk of colonialization. Their perception is that the Church of England spread as an adjunct of the British Empire and so any evangelistic activity is understood as an attempt to destroy identity, culture and family relationships, not simply persuading an individual to become a follower of Jesus.[5] There are strong historical grounds to support these fears, and Christians would do well to study the actions of their ancestors with sceptical and suspicious eyes, to understand how we are perceived by many in the world today.

It is therefore useful to find new language to talk about activities that, in fact, virtually every faith community is engaged in. Thus, rather than talk about mission or evangelism, I prefer to talk about intentional growth, as all faith communities do this, normally focusing on three distinct but interrelated areas of family expansion, recalling the lapsed faithful, and welcoming spiritual seekers. I will illustrate the point with reference to my experience of Jewish, Hindu, Muslim, Sikh, Pagan, Baha'i, Buddhist and Christian communities.

Taking Leicester's two Jewish congregations as my first example, the Orthodox community's growth strategy focuses primarily on the first two strands. The rabbi's family is a particular case in point. At the time of writing he has nine children and by the time you read this that number may well be greater. This is an example of growth through family expansion. He also sees part of his role to be calling lapsed Jews to greater religious observance, and is tireless in his efforts to do so. Although Leicester Hebrew Congregation has seen some growth through these two methods, they do not organize any programmes to welcome or attract spiritual seekers. By contrast, the Progressive Jewish community has also grown through all three methods, seeing a modest increase in families and lapsed Jews attending as well as a number of spiritual seekers deciding that this community is their spiritual home. The process of joining is long and deliberately contains a number of obstacles, and there is no formal plan or outreach strategy; people simply turn up. It is not easy to become Jewish, but you can if you are prepared to make the effort.

The Hindu community employs the same three strategies. Many mandirs (temples) focus primarily on the first two, that is, on encouraging families to bring up their children according to their particular understanding of Hindu life and thought, and becoming a prominent place within the community for those who wish to be more active in their devotional life. Some Hindu groups, of which the ISKCON (Hare Krishna) movement is probably the best known, are active in intentional outreach to spiritual seekers, running faith discovery courses and activities. In Leicester, I have attended their five-session Explore course, which was designed to encourage both lapsed Hindus and spiritual seekers to embrace the ISKCON understanding of Hinduism.[6]

Exactly the same could be said of the Muslim community. Many masjids (mosques) focus primarily on providing a madrassah, a place of education for children, as a means of attracting a congregation. *Dawa* (mission) focused organizations, such as Tablighi Jamaat, are mainly interested in encouraging cultural Muslims to become religiously active Muslims, knocking on doors and inviting Muslim men who have lapsed in mosque attendance to come to congregational prayers, especially for Jummah prayers on a Friday lunchtime.[7] Some groups are interested in calling anyone and everyone to Islamic faith, and run courses aimed at achieving this goal.[8] Such groups often run book tables in town centres over the weekend; the more strategically focused ensure that these tables are staffed by white British converts, to emphasize the point that anyone can embrace Islam. Interestingly, in my experience it is often those groups like the Hare Krishna and the *dawa* focused Muslims who are also particularly keen on interfaith engagement.

Some groups are less focused on all three areas, although most are interested in family and/or lapsed cultural adherents. I am not aware, for example, of a Sikh community group that is particularly focused on spiritual seekers from outside of the culturally Sikh community. Similarly, the Baha'i or the Pagan community are open to individuals joining them, but do not have forms of intentional outreach aimed specifically at spiritual seekers. Other groups are too small to put significant resources into all three areas. Some Buddhist groups, for example, focus primarily on growth through interaction with individual adults who want to develop their own Buddhist practice. Other Buddhist groups focus particularly on bringing up their own children to share their faith. It depends on the circumstances and resources of the individual community.

Christians likewise vary in which intentional growth strategies they follow. No Christian church wants to fade away, but equally not all have plans for 'seeker friendly services' or evangelistic outreach. Some suggest that the best strategy is to focus primarily on lapsed congregants. In one interfaith discussion I heard the Archbishop of Canterbury, Justin Welby, make this precise point. Asked about the Church of England's strategies for mission, he explained that the main focus was on encouraging those who are culturally Christian to become more active and involved, as well as encouraging those who say they are of no faith to take faith seriously.[9] Of course, there always will be some individuals who cross faith boundaries, but the numbers remain small.

This, then, is my perspective on intentional growth in a church context: we should divide our efforts among the three areas I have outlined. That is, we should encourage families to bring up their children as Christians; we should encourage lapsed Christians to take their faith more seriously; and we should be open and engaged with seekers. Where appropriate, this will involve intentional outreach that specifically calls people to become followers of Jesus Christ, and we must be open to the possibility that this will include people of all faiths and no faith.

A fuller explanation of my views is found in the short piece below, which I wrote in January 2014 in response to a comment by Justin Welby on New Year's Eve 2013.

Exploding joyfully? Reflections on urban ministry in an Anglican context

The situation in the contemporary urban Anglican Church is both depressing and exciting, and as [at the time of writing] I lead churches in this context, I find myself alternatively depressed and excited by what I see around me. In this short reflection, I will use the writings of missiologist Lesslie Newbigin to shape my own reflections on what I am (and am not) doing, and how close I come to fulfilling the great commission to go into all the world and make disciples of Jesus Christ. I ask three questions. First, what situation do we face? Second, what duty is incumbent upon us? Third, how do we do that? The answers will be drawn both from Newbigin's writing and from my own reflections on seven years of Anglican ministry in an urban context. Before I begin to answer the questions, a few sentences about myself: I am an evangelical minister, who served five years as a curate in a multicultural urban priority area with three churches, and [was in 2014] in my second year of leading two churches in a different multicultural urban priority area in another city.

What situation do we face?

Back in 1986, Newbigin described Britain as a pagan society, whose paganism, born out of rejecting Christianity, was more resistant to the gospel than pre-Christian paganism (1986, 20). That is to say, people think they know what Christianity is, and have rejected it as either irrelevant or deficient. I concur in part with Newbigin's assessment: the majority of the white British families with whom I have engaged in the course of ministry, notably through Anglican occasional offices of weddings, baptisms and funerals, think of Christianity primarily as dry and irrelevant rule-keeping. While they are happy to participate in accessible and engaging presentations of the Christian faith, enjoying, for example Doug Horley DVDs or use of the Brick Testament to tell Bible stories, this only very rarely results in continued and sustained engagement with the Church or a living Christian faith.

Quoting the Chinese writer Carver Yu, Newbigin also comments on British (Western) culture being characterized by 'technological optimism and literary despair', whereby we are both supremely optimistic that science and technology will improve our lives while at the same time our literature (which I take to include both visual and print media) is characterized by scepticism, nihilism and despair (1991, 19; 1995a, 46). This also rings true of my own context; urban areas are especially blighted by new initiatives, which rarely have the depth of knowledge or resource to make anything more than a superficial difference, and hence often deepen, rather than alleviate, the nihilism of local long-term residents.

My experience suggests that the picture in urban areas is not entirely negative, however. These areas tend to have a highly mobile population, with many economic migrants and asylum seekers passing through. Sometimes this can merely increase the overwhelming demands placed on scarce resources and heighten local tensions. At other times, these people bring either a fresh curiosity or a vibrant Christian faith, which energizes and enthuses a tired and weary congregation. Seeing a refugee from a Muslim background come to a living faith in Jesus is a tonic that energizes struggling evangelists. The vibrant faith of a Nigerian Anglican challenges the habitual church attendance of 'Sunday-only' Christians. Such experiences are unfortunately relatively rare, and so the overwhelming picture remains a challenging one.

What duty is incumbent upon us?

If this is the problem, then what duty is incumbent upon us? How should we respond? Put simply, we must proclaim the word of God, personally and corporately, to transform individuals and society. Newbigin is clear: we must both act and speak in the name of Jesus, but most importantly, we must be Christ's body in the world. He suggests that the congregation is the hermeneutic of the gospel, that is, the only credible way of displaying the gospel to the world is 'a congregation of men and women who believe it and live by it' (1989, 226). Everything else – preaching, distribution of literature, evangelistic campaigns, community clean-ups, debt counselling, food banks and credit unions – is secondary.

The primary duty of a minister, therefore, is to enable the church community to embody the presence of Jesus Christ as best they can. The urban context provides particular challenges: the proportion of the congregation who have multiple, complex needs is likely to be quite high, and meeting them is costly in terms of time, energy and resources. Two examples will illustrate. I vividly remember the dilemma of engaging with one lady who could neither read nor tell the time. How should one disciple such a person? The normal off-the-shelf methods were completely inappropriate, and her own chaotic and needy lifestyle further compounded the issues. Equally, a convert from Islam may desire to grow in faith but his lack of spoken English, uncertain residency status and multiple health issues caused by his flight from his country of origin make his path to Christian discipleship a steep one. I could go on, but the point is that where need is great and resource small, progress is likely to be similarly slow.

How should we do that?

Having identified the problem and the outline of the solution, I turn to the specifics: what we should do and what we might expect will happen. I have picked on some striking phrases Newbigin uses, as a challenge to myself and others in an urban context. Newbigin comments that when we examine the New Testament we see that 'mission begins with a kind of explosion of joy' (1989, 116). How many of us can describe our congregations as exhibiting a vast explosion of love, joy and hope (1995b, 3)? I have certainly experienced my fair share of explosions, normally from angry long-term church members at something I have done. But our lives often lack the attractive pull of joy, and that is perhaps why the Church struggles to grow either numerically or in depth of relationship with God and with each other. These explosions may be most evident in our Sunday gatherings, but they are rooted in a deep relationship with the Father through the Son in the power of the Holy Spirit. How does the urban church nourish this?

Newbigin also encourages what I have termed a 'prayerful remaining', commenting that while Paul does not exhort believers to be active in mission, he regularly exhorts them to remain faithful (1989, 119). This is, I think, important in an era where the Church is declining and there is increasing pressure for swift results and short-term solutions. It is important for more people to come to a personal relationship with Jesus and become active members of his body on earth; but, fundamentally:

> There is no room either for anxiety about our failure or for boasting about our success. There is room only for faithful witness to the one in whom the whole purpose of God for cosmic history has been revealed and effected, the crucified, risen and regnant Christ. (1989, 125)

Numerical growth is a good thing, and the New Testament celebrates such growth; but the triumph of God's reign does not depend on the numerical growth of the Church. Indeed, as Newbigin notes, thousands were baptized in South America at the time of the *conquistadores*, but was this a period when the Church was most faithful to her Lord? The language of success is dangerous, as it soon transports the Church into the world of the military campaign or the commercial sales drive (1995b, 124–7).

There are also dangers in exhorting faithfulness over success, primarily of complacency and laziness, but there are graver dangers in prioritizing success, not least in inculcating a false notion that mission is primarily our own activity, rather than the work of the Holy Spirit. The comment on

BBC Radio 4's *Today* programme on New Year's Eve 2013 by the current Archbishop of Canterbury, that 'where you have a good vicar, you will find growing churches', is, taken in isolation, an overly simplistic statement that is in danger of falling into this trap.

There is a subtler issue related to success and faithfulness. Ministering in urban churches where growth, while present, is very slow, it is easy to end up in many worthy and worthwhile projects, including school governance, urban regeneration, interfaith dialogue and community fun days. All these are good things, but do we involve ourselves in them primarily out of faithfulness to the gospel, or out of a desire for some quantifiable success to boost our own egos? Newbigin suggests that our primary calling in such activities is as undercover agents, subverting human scheming for the glory of God (1991, 82). The question I must continually ask myself, therefore, is how can I subvert this meeting, this project, for the glory of God in Jesus Christ?

If Newbigin is correct that the congregation is the primary hermeneutic of the gospel, and my experience suggests he is, then our main focus must remain on the slow and painful work of growing a community of believers who explode joyfully with the good news of Jesus, and subvert all things to his glory. Newbigin suggests six characteristics of this community (1989, 227–33).

First, it will be a community of praise. This is, of course, not about Sunday services, but about the attitude to life every day of the week. The prevailing attitude should not be of a hermeneutic of suspicion or of the cynicism of which the British are so fond. Rather we live to praise God and thank him for all he has blessed us with. I have found urban congregations often to be very good at this, but it remains a continual challenge.

Second, it will be a community of truth, speaking the truth of the Christian story to defeat the lies of the world. This is important in an urban context, as the majority of the congregation may well have been devalued by the world, and might lack the trappings of worldly success. But they are, as Paul reminds us, the weak ones of the world chosen to shame the strong (1 Corinthians 1.26–31). Our churches need to be places where people come to a true understanding of their personal and corporate standing before God, as sinners redeemed by the grace of God.

Third, it will be a community that does not live for itself but is deeply involved in the concerns of its neighbourhood, a specific church for the specific place where it is. There are at least two challenges for urban churches: the first is to help a small and threatened congregation feel secure enough to risk opening up to the outside world (and so this third characteristic is an outworking of the first two); the second is the need for discernment in responding to overwhelming need with limited resources. Newbigin reminds us that mission is primarily the work of the Holy Spirit, and that most advances of the kingdom come about because of the sovereign actions of God, not the strategies or resource allocation of the Church or missionaries (1995b, 64).

Fourth, it will be a community 'where men and women are prepared for and sustain the exercise of the priesthood in the world' (1989, 229). Newbigin is clear that the whole Church is called to be a royal priesthood (1 Peter 2.5, 9), standing before God on behalf of people and people on behalf of God. The priesthood in the world is nourished and sustained by the priesthood in the Church, meaning that congregations must be trained, supported and encouraged to exercise their ministry in the world. The different gifts of different congregations' members should be recognized and affirmed and encouraged to develop. In small urban churches this will probably be primarily in one-to-one relationships; bigger suburban churches may well develop specific groups and ministries that support teachers, lawyers, doctors and so forth.

Fifth, it will be a community of mutual responsibility, a new social order which challenges individualism. In my experience in the urban church people are often very clear that they cannot cope alone, and the challenge is to develop mutually supportive relationships, where everyone is growing, and the foundation is Christ, not an individual's needs or ego.

Sixth, it will be a community of hope. Urban areas can often be characterized by despair, especially the bleaker areas of some of our northern cities. Often the church is the only beacon of hope in an otherwise grey landscape. We can only continue to offer that hope if we remain faithful to our calling and growing in our relationship with the Father, through the Son in the power of the Spirit.

I began by commenting that urban ministry is both depressing and exciting. It is primarily depressing when we forget the business we are engaged in. Newbigin reminds us that we are stewards, not owners of the gospel (1995b, 188–9). We must not be lazy or hide the treasure from view. Instead, recognizing that it is only when we are weak that we are truly strong, we must graciously hold out the word of truth. When we are able to remain faithfully, explode with love, joy and hope, and subvert the world for the glory of Christ, then we will see God at work, and everything becomes exciting again.[10]

Conclusion

This chapter has begun to make the case that interfaith engagement is not simply a good thing to do, but that it can be a specifically Christian activity. For Christians, there is a creative tension between hospitality, service and proclamation which provides a framework for interfaith work. I have looked at some of the reasons why Christians do not engage in interfaith work, categorizing them as issues of fear, apathy or shortage. I have given four examples of how interfaith engagement has helped my growth as a follower of Jesus. Next, I introduced the type of interfaith engagement that might take place in Britain today, asking what it means for us to love those of other faiths as we love ourselves. The chapter closed with a brief reflection on intentional growth, including a more extensive discussion of Newbigin's vision of the Church 'exploding joyfully'.

Notes

1 A brief overview and timeline can be found at www.telegraph.co.uk/news/worldnews/europe/france/11341599/Prophet-Muhammad-cartoons-controversy-timeline.html (accessed 29 July 2018).

2 One of many charities engaged in supporting persecuted Christians is Open Doors (see www.opendoorsuk.org/). It is worth noting that Open Doors argue that Christians are persecuted in countries that identify as atheist, Muslim, Hindu, Buddhist and, especially in South America, even Christian.

3 See, for example, https://weare.tearfund.org/try-veggie-experiment/

4 See, for example, www.huffingtonpost.co.uk/2016/01/25/britain-first-luton-march-condemned_n_9067474.html?guccounter=1&guce_referrer_us=aHR0cHM6Ly93d3cuZ29vZ2xlLmNvbS88&guce_referrer_cs=J72woeI8Mkwg7kJ3dgLo2Q

5 A good example is found in the response of the National Council of Hindu Temples to a recent Government consultation about caste and discrimination. Full details can be found in the report which can be downloaded from the following website: See www.nchtuk.org/index.php?option=com_acymailing&ctrl=archive&task=view&mailid=161&key=zj5NFTBr&subid=693-89056d70f7aa979c549cea8a5736aob5&tmpl=component

6 See www.collegeofvedicstudiesleicester.com/courses

7 Dr Riyaz Timol's PhD thesis consists of an ethnographic study of Tablighi Jamaat in the UK and overseas. Some sample pages of the thesis can be viewed at www.academia.edu/35436083/PhD_thesis_sample_pages_

8 Such as www.onereason.org/

9 www.telegraph.co.uk/news/2016/05/21/dont-speak-about-your-faith-unless-youre-asked-to-says-archbisho/

10 This paper was first delivered in June 2014 at a conference on the theme *Missio Dei and the New Politics*, held at Chester University, www.chester.ac.uk/node/26740

2

Who engages in interfaith relations?

This chapter discusses who engages in interfaith relations and the types of approaches they might take. The chapter is divided into six parts. First, I introduce the 'three-fold typology' of exclusivist, inclusivist and plural-ist approaches to interfaith relations, before nuancing the typology, and examining the different emotional resonances of the positions, clarifying definitions, engaging with critiques of the typology and explaining its value as a pedagogical tool. The bulk of the chapter consists of an overview of the views of 12 different theologians, four for each position, to illus-trate the variety of views in more detail. The final section invites you, the reader, to begin to develop your own understanding of your motivation and expectations in relation to interfaith engagement.

The 'three-fold typology'

A standard introduction for Christians to interfaith relations will invari-ably suggest that one can take one of three possible positions in relation to the salvific status of human beings. The first is exclusivism, namely that it is only by explicitly acknowledging Jesus Christ as Lord and Saviour that one is saved. The second is inclusivism, namely that the death, resurrection and ascension of Jesus Christ is the means of salvation, but this does not have to be explicitly acknowledged for a person to be saved. Third is the pluralist position, namely that there are many routes to salvation, often likened to the many paths to the top of a mountain, or even that all routes lead to salvation. This three-fold paradigm was originally put forward by Alan Race (1983) and is discussed at some length in many different books, including *Only One Way?* (2011), in which Gavin D'Costa, Paul Knitter and Daniel Strange each present one of the views within the typology and dialogue with the other two views. I will summarize their views to illustrate the different positions further.

Taking the views in order of presentation, Gavin D'Costa begins by advocating the inclusivist position. Writing from the perspective of a

Roman Catholic theologian, he discusses two key Catholic teaching documents: *Nostra Aetate* and *Lumen Gentium*. His argument could be summarized as understanding non-Christian religions as valid in their own right, as a means by which the Holy Spirit can work, as a preparation for people to receive Christ, and as signs of God's work in the world. D'Costa explains that 'anything that is good, true and holy in the cultures of the world can and should be incorporated into the Church' (2011, 36). Other faiths have much to teach Christianity about how to relate to God, but Jesus Christ remains the ultimate route of salvation.

Paul Knitter offers the pluralist perspective. He has written elsewhere as a strong advocate of 'dual belonging' (that is, simultaneous membership of two religious traditions; see Knitter 2009). His reasons for adopting a pluralist position are, first, the presence of so many different religious traditions in the world, which he sees as given by God for the good of humanity; and second, the need to address human poverty, inequality and the myriad challenges of our age, which means that religions must not compete but cooperate (2011, 50–1). Knitter emphasizes the mystery of God, pointing out that we cannot fathom the depths of the divine, and arguing that limiting God to the revelation brought by Jesus is overly restrictive. Knitter does not believe in the crucifixion as an atoning sacrifice, arguing that 'a God who sacrifices his own Son in order to satisfy his sense of justice looks a lot like a petulant and even an abusive father' (2011, 69). Instead, Knitter believes that the crucifixion is sacramental, a revelation of divine love, which leaves room for other revelations in other religions (2011, 69–70). Christianity may be distinct, but it is not unique. There are many routes to relationship with God, and all of them are valid.

Daniel Strange presents the exclusivist perspective. His argument is that 'non-Christian religions are essentially an idolatrous refashioning of divine revelation, which are antithetical and yet parasitic on Christian truth, and of which the gospel of Jesus Christ is this "subversive fulfilment"' (2011, 93). Strange's argument is, in essence, that the Christian Church has always held an exclusive understanding of salvation, and although modern political sensibilities mean that this understanding is now much less popular, that does not make it any less true.

Nuancing the typology

The distinctions between the typology must be clarified further. First, exclusivism is salvific rather than epistemological. That is to say, each possible position (exclusivist, inclusivist or pluralist), if chosen, logically excludes the other two. Thus one cannot be both an exclusivist and a pluralist in relation to one's understanding of how people are saved.

Second, inclusivism is not 'hermeneutical inclusivism', whereby the religious categories of, say, Christianity are used in a discussion of Islam. Rather, inclusivism includes those outside the formal boundaries of a religion on that religion's terms, so a Christian inclusivist believes that Muslims can receive salvation on the basis of the death and resurrection of Christ, even if they do not profess faith in the salvific merits of these events.

Third, pluralism does not mean 'anything goes', and one does not have to be a pluralist to recognize that modern society must be as open as possible to a diversity of worldviews, convictions, lifestyles and so forth. One can be an exclusivist and still have a respectful and welcoming attitude to other religions. As noted above, Kaemingk is a salvific exclusivist who argues strongly in favour of pluralism (2018). Yong correctly observes that these are the three logical options, but 'most theologians are far too complex to fit neatly into exclusivist, inclusivist or pluralist camps' (2008, 66).

Different emotional resonances

The different positions also have different emotional resonances. Thus, an exclusivist position might have echoes of intolerance and/or arrogance. Exclusivism is regarded as arrogant because it presumes sole possession of truth. Saying 'Jesus is the only Way' can be heard by many in contemporary society as indicating that the speaker actively dislikes those who do not share this view, and questions their right to exist (a tension explored at length in Strhan 2015). Yet, as noted above, each of the three positions is epistemologically exclusivist, and so each has the potential to be expressed arrogantly. The issue of arrogance, therefore, is related primarily to how the attitude is held, shared and heard rather than which attitude it is. Thus some might find inclusivism to be arrogant. Consider this example: a Muslim faithfully fasts for 18 hours a day to fulfil the instructions God gave via Muhammad for how to observe Ramadan. A Christian inclusivist responds by commending them and adding that their fasting is acceptable to God via Jesus' death on the cross. How might the Muslim respond? The same could be said of the charge of intolerance; it is possible to be an illiberal liberal. Illiberal liberals are those who preclude all options other than their own liberal stance and are vitriolic in condemning those who do not conform to their own understanding of the world. There were at least hints of illiberal liberalism in David Cameron's injunction that the Church of England must 'get with the programme' when in 2012 the Church of England's General Synod blocked plans for women to become bishops.[1] I should be clear that I am not opposed to women being bishops, but I am opposed to the state selectively enforcing religious doctrine. It is noticeable that the Church of England was condemned for not allowing women to be bishops, but there is no state condemnation of the Roman Catholic Church for holding the view that only men can be ordained, or the view of many Muslims that only men can be imams. The question is not what theological position you hold, but how you engage with those whose views differ from your own.

For some people, an exclusivist understanding of salvation will have very positive emotional resonances; it might be described as 'simply being faithful to the gospel'. It is an uncomplicated binary stance, which means that you know exactly where you stand and where others stand. It does not require complex reasoning as to the extent to which, say, modern Pagans are responding to a general revelation of God when they engage in their rituals. It allows for certainty as to the boundaries of the Christian faith community, but for some lacks the sophistication to deal with the complexities of the real world.

The positive emotional resonances of inclusivism are that it allows one to hold to a clear Christian paradigm while also including those of other faiths. One famous proponent of this type of view, Karl Rahner, popularized the phrase 'anonymous Christians' (1966) to describe those who do not own the name Christian but are nevertheless saved on the basis of Jesus' atoning death. In an era that holds inclusion and mutual respect as important values there is much that is attractive in an inclusivist position. But it is open to a charge of colonialism, of defining how people are saved with no reference to the belief systems they hold to. To understand this emotional resonance, imagine being told that you are in fact a Muslim because you have submitted to God and thus are really saved because of your attempts, albeit partial and faltering, to follow Islam. Or think of yourself being described as a Hindu who was simply following your guru Jesus, one among many, your path to enlightenment, whose exclusive claims are only relevant to his own disciples. Although these analogies are limited, they give some idea of how an inclusivist understanding of Christianity might be perceived by those of other faiths.

Finally, pluralism is highly attractive to those who struggle with the concept of condemning all other world faiths. Strange's understanding of world faiths as 'idolatrous refashioning' of the divine revelation found in Christ is antithetical to some as it sounds very politically incorrect.

Many people who are not especially religious often take refuge in lowest common denominator agreement, presuming that all religions are the same anyway. While this view is attractive to some it is deeply offensive to others. It also ignores the reality of the massive disparity between different belief systems and worldviews. Buddhism, for example, does not, in the main, accept the existence of a divine being (Amida Buddhism differs here, but for the purpose of this argument can be treated as an exception that proves the rule). How then can Buddhism be equated with Christianity? Hinduism, which is perhaps best described as a worldview and a way of life, includes within it strong disagreement as to which being constitutes the supreme revelation of the divine. Muslims, Christians and Jews have inch-wide but mile-deep disagreements over the precise identity of Jesus of Nazareth, over what the term 'prophet' means, and who counts as a prophet, to give just a few examples.

There are thus both positive and negative aspects to all elements of the typology, which has increasingly been recognized as having only limited value. As Kaemingk points out, the typology is only interested in what happens when someone dies, not in how to treat them while they are alive (2018, 16; see also the extensive critique in Yong 2003). The Catholic theologian Michael Barnes SJ likens the three views to the theological virtues of faith, hope and love (2002, 8). He suggests that exclusivism speaks of what it knows through the specific tradition from which it originates; inclusivism hopes for the fulfilment of all authentically expressed religious truths and values; and pluralism expresses love to affirm all those present (2002, 184). Gaston develops this idea, arguing that the virtues shift the typology from a question of soteriology to one of discipleship in a multifaith world (2017, 11). The reality is that most people do not fit precisely and neatly into one of the three categories, exclusivist or inclusivist or pluralist, but it is nevertheless 'a useful pedagogical tool to enable reflection on attitudes to other faith traditions, and can be used to encourage intra-Christian theological engagement' (Gaston 2017, 4). This is primarily how the typology is used within this chapter: to enable readers to reflect on their own views. I will therefore be deliberately provocative in some of the examples used and positions explored, to enable a fuller exploration of the implications of a variety of different perspectives on the issue of relating to people of other faiths. In what follows, I engage further with the typology as a pedagogical device, using it to artificially group 12 different approaches to the question of interfaith engagement into the three categories of pluralist, inclusivist and exclusivist.

Examples of pluralist approaches

This section takes in the arguments of Michael Amaladoss, Kenneth Cracknell, John Hick and Perry Schmidt-Leukel. They are included to give a sample of possible pluralist approaches to interfaith engagement, as a stimulus for the reader.

Michael Amaladoss

The Indian Catholic theologian Michael Amaladoss' views of other faiths sit somewhere on the continuum between pluralism and inclusivism. Thus he states:

> The Spirit is the source of pluralism in the Christian tradition. The recognition of the presence and action of the Spirit in other religions may lead us to see the many Gods of different religious traditions as manifestations in history and culture as the One Absolute beyond name and form. (2017, 13)

By this Amaladoss means both that the Spirit is at work in various ways within the Church but that the same Spirit is also active outside of the Church. Elsewhere, he rejects the agnostic relativism of the pluralist John Hick (2017, 26), explaining that as a Christian he believes that in and through Jesus he possesses all truth (2017, 28–9). But at the same time, he recognizes that God may be at work in and through other religious traditions (2017, 30–4). Elsewhere, he argues that the presence and action of God may be observed in the sacred texts and ritual actions of other religions, but that not all religions are the same (2017, 38–9).

One of Amaladoss' motivations in writing is to challenge the violence that is done in the name of religion, arguing that there are invariably political and socio-economic causes for actions that are identified as being motivated solely by religious faith. Rather than violence, Amaladoss advocates dialogue between religions, as well as critiquing exclusivist understandings of faith as having the potential to be used to justify violence. He wants people of different faiths to work together for the good of all, in a public space that recognizes and supports the contributions of all religions (2017, 45–68). He develops this point at length, arguing about the danger of fundamentalism of any kind (he gives Christian, Muslim, Hindu and Buddhist examples) and in favour of working together, seeking to reconcile the multiple ethical frameworks of different religious traditions, without privileging one over the others (2017, 70–107).

What exactly does Amaladoss believe about other religions? He is a subtle and complex writer, and any short summary will not do full justice to the breadth and depth of his thought. On the one hand he talks about the need for dialogue between religions and between ideologies but on the other he suggests that one result of these dialogues will be the dissolution of the borders that exist between them. His position on the border of pluralism and inclusivism is seen in this statement:

> Christian theology has always recognized that people belonging to other religions could be saved by God if they are true to their conscience. What is new is that today we believe that God is reaching out to the people, not in spite of their religions, but in and through their religions. (2017, 118)

He goes on to argue that the religions of the world can be seen as 'different manifestations of the Word through the Spirit', which should not be limited to what God does through Jesus (2017, 121). This takes his argument closer to a pluralist view than an inclusivist one, although the case could be made either way.

Amaladoss encourages Christians to step out of their comfort zones, to engage with the religious other expecting to encounter God already at work. He advocates dialogue not just between religions but also between ideologies, such as the different types of capitalism or socialism that are present in the world (2017, 137). He is content for some to have a double religious identity, both Hindu and Christian, for example, arguing that this is not syncretism but a creative tension that is both integrated and inclusive. But while this may describe his own position, he does not leave behind his own Christianity, remaining firmly convinced that 'God's salvific plan for the universe has been manifested fully and in a unique manner in Jesus Christ (Eph. 1.3–10; Col. 1.15–20)' (2017, 221).

In an earlier work, Amaladoss argues that people and their religions are exclusive, but God is not. He suggests that God will work out how to bring all things together so that he will be God in all (2008, 42). This allows him also to argue for 'eucharistic hospitality', which means being 'open to the idea that a person could relate to Jesus Christ in a creative and meaningful way, even sacramentally, without being a formal member of the Church' (2008, 94).

The Indian context from which Amaladoss writes influences his perspective, as violent religious conflict between different religious groups, especially Hindus, Muslims, Sikhs and Christians, is a fact of modern Indian life. At the same time, there are many Indian villages where people of different faiths celebrate each other's festivals and make little of the doc-

trinal differences between them (on which see Swamy 2016). Amaladoss'
main concern is to advocate peaceful coexistence, and he believes that
a pluralist/inclusivist understanding of religious faith is a necessary pre-
cursor to achieving that goal. He is also shaped by an understanding of
truth that rejects the binary of *either-or* in favour of *both-and*, thus allowing him to claim both relationship with Christ and the full validity of the
Hindu tradition, and to argue against the need for strict borders between
religions, which in his view cause conflict and preclude harmonious
relationships (2008, 193–209).

Pause

What resonates with your understanding of the Christian faith? What
is different? Does this change or confirm your own perspective?

Kenneth Cracknell

Kenneth Cracknell is an academic and theologian with a wealth of
experience in both teaching and interreligious engagement. Initially
ordained as a Methodist minister, he worked in local churches, for the
British and World Council of Churches, primarily in interreligious engagement, and in theological education in both England and the USA. In what
follows, I discuss the arguments of *In Good and Generous Faith*, one
of his later works that brings together a lifetime of reflection on issues
of Christian engagement with other faith communities. Cracknell's core
argument is for a Christian pluralism that simultaneously holds a clear
Christian identity, and a 'good and generous' faith that responds to other
world faiths with courtesy, justice and love.

Cracknell's argument has five parts. First, his survey of salvation history proposes that God has always been speaking with all his children,
regardless of their religious, cultural or ethnic identity. The concept of
creation as a doctrine of grace is core to his case, especially when linked
with the concept of covenant, exemplified in the covenant with Noah,
which is argued to be for all people for all time. The case is supplemented
with positive references to 'the nations' throughout the Old Testament,
for example Psalm 102.21–2 or Isaiah 19.16–24. Cracknell also finds
reference to godliness among the nations in the New Testament, both in
Jesus' interactions with those outside ethnic Israel and in the growth of
the Early Church among the gentiles, before concluding by discussing the

vision of Revelation of a city where salvation is for all the peoples of God.

Second, Cracknell's Christology understands Jesus as a unique reve-lation of God, but does not preclude the possibility of the grace and love of God operating unnamed or under other names. The basis of his argument is New Testament teaching of the pre-existence of Christ, in particular the theology of Jesus as Logos or Word of God. He contends that the theology developed among the Greek Fathers of the Early Church recognized the work of the Word in the world before the incarnation and can be under-stood as much more pluralist than the views of the Latin Fathers.

Third, ethics are important for Cracknell. He discusses the approach to dialogue taken by Wilfred Cantwell Smith and Raimon Panikkar, arguing that friendship points towards pluralism because of the interdependence of humanity. Cracknell argues that dialogue is a face-to-face experience, where people talk about their beliefs and practices rather than listing the doctrines of their own or other faiths. He proposes that dialogue becomes the means by which people of all faiths can work together to serve their local community. Moreover, dialogue is the means by which personal faith can be genuinely and authentically shared.

Fourth, Cracknell's spirituality for interfaith engagement focuses on the notion of pilgrimage, being a fellow traveller, even if the roads are sometimes unfamiliar and ultimate destinations uncertain or different from what is initially expected. He calls for a balance of commitment and openness; commitment to personal faith in Jesus and openness – and love – towards others. He also suggests that it is important for Christians to be silent at times, engaging in personal meditation when in the presence of the worship of those of other faiths. Cracknell advocates a spirituality of enquiry, of willingness to learn to see the world as others do, entering as far as possible into the worldview of a Muslim or Hindu or Buddhist.

Finally, his missiology is one of quiet confidence, speaking out when asked. He explains that:

> Mission in the midst of religious pluralism is action in good and gener-ous faith for the sake of friendship: friendship among the peoples to be sure, but also and ultimately in relation to the God who was revealed in Jesus Christ and wills that all of us shall be his friends. (2005, 179)

Aspects of Cracknell's arguments sound more inclusivist than strictly pluralist, and indeed he describes his Christology and understanding of salvation history in those terms. I include him within the section on pluralism, however, primarily because I understand him to be arguing for salvation by means other than Christ. Cracknell writes out of his experience of decades of interfaith engagement and his approach is one of trying to blend his Christian faith with his close personal friendships with those of other faiths. It is difficult to be clear as to whether the result is inclusivist or pluralist, but that is more a recognition of the limit of the labels than anything else.

Pause

What resonates with your understanding of the Christian faith? What is different? Does this change or confirm your own perspective?

John Hick

John Hick is a well-known advocate of a pluralist understanding of religious faith who has written extensively on the subject of world religions and the relationships between them. What follows is a brief summary of a few of his works, included to give a sense of his arguments. Hick describes himself as having a penchant for 'problematic theology' which is always open to revision and seeking better ideas and explanations, questioning established teaching (1980, 1). In one of his earlier writings he explains that he does not see Jesus as divine but as someone who was so conscious of the divine that if we were in his presence 'we could catch something of that consciousness by spiritual contagion' (1977, 172). For Hick, the notion of an incarnation is meaningless when taken literally, but useful as a metaphor to aid spiritual development (1977, 177–8). Hick dismisses the idea that only those who have heard of Christ could be saved, regarding the idea as 'excessively parochial' and presenting God as a mere 'tribal deity' of the predominantly Christian West' (1977, 180). Instead, he favours an understanding of the Logos or Word of God as active behind all religious traditions, drawing all people to salvation. Hick is clear that this Logos is not to be equated with Jesus of Nazareth, who was only one of many points of contact between the human and the divine (1977, 181). He calls for a 'Copernican revolution' in our view of religions, explaining that the universe of faith centres on God, not Christianity, and that therefore all religions are different revelations of God (1980, 51–2).

Hick is fully convinced that there is a spiritual dimension to life, arguing that what happens in different places of worship is essentially the same, an encounter with the divine (1980, 45–9). He describes himself as a 'critical realist', aware that everyone's experience of reality is subjective, shaped by the culture, worldview and context in which they find themselves. This, he argues, includes religious experience; if you live in a theistic culture you think of the 'Ultimate' in one way, but if your culture focuses on a reality beyond god-figures, then you think of the Ultimate in those terms (2010, 67). Hick explains the implications of his beliefs for Christianity as meaning that he rejects most of the historic teaching of the Church, such as Jesus' Virgin conception or his bodily resurrection, and that Jesus was God incarnate. Hick sees religious traditions as both good and bad: good in that they have provided meaning and structure for countless millions of people, as well as being responsible for the founding of hospitals, schools, universities and much work for the good of humanity, but bad in that they have been used – and are still used – to justify violence, oppression and exploitation (2010, 122–3).

For all his scepticism about the historic teachings of Christianity, Hick remains convinced that there is a fifth, spiritual dimension to life. He is equally convinced that all religions are incomplete, contextually bound, attempts to attain the same goal, a relationship with the Ultimate or Transcendent, or the 'Real' as he prefers to call it (2004, 9). This is not a personal deity who intervenes in the created order but the fifth dimension of reality, which the fifth dimension of our own being yearns to relate to in some mystical way. For Hick, the existence of evil and suffering in the world mitigates against the notion of a personal deity, as such a being would be capricious and cruel to allow the suffering that is regularly experienced in our world today (2004, 17).

Hick argues in favour of the 'cosmic optimism' of religious traditions, believing that we can move on from the condition in which we presently find ourselves to a better condition, with the help of the Real, who is conceived of as having a benign attitude towards humanity.

Pause

What resonates with your understanding of the Christian faith? What is different? Does this change or confirm your own perspective?

Perry Schmidt-Leukel

The essence of Schmidt-Leukel's argument is that pluralism means that some, but not necessarily all, religions are equally valid paths to salvation. His most recent explanation of his views is found in *Religious Pluralism and Interreligious Theology*, a book based on two series of lectures he gave. He explains that his understanding of pluralism is not relativism, as he recognizes that there are valid criteria by which one can determine if a religion has a greater revelation of truth than others. He is also clear that pluralism is not toleration, as tolerance presumes a negative assessment of that which is tolerated; and moreover there are many things that should not be tolerated (2017, 4–5). He is also clear that pluralism is specific, arguing that one does not hold a general theory of pluralism, but rather is a Christian pluralist or a Buddhist pluralist or a Sikh pluralist and so forth (2017, 7–8).

The particular nature of pluralism is then demonstrated through a discussion of its Christian, Jewish, Islamic, Hindu, Buddhist and Chinese religious forms. For Christians, the questions revolve around how to understand the nature of God's love, of saving faith and divine revelation. For Jewish pluralists, the point of departure is the so-called 'Noahide Laws', that is, the commands God gave to Noah, which are taken as applying to all humanity. The more complex question concerns what it means for the Jews to be God's chosen people, with the response being variations on a theme of understanding God at work in different ways for different peoples. Within Islam, the primary justification for pluralism is Surah 2.62, which is quoted as follows:

> Those who believe and those who follow the Jews and the Christians and the Sabeans – any who believe in Allah and the Last Day, and work righteousness, shall have their reward with the Lord: on them shall be no fear, nor shall they grieve. (2017, 44)

A second verse, 5.69, which was revealed towards the end of Muhammad's life, is taken as further confirmation of the case. Sufi mysticism is also used to strengthen the Islamic case for pluralism.

Schmidt-Leukel argues that Hinduism has exhibited both pluralist and anti-pluralist tendencies in its history. The latter is particularly seen in the contemporary Hindutva movement, which has an exclusivist understanding of Hinduism. The pluralist impulse in Hinduism is most readily affirmed when *sanatana dharma* (eternal truth) is recognized as holding true for more than one specific historical or linguistic articulation of truth. Regarding Buddhism, Schmidt-Leukel explains that Buddhism tends to emphasize holding lightly to its teachings, but nevertheless those teachings of the Four Noble Truths and the Eightfold Noble Path are necessary to attain enlightenment, and thus there is a tendency towards an exclusivist understanding. But there are pluralist impulses within Buddhism. For

Theravada Buddhism, Schmidt-Leukel identifies teachings of the existence of multiple enlightened beings, and multiple incomplete religious truths. For Mahayana Buddhism, there are the teachings of the existence of both relative and absolute truth, and the doctrine of different religious ends for different religious actions, although Schmidt-Leukel regards this as more inclusivist than pluralist.

Finally, within Daoist understandings, all human beings are to live in accordance with *qi*, 'the vital energy as which the unfathomable *Dao* is manifest in life' (2017, 94). All religions can, therefore, be seen as useful or harmful depending on how they relate to this aspiration. Confucianism, like Daoism, values harmony, and so where religion leads to a healthy 'middle way' it is viewed positively, but where it leads to extremes it is understood negatively.

Schmidt-Leukel is clear that religious pluralism is not a theory above religions but a way of interpreting their diversity and encouraging interaction between them. He argues on this basis in favour of interreligious theology, by which he means reflection 'on the major themes of human life by drawing on the insights from more than one religious tradition' (2017, 113). For Schmidt-Leukel there are four key principles of interreligious theology. First is a theological credit of trust, which put in Christian terms is 'the assumption that revelation in the sense of divine self-communication is not limited to the people of the Judeo-Christian tradition' (2017, 131). Second is the unity of reality, which believes that all truth wherever and however it is discerned is compatible and coherent. Third, interreligious theology is tied to interreligious discourse; it is a project not of isolated individuals but one of collaboration and team working. Fourth, it is an open process, never complete, always changing and developing.

Schmidt-Leukel makes an intellectual and academic case for a pluralist understanding and a pluralist methodology of academic enquiry, which may appear far removed from the everyday interaction of peoples of different faiths. But the underlying pluralist principles could be applied to any sphere of life and integrated into any way of working.

Pause

What resonates with your understanding of the Christian faith? What is different? Does this change or confirm your own perspective?

The attraction of pluralism

One of the primary attractions of pluralism is that it is a position that fits with the spirit of our age, including and welcoming all people without standing in judgement over their views. As the above examples illustrate, those Christians who adopt a pluralist position are often strongly influenced by their experience of engaging with those of other faiths. They experience God at work in other religious traditions, and so refuse to limit the divine to Christianity. They are often especially taken by the mystery and unknowable nature of God, and some, such as John Hick, refuse to be limited by that term in order to include all faith perspectives. It is important to recognize that pluralists and atheists disagree, as even as radical a pluralist as John Hick believes in some form of supernatural reality.

Examples of inclusivist approaches

This section on inclusivist approaches discusses the views of Michael Barnes, Stephen B. Bevans and Roger P. Schroeder, Richard Sudworth, and Amos Yong. As before, the aim is to offer a range of views to challenge your thinking on the topic.

Michael Barnes SJ

One of the key concepts that Michael Barnes employs is the 'seeds of the Word'. Rooted in the theology of the Greek Fathers of the Early Church, the idea is that the divine Word (Logos) has scattered seeds throughout the garden of the world, and our job as faithful Christians is to discern where these plants are growing, and to nurture their growth. He notes the presence of many 'family resemblances' across the major faith traditions, and advocates the importance of listening and vulnerability when engaging with difference. Barnes' inclusivism is rooted in his understanding of the (Roman Catholic) Church as 'a community which exists not for itself but precisely *for others*; its identity is truly to be found only in and through the relationships it establishes with others' (2002, 35, emphasis original). That is, we cannot presume to know or understand everything about the other, but in building relationship we learn more about the other, about self and about God.

Writing as a Roman Catholic, Barnes unsurprisingly takes his lead from a significant teaching document of the Catholic Church, *Nostra Aetate*, which was first promulgated in 1965 after the Second Vatican

Council. This means that Barnes is initially concerned with the relationship between Christians and Jews, especially after the Holocaust. This leads him to recognize the twin tensions of being faithful to Christ as the way, the truth and the life, but also open to the truths and values of other faiths, making an ethical response to the legacy of the Holocaust. The concern is that any theological position that leads to a rejection or belittling of people of other faiths can potentially lead to passively standing by while atrocities are committed. It also means that Christians have to recognize the limits of their own knowledge, that others are strange to them and that it requires humility and effort to understand them more clearly.

Barnes recognizes that interfaith encounters are fraught with risk, but also that faith is marginal in contemporary society. Barnes discusses what it means to recognize someone as 'other', arguing that the recognition entails some form of relationship from which a clarification of the precise nature of difference can emerge. This is a task that requires humility and patience but also obedience to the revelation of God.

When Barnes discusses how to tell the Christian story in the context of other faiths, he recognizes the limits of language; any linguistic presentation of faith, whether our own or that of others, is fraught with difficulty and the possibility of misrepresentation. Faith can, of course, be adapted to a particular cultural and historical context, but this process must be undertaken with care. Christians are called, as noted above, to discern the 'seeds of the Word' wherever they may be found. Barnes believes that the grace of God is active in transforming the world, and the task of the Church is to discern where this is taking place and 'cooperate as companions of the Son' (2002, 148–9). He suggests that God may particularly be found in the other, the poor, the stranger, the marginalized, and through reflection on the experience of Dalit and other excluded Indian Christians he argues that this is where the Church ought to be especially active.

Barnes argues that an assumption of pluralism is that 'inter-religious encounter will enable a complete theory of meaning once the means and methods of communication have been clarified'. But, he counters, such an assumption ignores the 'irreducible mystery of otherness' (2002, 182), proposing that we can never fully understand the other, nor reach the religious equivalence that pluralism presumes. For Barnes, the Church can only speak of the possibility of God's action elsewhere on the basis of experience and knowledge of God's action in the 'school of faith' that is the Church (2002, 187). This means that the Church can expect God to be at work beyond her borders, presuming God to be drawing all people to himself.

Barnes argues that the Church should be a worshipping community formed and oriented for mission, equipped and empowered through the celebration of the Eucharist, which acts as a school that teaches the generous hospitality needed to discern the seeds of the Word in the world (2002, 203). Interfaith engagement is thus, at its heart, a process of contemplating the depths of God, of discerning the presence and activity of God's Spirit throughout the world. Christian identity is, Barnes proposes, only comprehensible in relation to other communities of faith. We understand both ourselves and the other who is different from us in the 'broken middle' of the relationship that exists between us. Through deepening that understanding we gain a clearer and deeper knowledge of the hospitable God who acts as both guest and host, and whose area and scope of work we cannot predict but can only discern and follow (2002, 250).

Pause

What resonates with your understanding of the Christian faith? What is different? Does this change or confirm your own perspective?

Stephen B. Bevans and Roger P. Schroeder

Bevans and Schroeder are Catholic theologians, members of the Society of the Divine Word (SVD), a male Catholic missionary order. They have developed the concept of 'prophetic dialogue', which they describe as a synthesis of three main theological teachings about mission: mission is participation in the action of the Triune God, it is liberating service of the reign of God, and it is proclamation of Jesus Christ as universal saviour (2005, 348–95; 2011). They also describe prophetic dialogue as an umbrella term that encompasses various aspects of missionary endeavour, notably 'witness and proclamation; liturgy; prayer and contemplation; justice, peace and the integrity of creation; interreligious dialogue; inculturation; and reconciliation' (2011, 2).

For Bevans and Schroeder, prophetic dialogue is not so much a technique as a form of spirituality, a holistic approach that shapes everything a missionary does. They suggest that God is best described as a verb, not a noun, a shorthand for indicating that God is always active and present in creation, that God is 'self-diffusive love, freely creating, redeeming, healing, challenging that creation' (2011, 10). Therefore we must join in that activity; the Church is most authentically itself when it is not concerned for its own growth, but when we are outside it, at work in the world, participating in God's great dance in the world (2011, 16).

Bevans and Schroeder explain their understanding of Christian mission as dialogue as a spiritual approach, a style of living in relationship with neighbours. They approvingly quote the Federation of Asian Bishops' Conferences' understanding of mission as dialogue with the poor, with local culture and with other religious traditions (2011, 27). They offer four images for dialogue: first, a treasure hunter, searching for riches already present; second, a guest who brings a blessing but must learn the etiquette of the context in which they are being hosted; third, a stranger who must act with care and respect in an unfamiliar context; and finally the idea of entering someone else's garden, learning how to care for and nurture what is found growing there, and only in time responding to invitations to teach. The notion of mission as prophecy is that of speaking forth the truth in God's name. This may take the form of prophetic action or it may be verbal proclamation. It may mean forming a counter-cultural community of 'resident aliens' (1 Peter 1.1) or it may mean speaking truth to power (2011, 31–4). They offer three images of mission as prophecy. First is a teacher who presents in a clear, accurate, interesting and relevant way, is open to questions, and is ready to learn. Second is a storyteller, sharing stories that bestow identity, and opening us up to our own deepest experiences. Third is a trail guide, one who knows the way and who knows how to read maps (2011, 40–52).

Although they do not all directly relate to interfaith work, it is worth expanding slightly on the six elements of mission that Bevans and Schroeder argue constitute prophetic dialogue. First, witness and proclamation are carried out at the personal, congregational, institutional and interdenominational levels. Second, liturgy, prayer and contemplation are understood not to be ends in and of themselves but preparation for life in the world. Third, work for justice, peace and the integrity of creation requires action on behalf of and living in solidarity with the poor and marginalized, but also needs to empower them to have their own voice. Fourth, inculturation means that the gospel must reflect local experience, context, history and socio-economic reality. Fifth, the Church must engage in reconciliation, at a personal, group and political level. The sixth element of prophetic dialogue is interreligious and secular dialogue. Bevans and Schroeder identify four aspects: the dialogue of life, that is, living alongside people of other faiths; the dialogue of social action, working together for common concerns; the dialogue of theological exchange; and dialogue of religious experience, with the primary example given being of people praying together, each in their own ways (2011, 64–71). They argue elsewhere that dialogue does not replace proclamation or the need to invite to Christian conversion, but rather that dialogue is the place to begin (2005, 378).

The Spirit is viewed as being active throughout the world, including in faith traditions outside the Catholic Church. Bevans and Schroeder develop the analogy of a garden at some length. The first question they ask is why enter someone else's garden, answering that they do so on the basis of 'a radical trust and belief in the power of God's Spirit at work in the lives and cultures of people' (2011, 75). They suggest that as Moses removed his sandals at the burning bush, the missionary comes in humility, wanting to learn, discerning what is of God, which is to be affirmed and what is not, which is to be challenged. This is the tension inherent in the approach. The prophetic aspect brings the challenge, confronting the failures of the world, the flesh and the devil, while the dialogical aspect brings affirmation and relationship.

Bevans and Schroeder are faithful to the main teachings of the Catholic Church; hence the approach is inclusivist in line with the main Catholic teaching documents, such as *Ad Gentes*, *Evangelii Nuntiandi*, *Redemptoris Missio* and *Dialogue and Proclamation*, which they discuss in turn (2011, 138–52). Elsewhere, Bevans argues at length that prophetic dialogue can be understood as a form of contextual theology (and vice versa, that contextual theology is a form of prophetic dialogue). The core arguments are that all cultures have something of God within them; and the gospel calls Christians to the heart of their own culture, offering a full expression of Christ through their lives (Bevans 2015).

Pause

What resonates with your understanding of the Christian faith? What is different? Does this change or confirm your own perspective?

Richard Sudworth

In *Distinctly Welcoming*, Sudworth sets out an introductory guide for Christians wishing to engage with multifaith society. He refuses to be constrained by the three-fold typology, arguing that it is overly simplistic, but admits that if pressed to pick one option, he is probably an inclusivist (2007, 33). He explains his understanding of the kingdom of God as having 'no limits, just edges'. That is to say, God sets the boundaries but there are clear distinctions between the kingdom of light and that of darkness

(2007, 41). Christians are called to live lives of worship, loving their neighbours as themselves, not getting overly concerned about establishing and maintaining the boundaries of the Church. Sudworth argues that Christians must develop a secure personal identity and it is through doing this that they are enabled to engage positively with those in other faith traditions. He emphasizes that interfaith encounter requires recognition of the distinctive nature of each faith, recognition that does not necessarily lead to agreement (2007, 45). Sudworth identifies seven core, distinctive beliefs of Christianity: that God is Creator, incarnate, a redeeming God, a God of grace, a God of resurrection and eternal life, a covenant God, and a triune God. These seven hallmarks of a distinctive Christian faith become, he proposes, the means and motivation for Christian engagement with the wider world (2007, 48).

Sudworth is positive about Christians engaging in evangelism with people of other faiths, provided it is 'infused with a spirit of listening, dialogue and inquiry' (2007, 62). He also argues for the importance of both giving and receiving hospitality; that Christians are called to be distinctly welcomed, allowing others to be the host. The advantage of this, he explains, is that we are then much better equipped to understand those we are talking with, and so able to communicate the good news of Jesus to them in ways they can actually hear.

Similarly, social action projects can be 'robustly Christian but rejoicing in the grace we find beyond our boundaries' (2007, 76). The seven core beliefs he identified are used to explain what a robustly Christian project would look like. Christians should seek creative solutions; we should recognize that the incarnation challenges us to live out our faith and get our hands dirty; we should seek to redeem all that is broken and lost; we should demonstrate gracious, unconditional love; we should offer resurrection hope in the social action we engage in; we should embody the covenant in our faithfulness and careful action; and, just as the Triune God is relational, so all our projects must be relational (2007, 48–9).

Sudworth is clear that Christians can, and should, conduct distinctly Christian youth work, based both in churches and in schools. But he also encourages Christians to think about how their actions would be perceived by people in other faith communities. Any approach should be carefully thought through and planned such that it does not seek to denigrate or belittle other faith communities but simply proclaims Christianity in as attractive and open a way as possible.

Sudworth argues that Christians can act as agents of unity in our diverse society. His vision of modelling the life of Christ in our interfaith relations is expressed as follows:

If we follow a relational God, who gives of himself, even to the extent of dying, if we follow a God who loves us freely and whose offer of life does not require that we be perfect or even better, if the God we worship reaches out, speaks and crosses boundaries ... then maybe we should, too! (2007, 108)

Sudworth's central argument is that God is actively at work beyond the boundaries of the Church. By constraining and limiting our expectation of the sphere of God's activity, we miss out on much of what God is doing. Our ultimate aim, Sudworth argues, should be to worship God and that will include reaching out beyond our comfort zones and normal boundaries.

Pause

What resonates with your understanding of the Christian faith? What is different? Does this change or confirm your own perspective?

Amos Yong

The Pentecostal theologian Amos Yong develops a pneumatological understanding of mission and of engagement with the world religions. One of his earliest reflections on the topic was entitled *Beyond the Impasse* (2003), a reference to the limited value of the three-fold typology that shapes this chapter. He argues that the world's religions must be engaged with first and foremost on their terms, and that while relationship with Christ is necessary for salvation, it is the Spirit who brings about that relationship and the Spirit blows where he wills. Although he does not fit any of the three categories within the typology, arguably inclusivism is the closest to his position, as he himself acknowledges:

Perhaps I am close to the inclusivist position that affirms the ontological normativity of Christ for salvation without insisting that persons who have never heard the gospel or verbally confess Christ have absolutely no hope of this great salvation. (Yong 2003, 27; see also Yong 2008, 65–98)

Hospitality is a central theme for Yong, who argues that God offers us hospitality in Christ by the Holy Spirit and also receives the hospitality

43

shown to Christ (2008, 105). Yong has four main theses that defend this position. His first is that Jesus Christ is both paradigmatic host who offers the redemptive hospitality of God and also the exemplary guest who travelled far from home. Second, the gift of the Holy Spirit is a sign of God's abundant hospitality to the whole world. Third, Christian hospitality must be characterized by the triune character of God, with no end to the hospitality both offered and received, and fourth, the triune nature of God means that we are invited to participate as both guests and hosts in the divine hospitality that Christ reveals in the power of the Holy Spirit (2008, 126–7). This means that when we encounter people of other religious traditions, 'hospitality opens up a "free space," where people of other faiths can enter', a process whereby strangers and enemies become friends and where hosts provide a space within which guests may change. Also, if we understand Christian mission through a paradigm of hospitality, we must not simply be hosts, we must also be guests, and hence we must risk being vulnerable to and with others (2008, 132).

Yong believes that God is universally present and active in the Spirit and that God's Spirit is the life-breath of his image in every human being, and is also the presupposition of all human communities and relationships (2003, 44–5). In a later book, he develops this into five key theses, which sum up his approach neatly. First, a viable contemporary theology of mission and evangelization is necessarily pneumatological. Second, a viable contemporary theology of interreligious ecumenism can be understood in part as an outgrowth of a pneumatological theology of intra-Christian ecumenism. Third, a pneumatological theology of mission and evangelization in an interreligious context is able to safeguard the perennial tension that exists between dialogue and proclamation. Fourth, a pneumatological theology of mission and evangelization will also enable a truly crucicentric and, hence, liberative solidarity to emerge in the interreligious encounter. Fifth, on a practical level, a pneumatological theology of mission and evangelization in a religiously plural world will need to be especially alert for what the Spirit is saying in and through the churches, be sensitive to the presence and activities of religious others, and be discerning about the broader context of Christian ministry (2014, 51–4). Yong is positive about the possibility of good relations across faith communities, arguing that:

> To the degree that other faiths inspire liberative actions by their adherents and urge initiatives of justice to address social, structural and systemic inequalities, to that same degree followers of Jesus as Messiah ought to partner with their co-religionists to address these latter realities

that often can only be confronted with coalitions across ideological (and religious) lines. (2015, 28)

Pause

What resonates with your understanding of the Christian faith? What is different? Does this change or confirm your own perspective?

The attraction of inclusivism

Inclusivism is attractive because it allows Christians to be clear in their own identity but at the same time not sit in judgement over other faith traditions. It makes space for the mystery of God, presuming he is active at work in the world in ways we cannot understand but need to discern. Inclusivism also builds on the experience of God in non-Christian contexts, looking for the seeds of the Word in the world, for the actions of the Spirit beyond the borders of the Church.

Examples of exclusivist approaches

The four exclusivist approaches discussed are those of Dewi Hughes, Harold A. Netland, Andrew Smith, and Daniel Strange. As before, they are selected as examples of this position.

Dewi Hughes

Hughes is the author of a short guide produced by the Evangelical Alliance entitled *The World on our Doorstep*, which sets out a paradigm for evangelical mission among people of other faith communities. It is primarily focused on practical advice, but includes some theological reflection.

Hughes explains that evangelical Christians believe they have good news to share with 'everyone including adherents of the religions' (2016, 29). He outlines the basis of faith of the Evangelical Alliance as having three main tenets. First is the human predicament: human beings are made in God's image to love, be holy and care for all creation, but have been corrupted by sin. Second is God's provision in Christ, affirming Jesus Christ as born of the virgin Mary, fully divine and fully human, who died on a cross as an atoning sacrifice, was resurrected bodily, ascended and is now seated and reigning at God's right hand. Third is human participation in that provision by God's grace, through the ministry of the Holy Spirit, leading us to repentance and faith (2016, 30). His exclusivism is clear: 'Atheists, humanists, nominal Christians, Hindus, Muslims etc. all come to God the Father, through Jesus in the power of the Spirit if we come at all' (2016, 31).

The framework he develops for understanding other religious traditions is based on biblical teaching about idolatry, with some discussion also of the demonic. He surveys instances of idolatry in the Old Testament and argues that although this teaches that all religions other than Christianity are idolatrous, the main aim of biblical reflection on idols is as a warning to God's people. Hughes explains that although idols are generally nothing, they can become gateways by which the demonic can impact devotees of that particular idol (2016, 38).

This does not lead to an entirely negative assessment of world religions. Hughes argues that every religion has aspects of truth to it, utilizing the concepts of 'common grace' and 'general revelation' to express this view. The former refers to God's continuing goodness to people despite their rebellion against him, and the latter says that the nature of God can be discerned from observation of creation (2016, 40–1). This means that Christians can, and should, learn about other faith traditions, building relationships of love and understanding, primarily for the purpose of enabling the most accurate and accessible communication of the gospel of Jesus Christ, through both word and action. Hughes discusses Justin Martyr's concept of the *Logos spermatikos*, the 'seeds of the Word' that some of the inclusivist or pluralist authors discussed above take to be present in all religious traditions as preparation for them to receive Christ. Hughes rejects this approach, noting that Justin Martyr failed to convince his Roman audience, and was indeed martyred for his faith (2016, 44–5).

In the course of an examination of the relationship between religion, faith and culture, Hughes argues that acceptance of the Christian faith potentially involves a radical redirection of lifestyle. Thus, Hughes suggests that while a Muslim who converts to Christianity might be able to continue using prayer beads to remind him of the names of God, other unspecified 'traditional practices' might be deemed unacceptable (2016, 50). Hughes is clear on the importance of contextualization, 'adapting the gospel to a non-Christian culture' (2016, 52), which includes, of course, modern British culture.

He gives examples of how contextualized outreach can be done, but the overriding imperative is that people must make a verbal profession of faith in Jesus, or else they are eternally lost. Hughes discusses the Mahaba network with approval, regarding it as a way of showing unconditional love to Muslims through prayer and outreach. He also notes the cultural barriers that many from other faith backgrounds would face on entering a church, such as not taking their shoes off, sitting on chairs not the floor, physical posture and the lack of reverence for holy books (2016, 65). Hughes goes on to examine the impact of conversion on the wider family, giving an example of the ostracism that converts experience and the role of 'insider movements' where people become followers of Jesus but do not leave their cultural tradition (2016, 82–3). He stresses the importance of hospitality for converts, of understanding their cultural background and working hard to care for them.

For Hughes, evangelical Christians can engage in dialogue but they must be clear that their aim should be both proclamation of Christ and also loving, respectful listening to the dialogue partner to understand and appreciate their perspective and position. Dialogue may be polemical, designed around the process known as Scriptural Reasoning, or to build community understanding and relationship. When he discusses education, Hughes calls for evangelical Christians to become more actively involved in the sector, and similarly when he reflects on politics he urges greater confidence and engagement at all levels of politics to ensure that an authentic evangelical Christian voice is heard among the many other competing voices.

Pause

What resonates with your understanding of the Christian faith? What is different? Does this change or confirm your own perspective?

Harold A. Netland

In his book *Dissonant Voices*, Harold Netland argues the case for an evangelical, exclusivist understanding of Christianity. He begins with a survey of the fact and nature of religious pluralism, including an extensive discussion of the shift within Christian theology from an exclusivist towards inclusivist and pluralist understandings of Christian faith. Netland sets out reasons why Christian exclusivism might be rejected and clarifies his understanding of the term, explaining that he does not regard all the claims of other religions as false, or that they are entirely without value. Netland proposes that Christian exclusivism is just one example of many types of religious exclusivism, illustrating his point with extensive discussion of Hindu, Buddhist, Islamic and Shinto views. Netland's argument is that not only do all four faiths make mutually incompatible claims about the nature of reality but that the difference is not simply doctrinal, it also relates to lifestyle and interaction with wider society. His argument is that evangelical Christian exclusivism is a more faithful exposition of Christian faith than inclusivist or pluralist views, and more intellectually honest because it recognizes its incompatibility with other worldviews.

Netland spends much of his volume discussing the nature of religious truth. He defends the view that propositional truth claims are fundamental to religious worldviews, arguing against the notion that personal truth is foundational. Netland develops ten criteria for evaluating religious truth claims, rejecting relativism in any form as logically and intellectually incoherent. His final main chapter discusses views about Jesus, and includes his categorization of four possible evangelical exclusivist views on the fate of those who do not accept Jesus as Lord and Saviour. These are, first, that only by consciously and explicitly responding to the proclaimed gospel of Jesus Christ can one be saved. Second is a theoretical understanding that some who have never heard the gospel can be saved, coupled with a refusal to speculate on who, choosing instead to leave it to the mystery of God's sovereign justice. Third is a willingness to speculate, encapsulated in an argument that just as some people were *chronologically* before Christ, others might be *informationally* before Christ, and so could potentially be saved. Fourth, those who die without having had an opportunity to respond to Christ are given a chance, either at death or immediately afterwards (1991, 265–77). Finally, Netland argues that evangelicals should participate in interreligious dialogue, especially in informal conversations with friends and neighbours, and in favour of tolerance, understood as respecting the right of others to practise their faith in freedom, without experiencing harassment or hostility. Throughout *Dissonant Voices*, Netland engages with a range of theological and philosophical positions that are at odds with his own. His most extensive interaction is with the writings of John Hick and Paul Knitter, demonstrating a willingness to engage in uncomfortable conversations.

Netland updates and expands his arguments in a later book, *Christianity and Religious Diversity*. He begins with a definitional discussion in relation to the concepts of religion, culture and worldview, before discussing secularization, globalization and religion from the Enlightenment onwards. Netland illustrates the changing nature of religions through a discussion of how Buddhism has developed and adapted to different contexts, both in Asia and in North America and Europe. His point is that no religion can be described as timeless or unchanging, a point he further illustrates through his discussion of a range of different perspectives on the person of Jesus.

In the second half of the book, Netland returns to the topic of *Dissonant Voices*. He engages in an extensive discussion of religious pluralism, which he rejects, primarily through a critical engagement with the writings of John Hick. Netland refreshes his arguments for Christianity as the one true religion, emphasizing that this is a truth claim, not a moral judgement, and explaining the Christological basis for his conviction. The final chapter brings the freshest material. Netland explains how he expects Christians to live in a multifaith world, living out both their commitment to the Lordship of Christ and also a desire to be sensitive and respectful to others as they share that belief. Netland argues that Christians must demonstrate God's love in how they treat others, acting with humility and moral integrity, engaging in interreligious dialogue as well as in proclamation of the Gospel.

Pause

What resonates with your understanding of the Christian faith? What is different? Does this change or confirm your own perspective?

Andrew Smith

In *Vibrant Christianity in Multifaith Britain* Andrew Smith begins by suggesting that many Christians view the world through what he terms 'the spiritual scale' which moves from good through neutral and dodgy to bad (2018, 12). Many activities, such as shopping or going on holiday, are viewed as neutral, while entering the place of worship of another faith community is dodgy at best and perhaps altogether bad, requiring prayer for spiritual protection. Smith explains that he is very happy for people to pray before entering a place of worship, but adds that in his experience visits to such places do not lead to people sliding into sin or experiencing spiritual attack. Moreover, he regards the spiritual scale as an inaccurate way to view the world, suggesting that reality is far more complex, with any action potentially having both spiritually positive and negative aspects.

Smith shapes his theological reflections around the two greatest commandments, to love God and love our neighbour. By holding the two in tension we can remain faithful to Jesus while also loving all those around us, regardless of their faith or belief background. Thus he suggests that the 'more we are confident in our love for God, the greater love we can have for our neighbours as we see them as made in the image of God and loved by him' (2018, 23). He is also clear that love will lead to action. We can respect someone at a distance, but if we genuinely love them then we will act in ways that benefit them, taking the initiative to reach out even if we are not loved back (2018, 24–5). Smith builds on the picture in Philippians 2 and John 13 of Jesus acting as a servant, noting that in Matthew 25, those who are commended simply acted for the good of those they served without expecting any result or reward.

Regarding issues of salvation, Smith moves from a binary world of us versus them, to a more nuanced, complex, messy picture. Drawing on passages such as Luke 10.25–37 and Matthew 25, Smith argues that the New Testament does not allow us to insist on binary categories, support- ing this claim with examples of profound experiences of God that he and others have had while in places of worship of other faith communities. The example he gives from his own experience is sitting in the Sikh Golden Temple in Amritsar at 11.30 p.m. watching volunteers enthusias- tically but silently cleaning the building thoroughly while listening to their fellow Sikhs singing from the Sikh scriptures, the Guru Granth Sahib. For Smith, this experience made him link the role of a servant with a life of worship in a way he had never managed to do before. He concludes his discussion of salvation by returning to the question of who is going to heaven, arguing that the decision is ultimately down to God, but salvation is guaranteed to those who have faith in Jesus, there is punishment for the wicked and there is 'the tantalising possibility of salvation for others who haven't heard or who are following Jesus' example without explicitly being a disciple of Jesus' (2018, 47).

Regarding evangelism, Smith was pivotal in producing the Christian Muslim Forum's guidelines for ethical witness (discussed in greater detail in Chapter 5 below). He advocates a friendship-based, conversational approach to evangelism, urging Christians to reflect on the impact con- version has on a family and worshipping community before they engage in trying to convert anyone to Christianity. Smith suggests that simply trying to win intellectual arguments will not make much of a difference; Christians should be primarily relational in their approach. He also advocates dialogue, and taking active steps to build peace among those who disagree with each other. He suggests that Christians should engage in peacemaking as a normal part of their discipleship, both within and between communities and groups they engage with. He recognizes that evangelism, dialogue and peacemaking are all interconnected activities that cannot necessarily be artificially distinguished from each other, but also suggests that each has distinctive aims and emphases.

Smith's main argument is that 'encountering, befriending and sharing faith with Sikhs, Hindus, Muslims and others is not a job just for professional interfaith workers or cross-cultural missionaries. It is a task for the whole Church, for leaders and congregations, young and old' (2018, 108). The expectation is that all will be engaged in a form of intentional outreach, sharing Jesus in a way that can genuinely be heard as good news.

Pause

What resonates with your understanding of the Christian faith? What is different? Does this change or confirm your own perspective?

Daniel Strange

Daniel Strange's book *For Their Rock is Not as Our Rock* is a reformed evangelical theology of religions relying heavily on the Dutch reformed scholars J. H. Bavinck, Hendrik Kraemer and Cornelius Van Til in particular. The central thesis of the book, which is regularly restated, is that:

> From the presupposition of an epistemologically authoritative biblical revelation, non-Christian religions are sovereignly directed, variegated and dynamic, collective human idolatrous responses to divine revelation behind which stand deceiving demonic forces. Being antithetically against yet parasitically dependent upon the truth of the Christian worldview, non-Christian religions are 'subversively fulfilled' in the gospel of Jesus Christ. (2014, 42)

Strange helpfully begins with a short autobiography, explaining his personal perspective, something I recognize as being crucial for establishing strong relationships within and across faith boundaries. Strange writes as an evangelical, for evangelicals, based on his conviction that evangelical theology of religions is underdeveloped and requires further work. He argues that the Christian God is distinct from creation, and that creation is dependent upon God for its continued existence; humanity is created in the image of God, which includes a religious nature that is only fulfilled by entering into relationship with the 'self-contained ontological Trinity, *the* living God of the Bible' (2014, 71, italics original). The fallen nature of humanity means the Creator–created distinction has become blurred, as people pull the divine down to their level and try to elevate themselves to the level of the divine.

Strange develops the concept of 'remnantal revelation' as a means of understanding other religious traditions; this partial glimpse of the divine, which has been distorted over time, explains why different faith and belief positions exhibit resonances with Christianity. The story of Babel provides Strange with the key theological resource, as he regards it as providing a historical and theological account of the origin and diversity of false religion. Strange also discusses the idolatry of the religious other in both the Old and New Testaments, arguing that 'idolatry is perhaps the hermeneutical master key with which to unlock the nature of non-Christian religion and religions' (2014, 156). Strange argues that this idolatry has four sources: 'imaginal' or 'intuitional' revelation, coming from the imago Dei; 'remnantal' revelation, rooted in humanity before the fall; 'influential' revelation, that is, the impact of the Judaeo-Christian worldview; and 'demonic' revelation (2014, 246–60). He develops his case that this idolatry is subversively fulfilled in the gospel of Jesus Christ, which contradicts, confronts and condemns all other religious perspectives. Strange argues that this understanding should act as motivation for Christians to be appropriately sensitive yet bold in their proclamation of the gospel. He utilizes Paul's experience in Athens as a biblical example of subversive fulfilment (2014, 285–94) and reinforces this with a contemporary example in his discussion of Sunni Islam (2014, 294–300). Strange concludes with a call to evangelical Christians both to increase their knowledge of lived world religions and to demonstrate their love for those who are part of those traditions.

Pause

What resonates with your understanding of the Christian faith? What is different? Does this change or confirm your own perspective?

The attraction of exclusivism

The strongest attraction of exclusivism is probably the certainty that it offers. The borders appear clear and the position stands on the historic teaching of the Church. God reveals himself in Christian Scripture and in the person of Jesus Christ. The rest is outside of his activity, and can be attributed to the world, the weakness of humanity or the demonic.

Conclusion

You may have found yourself very attracted to one of these three positions, of exclusivism, inclusivism or pluralism, or even to the work of one particular author. But you may find yourself still unsure as to what you think. That's fine. The point of this chapter is to help you begin to think a bit further, without forcing you to a settled opinion. Many of the authors discussed above do not fit into any of the three categories neatly. Other authors do not even try. To give one example, in *Deep Equality in an Era of Religious Diversity*, Lori Beaman argues that conceptions of accommodation and tolerance mask privilege and power. Hence, we must move beyond these superficial engagements to deep equality, which understands religious identity to be both fluid and contextual and makes space for those who have no religious worldview. Beaman argues that the day-to-day interactions of most 'ordinary' people tend not to emphasize religious difference, and hence religious identity is not even necessarily the primary marker of identity. She is critical of 'Christianity's tendency to imagine itself as representative of everyone, even when they themselves do not find themselves adequately or at all represented' (2017, 64), arguing that rather than engage in terms of similarity or difference, we must think in terms of deep equality. This will produce a shared solidarity that acts for the good of all, regardless of the power or status of any individual. Beaman's pluralism is not especially interested in questions of salvation but rather it is concerned with the pragmatic realities of daily life. Her argument for deep equality is centred on the subject of power; who is in charge, and how do they use that authority? She advocates understanding everyone on their own terms and building relationships of genuine reciprocity, recognizing that everyone has something to gain from the partnership.

Taking another perspective, Matthew Kaemingk, as shown in Chapter 1, is a salvific exclusivist who argues at length for political pluralism. In a not dissimilar way, Newbigin explains his own understanding in relation to the three-fold typology as follows:

The position which I have outlined is exclusivist in the sense that it affirms the unique truth of the revelation in Jesus Christ, but it is not exclusivist in the sense of denying the possibility of the salvation of the non-Christian. It is inclusivist in the sense that it refuses to limit the saving grace of God to members of the Christian church, but it rejects the inclusivism which regards the non-Christian religions as vehicles of salvation. It is pluralist in the sense of acknowledging the gracious work of God in the lives of all human beings, but it rejects a pluralism which denies the uniqueness and decisiveness of what God has done in Jesus Christ. (1989, 183)

The purpose of the above brief literature review has been to introduce a selection of contemporary Christian theological reflections on interfaith engagement, with the purpose of enabling the reader to reflect person-ally on the issue. The point about epistemological exclusivity should be abundantly clear. To illustrate with one example, while Strange argues that religions other than Christianity are 'sovereignly directed, variegated and dynamic, collective human idolatrous responses to divine revelation behind which stand deceiving demonic forces' (2014, 42), Yong declares that 'the religions of the world, like everything else that exists, are providentially sustained by the Spirit of God for divine purposes' since 'all human endeavours reflect either God's permissive or active will toward ultimately divine purposes centred around the full revelation of Jesus Christ and the impending kingdom of God' (2003, 46).

This is the fundamental question for deciding how to engage with people of other faiths. Do you believe that the faith they adhere to is guided and shaped by the Spirit of God? Or is it the realm of the demonic? Or to some extent both? For some Christians this is, of course, completely the wrong question, as not everyone engages with the world in such precise spiritual terms. For others, it misses the point by not being focused on relationships in the here-and-now. But it is nevertheless a question to reflect on, asking which position you hold and the implications of holding it. And whatever view you hold, how can you fulfil the two great commandments to love God and love your neighbour in relation to engagement with people of other faiths?

Note

1 www.independent.co.uk/news/uk/politics/get-with-the-programme-david-cameron-condemns-church-of-england-decision-to-block-women-bishops-8340352.html (accessed 17 June 2018).

3

What does the Bible say?

Having established something of the why and who of interfaith relations, in this chapter I turn to 'what': specifically, what the Bible says. I examine ten Bible passages, five from the Old Testament and five from the New, that are often used in discussions of interfaith relations. The threads of discussion are organized under the three themes of hospitality, service and proclamation introduced in Chapter 1, exploring the creative tension that exists between these themes. The ten passages are: Abram's call and his hospitality of the visitors at Mamre (Genesis 12 and 18); Ruth's acceptance into the people of God; Elijah's ministry, especially his care of the widow of Zarephath and his confrontation of the prophets of Baal (1 Kings 17–18); Elisha's healing and welcome of Naaman (2 Kings 5); Jonah's mission to Nineveh; Jesus and the centurion's servant (Matthew 8.5–13); the parable of the good Samaritan (Luke 10.25–37); Jesus' conversation with the Samaritan woman (John 4); John 14.6; and Paul in Athens (Acts 17) and his argument in Romans 9—11.

Abram/Abraham

Abram's call (Genesis 12)

Scholars debate the transition from Genesis 11 to Genesis 12. Some argue that there is a shift from a sort of 'proto-history' or foundational myths about the creation of the world to a more fully fledged historical narrative. Other scholars argue that Genesis 12 is just a natural progression of what came before. Thus Gordon Wenham (1987, 267) comments that 12.1 presumes the genealogical information supplied in 11.27–32. Whichever view you hold, most people would recognize the event recorded in the opening verses of Genesis 12 as being of incredible significance for the history of the world. More people on the planet today owe their religious faith to Abraham's decision to say 'yes' to God's call than to any other single event in the whole of human history.

First, notice the promise Abram receives. He will be blessed so that he in turn may become a blessing, he will receive in order to be able to give. This movement, from receipt to gift, from being blessed to blessing others, lies at the heart of all religious activity, not least how we engage with those whose faith is very different from our own. Everyone lives out their faith in their own particular way. All the great religions have teachings that the religion's followers adhere to. But each of us is a unique individual, born in particular circumstances, brought up in a particular way and now living in a particular place. Much of what most Christians do when they pray, for example, is similar but not necessarily identical. However we live out our faith, I believe that having been blessed, having received the grace of God, we should then share that grace with others.

Abram was obedient to God's call, even though it was costly. As a nomad, he was perhaps more able to travel than some people. But there is a difference between living out a nomadic lifestyle while still in relationship with your wider family and deliberately choosing to separate yourself from them by travelling hundreds of miles into unknown territory. As Wenham comments, 'Abram is to give up all he holds dearest for an unknown land promised by God' (1987, 274).

Abram heard the Lord calling him, recognized that this was God speaking and so chose to act. My challenge today is to discern when it is God who is calling me, and when it is the spirit of the age or my own selfish desires or another person's flawed understanding. How do I know that I am truly within God's will? If I am honest, I can never be completely certain whether some of my choices are the ones God wants me to make, but I can have a degree of certainty, and I can be aware if I am deliberately choosing to act outside of God's will. Maybe one of the key challenges of relating to people of other faiths is discerning what God is calling you to do, how he wants you to balance the Christian imperatives of hospitality, service and proclamation.

The purpose of this short series of reflections is to enable you to think a bit more about how God wants us to relate to people whose faith is not like ours. What happens when the people of God encounter those outside of God's people? What attitudes do they display? What problems do they face? What do they show us that we should imitate? Do they do anything that we would now see as problematic? We all live out our faith from our own perspective and our own experiences, and I have written these reflections from my own viewpoint. I am an evangelical Christian by conviction, convinced that the best thing anyone in the world can have is a relationship with God through Jesus Christ in the power of his Holy Spirit. I know that many people do not share this belief, and also that I have much to learn from everyone I encounter. These reflections are a part of my learning, as I read the Bible and reflect and pray on how it is that God would have me love my neighbour as myself.

Sometimes how Abram behaves towards those who are different from him is very indicative of the normal human emotions, for example fear in the face of the foreign. Thus when he goes to Egypt he instructs his wife Sarai to pretend that she is his sister (Genesis 12.10–13). Wenham suggests that Abram feared that as a migrant with no family connections he was particularly vulnerable to exploitation in a land where, in contrast to Canaan with its Semitic tongue, even the language was completely foreign to him (1987, 288). Is our natural first reaction to an encounter with difference to be afraid? Is there any possibility of our deciding to overcome our fear that those who are not like us will want to kill us because of who we are or what we have? Abram here seems all too human, all too frail, all too lacking in faith in the God who called him and who says Abram will be a father of many nations. Abram has no children yet, and for the Lord's promise to be fulfilled then both he and Sarai must survive. So Abram ought to have had some confidence that going to Egypt was not a death sentence. But he chose faith in himself, not God. Abram's motivation is unclear. Wenham suggests that he is pretending to be her brother in an attempt to fend off potential suitors by promises of marriage without actually giving her away (1987, 288), while John Walton (2001, 396) argues that we cannot understand Abram's motivation and it is foolish to speculate. I do not say that to rebuke Abram or to claim superiority, but rather to challenge myself. When I encounter those who are religiously or otherwise different from me, what do I do? Fortunately for Abram, things turned out better than he expected; Pharaoh's house is cursed when he tries to take Sarai as his own and so Pharaoh returns Sarai to Abram, who is free to go on his way (Genesis 12.14–20).

Turning to the three themes that guide my reflections on these passages, notice that Abram is afraid to become a guest; the normal conventions and rules of hospitality do not appear to apply. There is also no desire to serve anyone and a hope that proclamation can be avoided, but circumstances force Abram to be clear who it is he serves.

Pause

- What am I looking for when I encounter those who are very different from myself?

> • How does my instinct for self-preservation impair my ability to relate to others? Are there ways in which it is making a positive difference?
> • How can I be generous in how I receive others?

Abraham at Mamre (Genesis 18.1–8)

In time Abram became Abraham, and while the promise of blessing remained, he did not yet have a son. So Abram took matters into his own hands (or rather, into his wife's maidservant Hagar's womb) and Ishmael was born. Abram still had a lot to learn about how to live out trust in God's promises, a challenge I recognize in my own life as well. The debate over whether Isaac or Ishmael was the heir of blessing is an ongoing controversy that I will not tackle in this reflection. Indeed, Isaac has not yet been born in the passage we look at next. Rather, I reflect on Abraham's offer of hospitality, on how many people he encounters and what he teaches us about welcoming others.

The first thing I noticed about Genesis 18.1–8 is that these events take place in the heat of the day, the time when most people would be resting, doing little or nothing because it is too hot to be at all active. But Abraham is in a hurry, rushing because his guests must be cared for. Whoever they are, nothing but the best will do. There is a challenge to our casual attitudes to visitors, some of whom we may regard as more of an inconvenience than a blessing. When someone comes to see me and I am in a hurry, or busy, or it is not a good time to care for them, what do I do?

A second interpretative question is about exactly who it is that comes to visit Abraham. The first two sentences set up a puzzle. The Lord appears, and then Abraham looks and sees three men. Does this refer to two distinct groups? The former Chief Rabbi, Jonathan Sacks, suggests that it does and furthermore that Abraham keeps God waiting in order to be hospitable.[1] His view depends on how the Hebrew of Genesis 18.3 is translated, in particular whether *adonay* should be translated as 'my Lord' (as in God) or 'my lords' (as a reference to the three strangers). The verb *ta'abor*, to pass by, is in the singular, but the reference to washing feet and resting is plural. Sacks takes Abraham's comment as indicating a request that God wait while he attends to the needs of the three strangers who have just arrived. If this is right, then the challenge about hospitality becomes even more acute. The scenario is this: God has shown up, and at the same time so have three other visitors. Would I ask God to wait while

I run about in the heat of the day, putting my health at risk, in order to make sure my visitors have everything they need?

Not all commentators agree with Sacks' interpretation. There is a long Christian tradition of seeing the angel of the Lord within the concept of a 'Christophany', that is, an appearance of Jesus Christ in human form before he is incarnate as the Son of Mary. If you follow this interpretation, it is important to recognize that this is a Christian apologetic agenda being pushed onto the text, rather than the original intention of the author, who probably understood the angel of the Lord to serve as a representative of God (see discussion in Walton 2001, 462–6). This appearance at the oaks of Mamre may be one such Christophany, but it may also be the case that Yahweh has to wait while the physical needs of visitors are met.

The hospitality Abraham shows here is exemplary; he is a man of means who is prepared to give the best to his guests, even humbling himself in service of them. In this incident, there is no direct proclamation of the God whom Abraham serves; while the text has hints of theophany, there is no suggestion that Abraham is aware of this fact.

Pause

- Which interpretation of the identity of the visitors do you find most persuasive?
- What does this passage teach you about being host to those of other faiths?
- What does this passage teach you about being a guest to those of other faiths?

Ruth

The people of God are expected to show hospitality to those in need. The injunction to care for the widow, the orphan and the resident alien is a regular imperative of Old Testament law (for example in Leviticus 19.9–10, 33–34; Deuteronomy 10.18–19; 24.17–22). The assumption behind these laws is that since the people of Israel were themselves resident aliens in Egypt, they will remember that experience, and it will motivate a sympathetic response to those who are now in a similar plight (Baker 2009).

Ruth is from Moab, the widow of an Israelite, who returns to Israel with her Israelite mother-in-law. They have no means of support, so initially Ruth provides for them by gleaning, gathering the scraps of grain overlooked by those harvesting (in accordance with provision made in Deuteronomy 24.17–22). The field where she gathers grain belongs to Boaz, a close relative of her late husband. In accordance with the Levirate law (Deuteronomy 25.5–10), Boaz redeems Ruth and takes her as his wife after the only closer relative declines to take responsibility for her. As both a widow and a resident alien, Ruth fits two of the three categories selected for special concern, and thus her treatment indicates Israelite hospitality at its very best.

In contrast with the story of Abraham, Ruth takes the initiative to avail herself of Israelite hospitality. When her mother-in-law Naomi announces her intention to return from Moab, Ruth insists she will go with her, and that nothing will separate them, but Naomi's God will be Ruth's God (Ruth 1.16–17). Furthermore it is Ruth, having received guidance from Naomi, who takes the initiative in going to the field belonging to Boaz (chapter 2), and going to see him at night (chapter 3). Her nocturnal visit to Boaz is the subject of much speculation among commentators, but whatever the details of what went on, Ruth's actions emphasize a different aspect of hospitality, namely that sometimes the guest must show initiative and work to attract the attention of the host.

The story of Ruth presents the Christian reader with three significant challenges when read with interreligious relations in mind. The first is the character of Ruth. She is an outsider to the people of God, but her actions display a remarkable faith in Yahweh. Against all logic, she first chooses to travel with Naomi rather than stay in her home country and seek a husband there. When she comes to Bethlehem she is primarily interested in caring for Naomi, and is obedient to Naomi's plan. When she has the option of finding a second husband, she looks primarily for a godly man who displays integrity and faithfulness to Israel's God.

The second converse challenge comes from the unnamed character Boaz asks to see if he is interested in redeeming Naomi's land. The land is tempting, but the responsibility for Naomi and Ruth is not, and so he rejects his right to redeem (Ruth 4.1–8). Frederic Bush calls him 'Mr So-and-so' and suggests that he is left nameless because of his irrelevance to Ruth's redemption (1996, 196). He is a member of God's people, but his brief appearance suggests that he is not interested in obeying God's commandments. He is primarily interested in his own success and financial security. Ruth and this unnamed man together challenge the human tendency to pigeonhole people, to erect barriers and fences, to divide into 'us' and 'them'. These lines are easily drawn in interreligious relations, and not necessarily along the lines of a particular faith. For some Christians it is easier to find more in common with people of a different faith who are temperamentally like them than it is to relate to other Christians with whom they profoundly disagree. What lines am I drawing, and are they ones that would meet with divine approval?

The third and biggest challenge comes from the character of Boaz. Here is a godly man who is overwhelmingly generous, a man of peace who looks for where the Lord is working in the world, blesses that work and endeavours to become part of it. Where do I see the Lord at work in those around me, both those of the Christian tradition and those outside of it? How do I respond to that work?

None of this suggests syncretism nor a one size covers everything lowest common denominator pluralism. When I read Ruth I see a loyalty to the Lord's commands that is lived out by those who are nominally inside and nominally outside of the Lord's people. I also see a failure to follow those commands from those who ought to know better. The challenge from Ruth, as indeed from many interreligious friendships today, is that we can all too easily assume that we know where and how God is at work. We do know much of his character and therefore much of how we might expect him to work, but he does still have the capacity to surprise us by working in unexpected places. The story of Ruth also exemplifies hospitality and service at both their best and their worst. Ruth is unstinting in her service of Naomi, and Boaz in his hospitality of Ruth; yet Mr So-and-so (to use Bush's phrase) shows no hospitality towards nor service of his fellow Israelite Naomi. Finally, Ruth proclaims her faith in Yahweh not only in what she says to Naomi but also in how she lives out that commitment, putting herself at risk in order that her mother-in-law might be cared for.

Pause
- Have I encountered people outside the Christian family who display the character of Ruth?
- Have I behaved like Mr So-and-so to those outside the Christian family?
- Have I behaved like Boaz towards those outside the Christian family?

Elijah

I now examine two incidents that hold the themes of hospitality, service and proclamation in tension: the famine in 1 Kings 17 and the confrontation with the prophets of Baal in 1 Kings 18.

Famine in the land (1 Kings 17)

The abrupt appearance of Elijah at the start of 1 Kings 17 is a challenge to Ahab's devotion to Baal. He brings a stark message: the Lord is going to inflict the covenant curses upon Israel for her covenant breaking. Moses had warned the people:

> Be careful, or you will be enticed to turn away and worship other gods and bow down to them. Then the Lord's anger will burn against you, and he will shut up the heavens so that it will not rain and the ground will yield no produce, and you will soon perish from the good land the Lord is giving you. (Deuteronomy 11.16–17)

The absence of rain is a particular challenge to worshippers of Baal. As Aaron Chalmer points out:

> Baal was a great storm god who possessed power over the weather and was responsible for bringing the seasonal rains. By extension, he was considered to be in control of the fertility of the fields as this was dependent on the rain he supplied. (2012, 106)

The challenge of 1 Kings 17 is clear: is it Yahweh or Baal who controls the weather? The one who controls the rain is the one who should be worshipped. Although in the UK we like to moan when it rains, the reality is we would die without it. When I travelled in Uganda I was told that if it rains after you arrive somewhere you are said to have brought a blessing, because rain makes the crops grow, refills the water butts and streams and means that life is possible. In ancient Israel, as in modern Uganda, rain gives life, and a three-year drought spells death, the punishment for ignoring the Lord.

Having given his warning, Elijah then departs (1 Kings 17.1). Some might think this was because of a threat to his life. It is certainly true that Jezebel is a danger to true followers of Yahweh, but that has not yet become obvious in the text. It is likely that Elijah conceals himself as a sign that the Lord's word has departed from Israel (Davis 2003, 209).

They have chosen Baal, so they will be left in Baal's care. Yahweh's word – and his provision – remains with his prophet, who for the moment is safe and cared for in the Wadi Cherith (17.2–6).

Consider Elijah's situation. He is alone, with only a twice-daily visit from a raven for company. Presumably the bird carries food in its beak, and vomits it back to Elijah for him to eat. Even if it was somehow carried whole, it is unlikely to have been that appetizing. Elijah is provided for, but his situation is far from comfortable or easy. But he still has a task to complete for Yahweh, and so he is preserved.

When God's people desert him, the first duty of the true disciple is to remain faithful and to call those people to repentance. Proclamation of the good news of Jesus, by words and lifestyle, is the duty of every Christian disciple. But before reaching out, we must examine our own hearts and our own walk with the Lord, ensuring that we are committed to him above all else. God's word is not to be treated lightly, but must be taken seriously, for he controls all of creation. Having said that, we must be wary of equating natural disasters, or those of human making, as clear and direct consequences of a specific act of disobedience. Jesus makes that clear when he heals the man born blind (John 9.3). The Lord is sovereign over history, not us, and he directs events. The whole of the Elijah story has a subtext of the superiority of Yahweh, and the error of choosing to worship other gods. Yet at the same time Yahweh's chosen prophet, whose very name means 'My God is Yahweh', leaves Israel and goes to an adherent of another religion for shelter (1 Kings 17.7–24).

Zarephath, a small town seven miles south of Sidon, was in the heart of Phoenicia, where Baal was worshipped (Davis 2003, 213). Elijah leaves Israel, the land of those who serve Yahweh, and goes into foreign territory, to the land where Baal is said to rule. Here he receives aid from the most unlikely of sources. Widows were usually poor; with no man to bring in income, all this woman had left was whatever resources of her household remained. Hers are nearly at an end: she has only enough for one final meal before she and her son starve to death.

Notice that the widow answers in Yahweh's name. Maybe she has recognized Elijah as an Israelite. Maybe she has some incipient faith in the Lord before she meets Elijah, although she refers to Yahweh as Elijah's God, not her own. The text does not give a clear answer. What we do learn is that she trusts Elijah's word enough to do what he says, and her faith is rewarded. She and her son host Elijah and in return their own lives are preserved. This is not a one-off, but a miracle of continuous provision, and so of continuous faith and grace. Each day the widow, her son and Elijah rely solely on Yahweh's generosity to provide their daily bread.

But then tragedy strikes: her son dies. She assumes that the presence of a holy man of Yahweh has brought punishment upon her for her sins. Her fledgling faith in Yahweh stumbles and falls to the ground. Can she dare to believe in him? She has to trust. Elijah takes the boy from her. He has just died, his corpse still warm, and Elijah simply takes him away. She must have been in agony.

But upstairs, Elijah is praying. He cries out to Yahweh. He knows he can do nothing by himself, nothing in his own strength. It is Yahweh who gives life, Yahweh who takes it away. He begs for the boy's life, and his prayer is answered. His mother's faith soars again, on eagle's wings now, rising high. She has learnt that Yahweh's ways are beyond her understanding, but that he cares for her (Davis 2003, 213–27).

Jesus refers to this incident in his sermon at Nazareth. Reminding the crowd that prophets do not receive honour in their own country, he tells them:

> I assure you that there were many widows in Israel in Elijah's time, when the sky was shut for three and a half years and there was a severe famine throughout the land. Yet Elijah was not sent to any of them, but to a widow in Zarephath in the region of Sidon. (Luke 4.25–26)

The point is clear, and Jesus' audience understand it well enough as they try to stone him (Luke 4.28–29). The people of God rejected God's word, so his word went out beyond the borders of ethnic Israel to those who had faith in him. The Lord is not parochial or territorial. He gathers people to himself from many faiths and nations. But it seems to be entirely on the Lord's own terms. This nuances the discussion of hospitality; ultimately it is God who is providing for everyone's needs, and although the widow and Elijah serve each other, they do so with the gifts God has given them. Elijah also proclaims his faith by who he is as much as by what he says, and the widow responds with gratitude, but also with anger when her son dies.

Who is God in Israel? (1 Kings 18)

1 Kings 18 asks a simple question: who is God? It gives a simple answer: Yahweh (much of what follows below is based on the exposition in Davis 2003, 229–45). The chapter begins by introducing Obadiah, a faithful servant of the Lord in the most unlikely of places: Ahab's court. You might have expected that only those loyal to Baal would have dared to

serve there, but Obadiah is resolute. He defies Jezebel, Ahab's queen, and saves Yahweh's prophets at great personal risk.

Obadiah stands as a challenging contrast with Ahab. The king is only interested in preserving his possessions. Notice how he is prepared to go anywhere through the land and take anything he finds in order to ensure that his horses survive. No mention of caring for his subjects, he just looks after his own needs. Obadiah serves Yahweh from a difficult position in court, presenting us with an interesting paradigm to ponder. To what extent can a Christian work for those whose actions and motivations are antithetical to God's? Where should lines be drawn? What level of personal risk should we take?

I understand Obadiah's reluctance to go to Ahab to mean that he is unsure whether Elijah will still be there when he gets back with Ahab. I do not think Obadiah is afraid of death so much as of a needless death. He asks, why should I go and tell Ahab where you are if I am not certain you'll still be here? Won't Yahweh's Spirit spirit you away? Then I'll be executed for no reason. I have not walked this tightrope for so long, saved all those prophets just to throw it all away, he seems to imply. I will stand up to the king, but I only take carefully calculated risks, not silly ones, Obadiah explains. I take that as a personal challenge: to not shy away from calculated risks for God's glory, but also to invest the time to do the calculating. It echoes Jesus' command to us to be as wise as serpents and as innocent as a dove as we are sent out like lambs among wolves (Matthew 10.16). As I noted in Chapter 1, Lesslie Newbigin talks about subverting activities for the gospel, and perhaps this is how Obadiah lived and how we are called to live.

In this case, the risk proves to be worth it. Elijah is as good as his word, faithful to his promise (modelling Yahweh's faithfulness perhaps?), and appears before Ahab. They debate who the cause of the problem is, and agree to a public showdown, with 450 of Baal's prophets on one side, Elijah the sole one of Yahweh's prophets on the other. The question is clear: who do you think is God? Make a choice.

At this point, Elijah seems quite open-minded. He simply wants the people to choose: Baal or Yahweh. The limping indecision is the problem: there should be a wholehearted commitment. A test of fire will give the answer. Remember that Elijah has come from Zarephath in Sidon, the heart of Baal worship. Davis suggests that Mount Carmel might well have been ground made sacred to Baal, which brings the challenge into sharper relief (2003, 237). The region was fertile, a logical place to challenge the identity of the real fertility god.

Once the competition is under way, Elijah becomes more sarcastic. His question about Baal being on a journey or asleep probably refers to the cult's rituals (18.27). It was believed that Baal died in the heat of summer and then blood-letting by his prophets would act as imitative magic to prompt the rain to fall. But it is all in vain. The question about him being on the toilet is a simple sarcastic put-down: who worships a deity too busy defecating to answer the frantic prayers of the faithful (see Davis 2003, 239)?

When his turn comes, Elijah is calm. He calls the people near, bringing them back into close relationship with Yahweh. They are Israel, those who struggle with God, and they must come back to him. He rebuilds their altar, timing his actions to coincide with the appointed hour for the evening sacrifice in the temple. The 12 stones and ritual dousing with water recall the 12 tribes and the crossing of the Jordan. Elijah, following the instructions given by Yahweh, offers a sacrifice. Yahweh answers with fire, and then with rain, proving his power over nature and his complete mastery of the situation. The chapter ends with a reminder to Ahab of his proper function: Elijah runs ahead of him, indicating his role serving the king. Ahab should come back to Yahweh and serve him as the anointed king of Israel.

The first challenge I draw from the text concerns religious activity. Elijah resists all showmanship. He is calm, completely trusting in Yahweh. We do not tend to dance wildly or cut ourselves to get God's attention as the prophets of Baal did (18.28), but do we sometimes try to bargain with him? Perhaps if I pray more, get more involved in church, have more singing in a service, give more to charity, then God will bless me more (see Davis 2003, 240)? Elijah lives out his faith: he knows Yahweh is faithful, not just in his head but in his heart, with his actions, in the face of a hostile crowd. How easily do I shy away from a proper confidence in Jesus when I am living and working among those who do not call him Lord?

Second, what do we make of Elijah's instruction to slaughter Baal's prophets? Davis suggests that we must understand this as Yahweh's uncompromising holiness: he will stop at nothing to draw his people to himself (2003, 244). What does this say to us today? We do not hear Yahweh's direct word to us telling us to slaughter anyone; and certainly in the New Testament Jesus does not display violent hostility towards those of other faiths whom he encounters. But the text does force us to acknowledge the reality of violence done in the name of religion, even Christianity. As Christians, do we want to distinguish between Elijah's actions, which could be regarded as somehow being sanctioned by God, and other acts of violence done in the name of Christianity, be they the crusades or any other religious violence? (See Gaston 2017, 60–5 for an account of the

Walk of Reconciliation in which Christians travelled through the Middle East apologizing for the devastation of the crusades.) I think we must repent of calls for violence, turning away from such actions, but we must hold a desire for peaceful relations with our neighbours in tension with a desire to seek God's glory above all else. Keeping the peace for the sake of lowest common denominator fuzziness has no real place in Christian discipleship.

This chapter stands in marked contrast to the one before. Obadiah's faithful service of Yahweh's prophets challenges us to think about how we serve God and his people in a complex multicultural, pluralist world. But there are no hints of hospitality in Elijah's actions here, only uncompromising proclamation through both word and action.

Pause

- What can we learn from Elijah's care of the widow and her son in 1 Kings 17?
- What can we learn from Elijah's confrontation with the prophets of Baal in 1 Kings 18?
- How do we hold these two passages in tension?

Elisha

The story of Elisha's healing of Naaman (2 Kings 5) provides a further paradigm for hospitality. Naaman is an Aramite general who is afflicted with leprosy. An Israelite slave girl suggests to Naaman's wife that if only he were to go to see the prophet Elisha in Samaria, then he would be cured. Naaman accepts the recommendation, and goes first to the capital, bearing a letter from his master, the king of Aram. The king of Israel is distraught, knowing that he cannot do anything to cure Naaman, and fears ruin and destruction will come to his kingdom. But Elisha sends for Naaman, who duly comes to his home. Yet when Naaman arrives, Elisha does not go out to greet him, flouting all the expected protocols and duties of hospitality. Instead he orders him to go and wash in the River Jordan seven times. At first Naaman is indignant and refuses to do so, but is persuaded by his servants to comply. When he has washed, he is completely healed, his skin becoming like that of a young boy.

Naaman returns to Elisha's house, and offers him all manner of gifts, which Elisha refuses. Then Naaman makes the following request:

'If you will not,' said Naaman, 'please let me, your servant, be given as much earth as a pair of mules can carry, for your servant will never again make burnt offerings and sacrifices to any other god but the Lord. But may the Lord forgive your servant for this one thing: When my master enters the temple of Rimmon to bow down and he is leaning on my arm and I have to bow there also – when I bow down in the temple of Rimmon, may the Lord forgive your servant for this.'

'Go in peace,' Elisha said. (2 Kings 5.17–19)

Commentators are divided as to the meaning behind both Naaman's request and Elisha's response. Some, for example Barrick (2000, 30–1) and Cohn (1983, 178), argue that this indicates that Naaman is now 'fully converted' and has become a worshipper of Yahweh, the God of Israel, although Briggs (2010, 159) questions whether language of 'conversion' is appropriate. Brueggemann (2007, 271) contends that Naaman is still vacillating between Yahweh and Rimmon, while Effa (2007, 309–11) and Nwaoru (2008, 36) suggest that he is as committed to Yahweh as is practical, and his requests indicate the pragmatic response of a realist who knows the level of worship he will be able to offer. I find this final alternative the most convincing and propose that Naaman, having been healed, now has a new understanding of Yahweh and is committing to him, and he is in the process of working out how he can display this commitment in his everyday life.

The commentators all agree that Elisha did not explicitly condone Naaman's requests, but some (Effa 2007, 311; Briggs 2010, 155; Ngan 1997, 593) argue that a blessing of God's peace indicates tacit approval at least, a view with which I would concur. Naaman did not come to Elisha filled with peace, but now he goes away in peace, physically healed and so able to participate fully in society, in a right relationship with both Elisha and with Yahweh, the God Elisha serves.

This story is used by some Christian missiologists (for example Barrick 2000; Effa 2007; Nwaoru 2008) to argue that Christian missionaries should neither impose nor prohibit particular practices on converts to Christianity, which is therefore understood more in terms of orthodoxy than orthopraxy. This has implications for how Christians might engage in outreach with those of other faiths, suggesting that we must allow seekers to engage at whatever level they see fit (see the discussion in Greenlee 2013 in relation to Muslim converts to Christianity). Just as Naaman decides how he will engage with Yahweh, so too those who come to church are left free to choose how to engage with the Christianity they encounter. Furthermore, just as Naaman receives healing before he makes any declaration of any sort of faith, so all who come to us receive the best possible care regardless of their stance towards Christianity. Thus Christian hospitality is practised: the guests receive what they have come to the host for, but by entering into relationship with the host they also have access to other areas of the host's life, in particular Christian worship. This story balances all three themes that are being used to guide these reflections. Elisha does serve Naaman, and offers him the hospitality he needs rather than what he wants. And as he does so Elisha also proclaims Yahweh as God, in a way that Naaman responds to in faith.

The significance of the Naaman story for Christians is emphasized in Jesus' use of Naaman as an example of a righteous foreigner. When he is explaining his mission in his 'Nazareth manifesto' Jesus observes that there were many lepers in Israel at the time of Elisha, but the only one who was cleansed was Naaman (Luke 4.27). Luke uses this example as one among many indicating that the kingdom of God is not solely the provenance of ethnic Israel, but of all who are 'God fearing'.

Pause

- What does the story of Naaman, and in particular his request to Elisha, teach us about how to engage with those of other faiths?
- Which view of Naaman's behaviour do you find the most convincing?
- What impact will this have on how you 'do church'?

Jonah

Although only a short book, Jonah presents scholars with numerous challenges. There are a number of views of the main theme. Okoye (2010) suggests four: the traditional Jewish reading of the value of repentance; a challenge to particularism, which excluded all gentiles from contact with God; a satire against prophecy; and a record of the conflict between Jonah and God. Doubtless elements of all these are present, and perhaps it is foolish simply to decide on one main theme. The book of Jonah is a lesson in the freedom and compassion of God, and a challenge to us to respond appropriately. In terms of the interpretative lenses being used in this chapter, it forces us to question our motivations and expectations related to the proclamation of God's word, and our attitude, including our desire to serve or be hospitable, towards those outside the family of faith.

The basic story of Jonah is well known: he is told to preach judgement and the need for repentance in Nineveh, but instead of heading west towards Nineveh he goes east, boarding a ship for Tarshish. A great storm arises; he admits to the sailors that he is the cause of the storm, and asks to be thrown into the sea. The sailors reluctantly agree, and do so, having prayed to the Lord asking for forgiveness for this action. The Lord provides a great fish to swallow Jonah, who repents while in the fish's stomach, and is duly vomited onto a beach. Then he goes to Nineveh. He preaches to the people, who repent and cry to God for mercy. God is merciful, but Jonah is outraged: he wanted to witness destruction. He goes to the outskirts of the city and sits down to wait. God provides a plant to shade him, but that night he provides a worm, which eats up the plant. Jonah is outraged at the destruction of the plant, which provides God with the opportunity of an object lesson: Jonah neither grew nor nurtured the plant yet he was angry. Should not God, who both grew and nurtured the people of Nineveh, care for them in their ignorance and repentance?

Jonah's experience reminds us of divine freedom, but also of God's character. He shows compassion and mercy on those who repent, and also to Jonah who stubbornly refuses to repent and accept God's plan. The book presents a great challenge to those who are secure in their own faith community and in their attitude towards those outside. The sailors' prayer for forgiveness and the Ninevites' repentance suggest some sort of relationship with the God of Israel, although the question remains as to how much this is pragmatic survival instinct and how much is devout faith (Allen 1976, 212, 223–5); Douglas Stuart notes that the sailors are not necessarily monotheists (1987, 455). It seems that those who are expected to have no faith teach the one who should have faith how to relate to God. As Stuart points out, the book is not universalistic, as it insists on repentance to avoid divine punishment (1987, 434). Jonah himself is a complex character: he is willing to be thrown to his death in the sea to spare the sailors, but refuses to accept the divine right to be merciful to the city of Nineveh.

Pause

- What does the book of Jonah teach about the freedom and compassion of God, and about how God works outside the borders of the Church?
- What does it say to the Church about how we view those who are not part of our community?

The centurion's servant (Matthew 8.5–13; Luke 7.1–10)

In discussing this miracle, where Jesus heals the centurion's servant merely by speaking a word of healing at a distance, I concentrate on the interaction between the centurion and Jesus, and not on the textual issues raised by this story regarding the identity of the one who is healed (that is, whether he is son or servant), or the relationship between the different accounts (including John 4.46–54, although it should be noted that I concur with R. T. France (2007, 309 n.28) that John records a separate incident). The core of the story, namely the great faith of a gentile, is the focal point for my analysis. It presents a challenging paradigm for hospitality, service and proclamation.

As Craig Keener (1999, 264–5) points out, a centurion would not have been a popular figure among the Jews. Keener moreover suggests that many of Matthew's first audience would have had relatives or friends who had died in the siege of Jerusalem in AD 70 or been enslaved soon afterwards. Therefore, the encounter between Jesus and the centurion is a practical outworking of Jesus' teaching that his followers should bless their enemies and pray for those who persecute them (Matthew 5.43–48; Luke 6.27–31). This context makes the encounter all the more startling. In Matthew's account, Jesus is surprised at the request that he come and bring healing, questioning the centurion, asking, 'Shall I come and heal him?' (8.7, as suggested by France 2007, 313; Keener 1999, 266; the NRSV has 8.7 as a statement of intent, but I agree with France and Keener that a question is more appropriate). In Luke there is less of a sense of surprise at the request, but both Luke and Matthew emphasize Jesus' amazement at the centurion's faith.

Two points should be clarified: why does Jesus not go to the centurion's house, and what is the exact nature of the centurion's faith? First, it seems probable that the centurion was concerned about Jewish purity laws. Not only was he a gentile, but there could potentially soon be a corpse in his house, if Jesus arrived too late (Green 1997, 284). The centurion therefore does not wish Jesus to contaminate himself through contact with two potential sources of uncleanness. Although Jesus is willing to break the social and religious taboos associated with going to the centurion's house this is unnecessary because of the man's faith.

Second, the centurion's faith is probably less about Jesus as saviour and more about Jesus as one with authority to heal, hence his analogy with his own position (France 2007, 315). He is a striking example of one who has recognized that God is at work in Jesus (Nolland 2005, 353) and would like to be part of that work.

This presents much food for reflecting on the three themes of hospitality, service and proclamation. There is some confusion in the passage as to who is guest and who is host, or to put the question differently, exactly who is serving whom. Is the centurion the host, caring for his guest's needs by saying that Jesus does not need to travel? Or is Jesus the host, welcoming the centurion into the family of God through healing the sick member of his household? Jesus undoubtedly serves the centurion through his gift of healing, but arguably the centurion also serves Jesus by not requiring him to travel and being concerned for his ritual purity. The lack of clear boundaries reflects the reality of many interfaith encounters today, when at times one may serve the other but at different times be served by the other. To give an example from my recent experience, St Philip's Church, next door to my current office in the St Philip's Centre, suffered a break-in during 2017. Very little was taken but a lot of mess created, and it was members of Masjid Umar, the mosque across the road, who came to help clear up. But earlier in the year it had been members of the church who, among others, had come to show their support and solidarity with the local Muslim community in condemning the suicide bombing at a pop concert in Manchester Arena on 22 May 2017. This is, of course, in many ways different from the healing narrative under discussion but the blurring of the distinction between guest and host is common to both.

Finally, the request for healing becomes an opportunity for proclamation and challenge. The example of the centurion's faith is a rebuke to those who ought to have known better. Jesus warns that 'the subjects of the kingdom' (that is, Jewish people) will not all be able to take their places at the feast in the kingdom of heaven where Abraham, Isaac and Jacob are present, but instead will be thrown out into the darkness where there is weeping and gnashing of teeth (Matthew 8.11–12). This has traditionally been understood as Jesus rebuking his Jewish audience by stating that the faith of a gentile is greater than theirs. The warning is that gentiles will be included in the eschatological banquet in the kingdom of heaven, but some Jewish people who might have expected to be included will in fact be excluded (see France 2007, 316–18). This raises an interesting question to reflect upon. Does it mean that those who are not formally identified as Christians but who have a living faith in Jesus are included in his kingdom, while those who say that they have faith but whose actions betray a lack of faith will be excluded? This is an extrapolation of what the text implies rather than a clear statement derived directly from it, but it is worth considering nonetheless, not least in relation to Jesus' comments in Matthew 7.21–23.

Pause

- What are people looking for when they come to Christians for help today?
- We are not the same as Jesus, so what does this passage teach us about him, and what does it teach us about our responsibilities?
- What does this passage suggest about the balance of hospitality, service and proclamation?

The good Samaritan (Luke 10.25–37)

The road from Jerusalem to Jericho descends 3,300 feet in 17 miles. It runs through desert and rocky country, and was known to be dangerous (Marshall, 1978, 447). It was an obvious context for Jesus' parable. The focus of the discussion is on praxis not intellectual belief. The lawyer wants to know what he should do, and is given an example to imitate, not contemplate, as Jesus emphasizes his view that love of neighbours knows no limits.

This was a contested point in Jesus' day. The Jews had endured successive waves of Hellenistic and Roman imperialism in recent decades, and were themselves split into numerous factions. The idea that God's love should be unconditionally shown to everyone was controversial, to say the least. Jesus' choice of characters for the story is significant. As Joel Green notes, the priest and the Levite

> epitomize a worldview of tribal consciousness, concerned with relative status and us-them cataloguing. Within their world, their association with the temple commends them as persons of exemplary piety whose actions would be regarded as self-evidently righteous. (1997, 431)

The Samaritan thus comes as a shocking contrast. He stops and helps at personal risk, and gives of himself. He is the character the crowd would have understood as the enemy, but Jesus has him play the role of hero, indicating that he expected his followers to love their enemies and pray for those who persecute them (as he taught in Luke 6.27–36). The paradigm for hospitality is clear: everyone should be welcomed, perhaps especially enemies and strangers we are frightened of, because it is only through welcoming enemies and strangers that they can become our friends (Pineda 2010). If we use the metaphor of service, then a similar point can be made;

the enemy, at personal cost, offers service to one who is in no position to repay him. The implication of Jesus' command to 'go and do likewise' is that Christians should serve their enemies regardless of the long-term consequences. The issue of proclamation is more subtle. The gospel is not spoken within the parable, but the parable itself encapsulates a core gospel message, suggesting that sometimes proclamation is through action not words.

This parable is one of the obvious ones that Christians utilize when participating in interfaith events. Jesus tells it in response to the question 'Who is my neighbour?', demonstrating that Christianity is concerned with radical love that crosses boundaries and includes those who are normally thought of as outcasts. But my experience suggests that it is important for anyone who utilizes it to be careful in precisely what they say, since as the American Jewish New Testament scholar Amy-Jill Levine notes, while she found much within Christian Scripture that resonated with her, she did not 'like the fact that the Levite in the parable of the good Samaritan was a bad guy. I am a Levite; I took that parable personally' (2006, 4). Two examples of how I have seen the parable used will illustrate the point further.

The first incident occurred at a celebration event for a faith and community group small grants programme. There were people from a wide variety of faith communities present, marking the good work that had been done all over England that year and looking forward to more of the same in the future, championing neighbours of all faiths and none working together for the good of all. At this particular celebration event, the opening keynote was given by a bishop, who told the story of the good Samaritan. It was an obvious choice, since it is about being a neighbour and the event was a celebration of a programme about neighbours working together. Unfortunately, the bishop in question had not registered quite how offensive this story was to many of the Jewish members of the audience. They heard it as an attack on Judaism, portraying their faith as legalistic, disinterested in people and lacking in mercy. Whether this was Jesus' original intention in telling the parable is beside the point. My observation is simply that if this story is told without any nuance then not everyone will hear it in the spirit of inclusion and care for all that the contemporary speaker may have intended.

The second incident illustrates how the story can be told. This was a different interfaith gathering, with a different bishop speaking. This time, rather than reading the story from a Bible, it was retold, with the negative focus clearly on the speaker. So the first indifferent passer-by was introduced as a bishop, with a joke about bishops not being much practical use. The second passer-by was a lawyer, with a joke about the speaker's past life as a lawyer, and a further comment that lawyers are not always that useful. By clearly making himself the negative focus of the story, the speaker ensured that the Jewish members of the audience heard it in the spirit it was intended. This point applies to any of the passages in this chapter. Retelling, and including appropriate interpretative glosses, may well be a safer way to communicate these stories to a mixed faith audience.

Pause

- How would you use this story in an interfaith context?
- Who are the 'Samaritans' in your context?
- How can you build relationships of care and love with these people?

The woman at the well (John 4.1–42)

Jesus' encounters with Samaritans during his ministry also raise questions about engagement with those of other faiths. Samaritans were tradition-ally regarded as sworn enemies of the Jews (Keener 2003a, 588–9; see also Robinson 2012, 167–75). The dispute had a long history, going back to the origins of the Samaritans as a mixed race, settled in the northern king-dom of Israel by the king of Assyria (see the account in 2 Kings 17.24–41). Despite these differences, the Samaritans nevertheless viewed themselves as true Israel, and heirs to the promises of God to Israel, and regarded their version of the Pentateuch, which had significant differences from the Jewish one, as the original one, direct from Moses (Beasley-Murray, 1999, 60–1).

When Jesus encounters the Samaritan woman at Jacob's well, he crosses a number of boundaries. As a devout Jewish male, and a rabbi at that, social convention dictated that he should not talk with a Samaritan woman of dubious social standing (Klink 2007, 196–8). Yet Jesus ignored these conventions and engaged with her, both in religious debate and also speaking into her personal circumstances (Ling 2006, 187–97). For Jesus' disciples in particular, it is the fact that he talked alone with a woman that was most shocking. They themselves had visited the Samaritan town to buy provisions, so their discomfort is about the gender of Jesus' conversa-tional protagonist, not her race (Michaels 2010, 239).

The interaction between Jesus and the unnamed woman is striking when considered through the three analytical lenses I am using. As with the centurion, notice the blurring of the distinction between guest and host, between server and served. Jesus makes himself vulnerable, asking the woman to provide him with water. In this sense he makes himself the guest and the woman the host; he is the served, she is the servant. But he does so against social convention, causing confusion and the subsequent conversation. The position is then reversed, as Jesus offers her 'living water', that is, the gift of the Holy Spirit (not clear from 4.14 but more so in 7.37–39). Now Jesus is the host and she the guest, and an uncomfortable one at that, as the conversation moves into personal territory. Yet somehow that discussion of her personal history, about which the text is vague and it would be unwise to speculate, becomes a proclamation of Jesus' identity. Having learnt that he knows everything she ever did (4.17–18, 39) and that he encourages worship in spirit and truth, not in a geographical location (4.21–24), the woman proclaims Jesus to her community. He himself declares his identity in response to her questions (4.25–26) and that, combined with what he says about her life, is enough for her to begin to have faith in him.

The text also blends personal history with theological controversy. It seems that the woman invokes the latter as a defence against too much discussion of the former (4.16–24), but Jesus is happy to take the conversation as it comes. He is clear about what he believes but in this incident he does not condemn Samaritan practice, although he offers an alternative future to the one she expects. It is probably unwise to try to draw too many parallels from this conversation to our contemporary context. Bob Robinson (2012, 200–27) tries to draw implications from Jesus' encounters with Samaritans for contemporary encounters with Islam. He finds 13 parallels between Samaritanism, Judaism and Islam. Some have merit: all three faiths are scripturally based religions of revelation, are monotheistic, and have distinctive prophetic and eschatological expectations. Some are more tenuous; the nature of 'clear distinctions between male and female space and functions' (2012, 205) depends on the time period under consideration and who is interpreting it, as some Muslims would argue that men and women both prayed together in the first mosque at Medina. Robinson recognizes the limits of the parallels. His point is that the encounter between Jesus and the Samaritans provides us with some questions to consider in how we relate to Muslims. These include, first, a refusal to blame or denigrate; second, a desire to receive hospitality from the other; third, the importance of respectful, constructive and practical dialogue; fourth, the fact that outsiders (that is, Muslims) may grasp what insiders fail to grasp; leading to, fifth, to the possibility of redefining the boundaries of the people of God (2012, 213–20).

Jesus does not engage with just this one woman but with the whole community, and he does so because they encounter each other almost by chance. I suggest that it was pragmatism rather than an overtly theological agenda that caused Jesus to pass this village: it was on the shortest route from Jerusalem to Galilee, and Jesus stopped there simply because he was tired and thirsty (Michaels 2010, 235, 238). The questions that flow from this episode centre on our attitude towards those we happen to encounter in our daily business. Jesus was not above crossing social and religious boundaries, and he was happy to make himself vulnerable and ask for help. He does not shy away from either personal or theological controversy, but engages in a patient and caring way. There is much food for reflection in this section on the nature of our hospitality to others who are very different from us.

Pause

- What does this story teach us about becoming guests of people of other faiths?
- What does it teach us about engaging in religious and theological controversy?
- How do those lessons apply in your context?

John 14.6

A friend once described John 14.6 as a 'Christian clobber text'. By this he meant that it is the sort of proof text used to clobber anyone who disagrees with the speaker's view about the salvation of those who have not explicitly confessed faith in Jesus Christ as Lord and Saviour. At first reading this is certainly the case. Jesus is uncompromising as he states: 'I am the way and the truth and the life. No-one comes to the Father except through me.' How else can this text be understood?

Some have tried to explain the text away. Thus, James Charlesworth suggests that 14.6 should be understood as 'two grammatically independent sentences'. The first is, he argues, positive and may well be authentic to Jesus. The second, negative, exclusivist statement that 'no one comes to the Father except through me' is a product of a later writer, who added it as a sign of his opposition towards those who were outside the immediate circle of Johannine Christians for whom the Gospel was written (2001, 260).[2] Others remain committed to an exclusivist understanding.

Don Carson argues that the exclusivism of John 14.6 points in two directions. First is the salvation-historical context: now that Jesus has come,
'it is totally inadequate to claim that one knows God, on the basis of the
antecedent revelation of bygone epochs, while disowning Jesus Christ'.
Second, this is not a statement of the effectiveness of Christianity as one
religion among many, but rather an affirmation that Christianity is the
only choice (1991, 491–2). In dialogue with Hindu friends, they have
understood this claim as the exclusive loyalty that any guru demands of
his disciple; that is, John 14.6 is an exclusivist claim but only applies to
those who choose to make it relevant to themselves. It has no impact, the
argument goes, on those who have not already identified Jesus as their
teacher and master; but for those who do, it demands complete loyalty
and obedience.

In his commentary, Craig Keener discusses John 14.6 at some length
(2003b, 939–43). He argues that 'the Way' means the way into the
Father's presence, a way that Jesus travels by virtue of his identity and
character. The disciples come to the Father by means of Jesus and their
participation in him. Keener proposes that 'way' be understood not so
much as a route for heavenly ascent as 'the way of righteousness and
wisdom', citing texts such as Exodus 18.20, Deuteronomy 8.6 and 10.12,
and Isaiah 55.7–9, as well as numerous references in Proverbs to support
his argument. Regarding the exclusivism of the text, Keener understands
the text as both ethical and Christological, suggesting that it shows Jesus
to be the 'sole adequate revealer of God' (941); just as Judaism drew
boundaries to indicate the existence of only One God, so the early Christians tightened that boundary to indicate that Jesus was the only way to
the One God. Keener rejects pluralistic interpretations, such as that of
Charlesworth above, arguing that for the author and first audience the
text was intended in an exclusivist, boundary-setting way. Early Christians
may have been ethically universalist, seeing good actions on the part of
many, but salvifically they were exclusivist, seeing their way as normative
for everyone.

In his discussion of John 14.6, Kenneth Cracknell sets out four ways of
engaging with the text that open up conversation and engagement with
people of other faith communities (2005, 55–93). First, he notes that this
text is an answer to Thomas' question in 14.5, where he asks how he can
know the way, not whether people of other faiths will be saved. Cracknell
proposes that Thomas is a positive figure in John's Gospel, who represents
a believing faithful disciple who is fully committed to Jesus. Thus, in John
11.16, Thomas states that he is ready to travel with Jesus back to Lazarus'
house and if necessary die there with him, and later in 20.28 makes the

declaration that Jesus is 'My Lord and my God', arguably the high point of the Gospel. Cracknell suggests that Thomas' question in 20.25 was one seeking assurance about the reality of suffering and death, confirming that it was indeed Jesus whom he knew to have died that God had raised from the dead. This picture of Thomas as a faith-filled disciple who also wants to understand the nature of redemption means that his question in 14.6 can be understood, Cracknell argues, as a question about Jesus' ultimate intentions and how those intentions are to be achieved. Yet this question is difficult to answer. Cracknell's analogy is of attempts to explain poetry through prose; if this could be done, then the poem would never have been written in the first place. Thus, our engagement with the answer to Thomas ought to point 'to the recognition of pain and perplexity, ambiguity and suffering, sacrifice and self-emptying', rather than a triumphalist doctrinal certainty (2005, 60).

Second, Cracknell engages with what Jesus means by stating that he is 'the Way'. This leads him to discuss the doctrinal teaching of the Council of Chalcedon, which affirmed that Jesus Christ is fully human, fully God, one Person who is 'ultimately related to the more general action, presence and revelation of God in his world' (2005, 61). For Cracknell, recognition of Jesus as 'the Way' understood in the terms outlined above opens up the possibility of conversation with other religious traditions that also utilize the concept of 'the way' or 'the path'. For Hindus, the three paths to salvation are the *jnana marga*, or path of knowledge, the *karma marga*, or path of good works, and the *bhakti marga*, or path of devotion. For Muslims, the opening sura of the Qur'an states:

> In the Name of God, the Merciful, the Compassionate.
> Praise be to God, Lord of the worlds, the Merciful, the Compassionate, Master of the Day of Judgement. You we serve and You we seek for help. Guide us to the straight path: the path of those whom You have blessed, not (the path) of those on whom (Your) anger falls, nor of those who go astray. (Droge, 2013, 1)

Similar arguments could be made in relation to the eightfold path of Buddhism or Jewish concern with *halakhah*, which means literally 'walking' in the way of God. For Cracknell, this common metaphor means that Christians must become more conscious of talking of their way, their path, as one path among many, although he caveats that by noting that for Christians the 'Way of God has been most clearly discerned in the way that Jesus followed – the path of rejection and suffering, abandonment and death' (2005, 71).

Third, Cracknell examines what 'coming to the Father' might mean. He recaps the Christian argument that the Fatherly love of God that Jesus taught, shown for example in the parables in Luke 15, is unique and unsurpassable. Cracknell proposes that this argument must be nuanced, not least by the rich Jewish tradition of engaging with God as Father, both in biblical texts such as Exodus 4.22, Deuteronomy 32.6 and Psalm 103.13–14 and in extra-biblical ones such as the Testament of the Twelve Patriarchs.[3] Modern Judaism also recognizes the Fatherhood of God, as do many other faith traditions. Cracknell gives three examples. In Sikhi, God is sometimes described as Father, such as in this prayer from the tenth Guru, Gobind Singh, which begins, 'O kind Father, loving Father, through thy mercy we have spent our days in peace and happiness; grant that we may, according to Thy will, do what is right' (2005, 78). The *bhakti* (devotional) tradition of Hinduism describes God as Father, and many traditional African religions also pray to God as Father. Cracknell cites five examples, of which one has the words: 'Our Father, it is thy universe, it is thy will, let us be at peace, let the souls of the people be cool; thou art our Father, remove all evil from our path' (2005, 83).

Fourth, Cracknell argues that John 14.6 must be understood in the context of the Fourth Gospel's concept of Jesus as the Logos, or Word, of God. The opening verses of John describe the role of the Word in both creation and redemption. Cracknell suggests that these verses use a concept common to the day in order to make connections with the wider, non-Christian audience for whom the Gospel was written as a missionary document. In the contemporary Stoic Greek philosophy, the Logos, or Word, was seen as the divine principle that was active throughout the created order. This in turn enables Cracknell to propose that the Word, although limited for a time in the incarnation of Jesus, was active before that in other ways and remains active in the ascended and exalted Christ, such that men and women of other faiths 'are touched by, illuminated by the Logos', and 'in their response actually "come to the Father"', a process Cracknell believes comes about through Jesus Christ (2005, 93).

John 14.6 is a text that primarily concerns proclamation of Jesus Christ. As seen above, some argue that this can be read inclusively, or even pluralistically, but many would see it as a simple exclusivist claim, although perhaps of limited scope. There is a danger in taking any text out of its narrative context; the reference to the Father's house having many rooms and Jesus going to prepare a place (14.2) is perhaps much more inclusivist (or even pluralist), although that depends on who you think Jesus is addressing. Underlying Jesus' words is the concept that he is the gracious host, preparing space for his followers, and welcoming them in. He serves his disciples, as he has demonstrated by washing their feet (John 13.1–17), reminding Peter that he must be served by Jesus if he is to become part of him (13.6–10).

Pause

- Of the various different understandings of John 14.6 outlined above, which do you find most persuasive?
- How does this affect how you choose to relate to people of other faith communities?

Paul in Athens and writing to Rome

What does the apostle Paul have to teach us about interfaith engagement? As the examples above have shown, it is quite possible to build a narrative based on Jesus' actions that is in favour of crossing boundaries, meeting with those who are different and building relationship with them. Paul's example is a bit harder to use, although the fact that most of his engagements with synagogues in Acts result in his expulsion and persecution is in itself food for thought.

The most likely place to turn is Paul's experience in Athens. In Acts 17, Luke records how Paul spent some time in Athens alone, and this included speaking at a meeting of the Areopagus, where he said to the assembled crowd:

> People of Athens! I see that in every way you are very religious. For as I walked around and looked carefully at your objects of worship, I even found an altar with this inscription: To an unknown God. So you are ignorant of the very thing you worship – and this is what I am going to proclaim to you. (Acts 17.22–23)

As Ben Witherington (1998, 521–3) notes, it is impossible to come to a conclusive historical certainty about whether such an altar actually existed. For our purposes, it is not an especially relevant question. The point is that Paul's rhetorical aim is to move from a familiar starting point to a proclamation of Jesus Christ. In his discussion of this speech, Ajith Fernando suggests that Paul found elements of Athenian belief he could agree with 'and used those elements as stepping-stones to presenting the gospel' (1998, 479). For Fernando, Paul's example is one of 'restrained provocation', that is, presenting Christianity clearly but in a way that does not cause unnecessary offence or focus on condemning practices of which one disapproves, since Paul does not condemn the worship of idols he would have witnessed at the Areopagus. Cracknell concurs, rejecting older interpretations of the text that regarded Paul's speech in Athens as a failure. For Cracknell, this is Paul utilizing the Stoic philosophical concept of the *logos spermatikos*, the seeds of the Word, to establish connections between the Logos, Jesus and the teachings of the Athenian philosophers. He suggests that Paul is utilizing philosophical ideas that the Stoics and Epicurean teachers would also have used, even quoting them before giving his own message, which was more controversial and which only a few believed (2005, 30–4).

Thus Paul establishes points of connection between what his audience is familiar with in order to present Christianity to them. This is, arguably, the strategy that Paul employs throughout his missionary journeys. Turning to his time in Corinth, it is a fairly commonplace observation that here as elsewhere Paul begins in the synagogue, presenting Jesus to those he might expect to be most open to his message. While some accept his message, many reject him, and so he leaves the synagogue, focusing instead on preaching to the gentiles. This strategy is one he applies in most of the places he visits, with differing results.

Turning briefly to Paul's letters, it is hard to construct anything other than an exclusivist understanding of Christianity from them, especially given the fact that many of them are written in order to persuade the audience of the truth of Christianity and the importance of sticking closely to it rather than returning to previous religious practices. Paul's letter to the Romans perhaps provides the most food for thought. The statement in Romans 1.20 that Creation witnesses to the glory of God could be taken as indicating that there is some form of revelation of God in all world religions, and the statement in 2.14–15 about gentiles following the law written in their hearts might support either inclusivist or exclusivist understanding depending on precisely how Paul's words are explained. The most complex passages are in chapters 9 to 11, where Paul discusses the fate of Jewish people who have not (yet) accepted Jesus of Nazareth as the Messiah.

Douglas Moo describes these chapters as Paul's 'anguished wrestling with the problem of Israel's unbelief' (1996, 547). Tom Wright concurs, seeing the focus of the chapters as Christological, as Paul answers the double problem of Israel's rejection of Jesus and the gospel that Paul preached (2013, 1161–3). These chapters have engendered much exegetical and theological controversy, and here I limit myself to a few brief comments on two points: first, how these chapters fit into Romans as a whole, and second, whether what they teach there is a special way of salvation for the Jews.

Scholars of previous generations have argued that Romans 9—11 are an aside, a distraction from the main argument that flows seamlessly from chapter 8 to chapter 12. This view has lost popularity in more recent times. Wright suggests that a key issue for the letter as a whole is responding to gentile belief that Jews can no longer be saved, noting that the 'normal Roman view of the Jews was disdainful or dismissive at best and angrily prejudiced at worst' (2013, 1217). The main argument is thus a demonstration of continuity and discontinuity with previous revelation in the Old Testament. God has not changed, neither has the covenant, but there is a new way of including people into God's family: belief in Jesus as the Messiah (Moo 1996, 550). Romans 9—11 is therefore integral to the letter as a whole, which is a carefully structured and precisely argued exposition of Paul's understanding of God and how he is at work in the world, written to an audience in Rome both as an introduction to Paul himself and as a way of encouraging Christians in Rome to unite behind this understanding of the gospel.

Turning to issues of interpretation relevant to these chapters, some have argued that Romans 9—11 can be interpreted as teaching that Jews can be saved without faith in Christ. There are hints of this understanding within the exposition in *Nostra Aetate*, but I find it unpersuasive. I will discuss two sections of Romans that are of particular relevance: the metaphor of the olive tree (11.17–24) and the statement that 'all Israel' will be saved (11.26).

The metaphor of the olive tree excites much speculation among commentators. I concur with Wright: Paul knows that his metaphor works against expected practice (2013, 1217). It would be normal to graft cultivated olive shoots onto a wild tree in order to harness the energy of the wild tree into growing more fruitful olives. But Paul argues the reverse, that wild branches (the gentiles) are grafted onto an established tree, Israel (see Psalms 1.3; 52.8; 128.3; Jeremiah 11.16; Hosea 14.6 for references to Israel as an olive tree). Paul does this deliberately as a challenge to the pride of the gentiles, reminding them that their new-found faith is established on the roots of the patriarchs and God's covenant with Israel (Kruse 2012, 440; Moo 1996, 704). The point is not to establish two covenants, one where Israel is saved through obedience to the law and another where gentiles are saved through faith in Christ, but rather to be clear that new branches are being added on, and older ones have died, as faith in Christ applies to all (Wright 2013, 1213–14).

Paul's statement that 'all Israel will be saved' (11.26) is taken by some as indicating that Jewish people have no need of faith in Christ. Commentators are divided as to the precise identity of 'all Israel'. Wright suggests that it refers to both Messiah-believing Jews and Messiah-believing gentiles, but excludes those Jews who have not accepted Jesus as the Messiah (2013, 1244). Kruse states that it indicates all the elect of Israel, that is, Jewish people, from all time (2012, 448–51), while Moo sees it as indicating 'the corporate entity of the nation of Israel as it exists at a particular point in time', referring not to every single person but to the nation generally (1996, 723). Although their precise definitions are different, all three commentators are united in believing that this passage is not universalist but remains particularist in its understanding of salvation; that is to say, it is understood as remaining within the context of Paul's oft-stated view that faith in Jesus is needed for salvation.

Wright helpfully points out that Paul is addressing different questions from the ones we face:

> The key question is not, Are the various religions equally valid ways to a distant deity? Nor is it, How can Christians affirm the 'civil rights' of Jewish people in the Post-holocaust world? The question Paul addresses follows on from the apparent failure of Israel described in 9.30–10.13. It comes, as we saw, in two stages: first (11.1–10), can any Jews at all be saved? and second, as in 11.11–24, can any *more* Jews be saved? 'Salvation' here, exactly as set out in 10.1–13, is correlated with the Messiah, and with the faith that believes his resurrection. (2013, 1221)

As this brief discussion has shown, Paul's letters lend themselves most easily to an exclusivist understanding of soteriology. That is not to say that this is the only possible interpretation, but that others require more exegetical work. In this, as in many other areas of Christian debate, questions both of the authority of scripture and how we expound uncomfortable or challenging teaching in public are foundational to the approach we might take. Paul's teaching is focused primarily on proclamation; his interest in service, which is a thread throughout his letters, is mainly for the fledgling Church, especially in Jerusalem. He balances his need to be a guest with refusal to do so when he feels that this would compromise his integrity as a messenger of the gospel.

Pause

- What does Paul's strategy in Athens (Acts 17.16–34) teach you about interfaith engagement?
- How do you understand Paul's argument in Romans 9—11? What implications does it have for engagement with Jewish people today? And with those of other faith communities?

Conclusion

We all read the Bible from within our own contexts; any self-reflexive interpreter must be aware of the tension between looking for confirmation of ideas already held and being open to having those ideas challenged and changed by the biblical text. In this series of reflections, I have tried to show that reading the Bible with interfaith engagement in mind is a rewarding and stimulating exercise. There are plenty of passages that reinforce the importance of proclamation of the Christian faith, but also a number that support the importance of offering hospitality to people of all faiths and none, and of acts of selfless service. The challenge of defining boundaries is reminiscent of Sudworth's observation that the kingdom of God has no limits, just edges (2007, 41), encouraging us to be alert to where the Spirit is at work in the world.

Notes

1 See http://rabbisacks.org/covenant-conversation-5767-vayera/

2 More specifically, Charlesworth argues that the redaction of the text of John's Gospel is indicative of the hardening of the opposition between the Johannine community and the Jewish people.

3 Cracknell quotes the *Testament of Judah* 24:1–2, which states, 'And after this there shall arise for you a star from Jacob in peace; and a man shall arise from my posterity like the Sun of righteousness ... and the heavens will be opened upon him to pour out the spirit as a blessing of the Holy Father.'

4

When and where does interfaith engagement take place?

This chapter begins with a brief consideration of when interfaith engagement might take place, followed by a more detailed discussion of the question of where. Having first noted three examples of formal, set-piece engagement (at the international level, as part of the civic life of a city, and as a specialist interest), the bulk of the chapter examines four different places where Christians might engage with people of other faiths: in a church context; in school; in other places of worship; and in the home. Finally, I discuss engagement in the civic space or over a shared issue, where faith communities are only a part of a wider collective effort. This includes treatment of the particular case of vigils after a tragedy.

When?

The simplest answer to the question of when interfaith engagement might take place is that it should be at a time that works for all those who are taking part. The challenge comes in finding that time. Every faith community has a rhythm to its year, which includes both times of intense religious activity and quieter times. The former can both preclude and also invite interfaith engagement, providing that care and sensitivity are exercised. Consider the Christian calendar. The degree to which Christians engage with the concept of a liturgical year varies considerably, but virtually all Christians increase their level of activity in the run-up to Christmas. Christmas carol services, Christingle services, nativity plays, Messy Christmas events and so forth all provide opportunities to engage with the community outside the core congregation. This is an obvious opportunity for interfaith engagement, although some sensitivity needs to be exercised, for example ensuring that suitable refreshments are available. Easter, although the high point of the Christian year, is perhaps harder to make into an occasion focused specifically on interfaith hospitality. This is because Easter is a season of proclamation of the crucified Messiah, a truth claim that is at odds with those held by other faith traditions. As noted below, in the example of a church engaging with the local Sikh community, Harvest provides an easy opportunity to invite others to participate in church activity.

As anyone engaged in interfaith activity soon learns, other faith communities also have a rhythm to their year that includes times when engagement would be easy and times when it would be more difficult. For the Jewish community, the ten days of the High Holy Days are a busy period during which they are unlikely to have much time for other engagement. The festival of Pesach (Passover) may include an opportunity to have an open Seder meal, to which members of other faith communities are invited. Others choose different festivals such as Purim or Lag B'Omer as times to engage with other faiths. Hanukkah, as a festival that celebrates light (in Judaism specifically the miraculous burning of the lamp for eight nights during the rededication of the temple at the end of the Maccabean revolt in 165 BC), is often used as point of engagement, although the fact that it sometimes falls at a similar time to Christmas can make the practicalities of this a challenge (in 2016, Hanukkah started on Saturday 24 December and concluded on Sunday 1 January 2017). Holocaust Memorial Day, it should be noted, is not a Jewish festival; in Israel the Holocaust is marked on Yom Ha Shoah (held on 27th of Nisan, a Jewish month roughly equivalent to April or May in Western calendars), and Jewish communities in the United Kingdom also mark this day. There will be significant Jewish participation in HMD but it is most likely to be a civic affair.

Ramadan is the most significant month in the Islamic year. When it falls in the summer months, the long days of fasting mean that most Muslims do not have much energy for other activities and so their willingness to be involved in interfaith activities is limited. Many Muslim communities organize interfaith iftars (the meal that breaks the fast), and sometimes other communities do the same, but there are challenges to this, especially if Christians end up offering hospitality to an event marking a Muslim religious observance (a point I return to below). Eid celebrations are perhaps easier to join in with as the religious element is clearly distinguished from the party.

For Hindus, Diwali is the most significant festival, but there are many others, especially Holi (a spring festival of colours) and Janmashtami (celebrating the birth of Krishna). Diwali is celebrated by Hindus, Sikhs and Jains, although each faith community associates a different story with the festival. For Hindus, the most common story is associated with

Lord Ram, his wife Sita, and brother Lakshmana, and the lighting of their triumphant path of return from exile with diva lamps, a symbol of the triumph of good over evil. For Sikhs, the story is of Guru Har Gobind freeing himself and Hindu leaders from imprisonment and returning to the Golden Temple in Amritsar. For Jains, the significance is that on this day Lord Mahavira attained Nirvana. Diwali celebrations often involve fireworks, lights and food, elements most people are happy to enjoy. For Sikhs, Vaisakhi marks the formation of the Sikh khalsa panth of warriors under Guru Gobind Singh in 1699, and is normally marked with a parade that commemorates the formation of a distinct Sikh people.

These are invariably large public occasions; it is easy to go and watch them and take part as far as you feel comfortable. Often the crowds attending are very large, so if you want a friend in that faith community to know that you are attending it is best to warn them in advance. I can well remember visiting one Hindu mandir during Diwali and my host commenting that I should leave my shoes in a certain place and hope that they would be there when we got back, but he could not guarantee it. This was a joke, but a joke based on a previous experience of another guest whose shoes took some time to locate when he wanted to leave!

As well as the rhythm of the year of different faith communities, it is also important to think about the rhythm of the academic year. Some communities are very shaped by what is happening in schools while others are not so concerned. Academic communities can only really engage in interfaith events when it suits their own timetables; exam season may preclude pretty much everything else, for example. Finally, it is also worth considering the rhythm of the working week. Some Christians who engage in interfaith work do so as all or part of their employment, but this is not the case for everyone you may want to engage with. Religious leaders may be able to make time to meet during the day, but others have commitments to be present at their place of worship to meet with devotees, or have other full-time work and so are only available at weekends or during the evening. The fact that different communities have different days as their holy day also complicates the picture: Fridays for Muslims, Saturdays for Jews and Sundays for Christians.

Having said all of that, pragmatism often has to take priority; if we waited for a time when everyone was guaranteed to be available, then we would be waiting a very long time. After all, if people consider something to be a priority, then they will make time for it.

Where?

Interfaith engagement takes place in all types of places at all kinds of levels. First, it might be part of formal interaction at an international level. From 25 to 27 January 2016, King Muhammad VI of Morocco hosted a conference in Marrakesh, jointly organized by the Ministry of Endowments and Islamic Affairs of the Kingdom of Morocco and the Forum for Promoting Peace in Muslim Societies, which is based in the United Arab Emirates. The majority of those who gathered were Muslims from all around the globe, but those from other faiths were also present. The focus of the conference was to examine the rights of religious minorities in Muslim lands, and resulted in a declaration affirming those rights and calling on Muslim majority countries to take active steps to implement them.[1]

Second, interfaith engagement may be a set piece as part of the civic life of a city. To give two examples from Leicester, the City Mayor hosts a quarterly 'faiths and communities forum' where faith community groups can, in the words of the official who organizes the gatherings, 'have an unmediated conversation with the City Mayor'. Once a year Leicester's Orthodox Jewish Community hosts a celebration marking Hanukkah in the town hall. Both of these occasions, and countless others like them, involve civic officials (both elected and officers) as well as those with leadership positions in the faith communities.

Third, interfaith engagement may be a specialist interest. This could be a bilateral group, such as the Council of Christians and Jews or Nisa-Nashim, a Jewish-Muslim women's gathering. It might be a gathering around a particular topic or concern, such as the Forum for Discussion of Israel and Palestine (FODIP), or the Feast, a Christian charity based in Birmingham that works nationally and internationally to promote community cohesion and interaction among young people of different faiths and cultures.

These three examples suggest that interfaith engagement is the focus of specialists, that it requires deep theological training, a lot of time and resources and great care in the preparation and delivery of show-piece events. This is indeed one important type of interfaith engagement. Each of the three examples above makes a significant contribution. The Marrakesh declaration indicates the willingness of at least some in power in the Muslim world to take the rights of minorities seriously. The inclusion of different types of engagement between civic authorities and faith groups as a matter of routine is important in building resilience to enable swift responses in times of crisis. London experienced four separate terrorist incidents in 2017, perpetrated by individuals with a variety of motives.

The different civic interfaith responses often involved (or were coordinated by) people who had a long history of engagement with each other. Specialist interests enable sustained focus on complex issues. FODIP, for example, encourages young people from Jewish, Christian and Muslim backgrounds to engage with the different narratives that come out of the conflict in Israel-Palestine. But while these are all important forms of engagement, they are a minority of the interactions that take place. Most interfaith engagement is not formally labelled as such; much of it is not scheduled but is spontaneous, spur of the moment and responsive. Often interfaith engagement is the by-product of social action, the sharing of a common concern or interest.

The three lenses of hospitality, service and proclamation are all relevant to the discussion of where interfaith engagement takes place. The context is normally crucial in determining how these three are to be balanced. To overemphasize in order to make the point, a vigil marking a joint community response to a national act of terrorism is hardly the place for explicit proclamation of the gospel, but it is the place to be generous in our service of those in need. By contrast, if people come to a church service then we ought, with appropriate sensitivity, to be confident in proclaiming our faith in Jesus Christ. In one sense this chapter is an extended theological reflection on how to balance two Christian imperatives. On the one hand, Christians are called to love and care for our friends and neighbours, regardless of their faith or ethnicity, an imperative I examine using the shorthand of hospitality and service. On the other hand, Christians are expected to be clear and unequivocal in their faith in Jesus Christ, not being unnecessarily offensive while recognizing that the message of the gospel is offensive or foolish to some. This is the imperative of proclamation, through both what we say and what we do. The challenge of balancing these two imperatives guides much of the reflection that follows.

Interfaith engagement in a church context

In this section I examine three types of interfaith engagement: those who turn up; set-piece engagement; and church-led social action.

Those who turn up

In 2016, those involved with the Church of England's Presence and Engagement network conducted research into clergy experience of evangelism and witness in multifaith contexts.[2] Five focus groups were conducted, in Leicester, Birmingham, London, Manchester and Bradford, all under Chatham House rules. One of the themes that emerged from all five conversations was engagement with refugees and asylum seekers as a catalyst for church growth. These people would often simply turn up at a church, looking for a community to belong to. Sometimes this was only a single individual but in other places hundreds have been drawn to the same church community, often by word of mouth. To give one example, Liverpool Cathedral has a weekly service, Sepas, which caters for the Farsi-speaking congregation and meets on a Sunday afternoon.[3] When I visited in 2017, I was told that the average attendance at Sepas is between 100 and 200 people. Many other places can tell a similar story; while they may not be ministering exclusively to Farsi speakers, they may have Farsi speakers as a significant group in a congregation that includes many nationalities. Examples of this trend include Stockton Parish Church,[4] St Stephen's in Hyson Green, Nottingham,[5] and St Mark's in Stoke-on-Trent.[6] These churches tell a story of significant growth as a result of people, often born into and having grown up following a different faith, choosing to become Christian and joining their local church. The examples above are all Anglican churches because that is the part of the Church I know best. But that does not mean it is only Anglican churches that are growing in this way, far from it. The reality is that many churches, of a huge variety of theological perspectives from High Catholic to independent conservative evangelical or charismatic, are growing, changing and developing as people of all faith backgrounds choose to start attending.

This phenomenon of people coming in ones or twos, in their dozens or even in their hundreds to a church looking to learn more about Jesus can be understood through the lenses of hospitality, service, and also proclamation. If these people come from a culture that is very different from white British culture, then their expectations of what being a member of a worshipping church community entails may also be very different. Minor issues might include whether shoes should be worn inside a place of worship; more significant ones might include how often people visit each other in their homes for meals and how long a visitor might be expected to stay, and what language(s) to use within a church service. A generous and welcoming host would adapt her behaviour to enable guests to feel at ease; might this include encouraging a congregation that is used to wearing shoes to church that, since the floor is carpeted and there is underfloor heating, actually you could remove your shoes on arrival? The question of motives is also relevant here; when we offer hospitality to those who turn up, do we do so regardless of how they respond, or is our hospitality conditional on a desire on the part of the guest to become a Christian? I return to this point below in my discussion of church-led social action.

The issue of proclamation is an interesting one. Sometimes converts to Christianity from Islam (or across any faith boundary for that matter) may be converting, at least in part, because of their negative experience of the faith they are leaving. This can result in open hostility towards the whole of the faith community they are leaving; the challenge is to help the convert to embrace their new-found Christian faith while at the same time retaining at least civil relationships with adherents of the faith they have left. Geography also plays a part here; someone may have left Islam, say in Iran, for reasons that are not of direct relevance to how that faith is practised in the UK. A church that sees significant numerical growth through those of other faiths becoming Christian will have to think through how to relate to local communities of other faiths.

A second aspect of the phenomenon of people simply turning up to a church is primarily related to those of dharmic faiths, especially Hinduism and Sikhism. I often attend the Leicester Diocesan Eucharist held in Leicester Cathedral at 8.30 on a Monday morning. During this short service it is quite common to see a Sikh gentleman come in, pray at one of the side altars and then leave. Cathedrals are well known for this type of individual faith engagement and no one really remarks upon it, especially when a person is engaged in personal prayer rather than participating in the Eucharist itself. Those with a pluralist understanding of faith may see a church building as simply one of many places in which to pray.

Sometimes people of other faiths do come to church specifically to participate in a service of the Eucharist. This is particularly noticeable on Christmas Eve. Colleagues across Leicester have told me of Sikh and Hindu families in particular who come to their local parish church every year for the service of Midnight Mass. What is the appropriate Christian response to this? Should we practise an 'open table' where all are welcome to participate, receiving bread and wine if they choose to? Or should we restrict access to those we know to be Christian? If we choose the latter policy, how do we know? For it is little short of racist to presume that because someone is white then she must be a Christian but if someone is brown-skinned then she is not. What if someone is a 'secret believer', one who follows Jesus privately while publicly remaining an adherent of another faith tradition? Attendance at Midnight Mass may be their only chance in the year to attend a Christian service. The point of distribution of the elements is hardly the occasion for a deep theological discussion, and if someone responds to the invitation that says 'all who know and love the Lord Jesus are welcome to receive' then who are we to refuse them?

What, then, is an appropriate eucharistic theology of hospitality? The point of distribution of the bread and the wine in some churches can be quite chaotic, while in others this is carried out in reverent silence. Either way, it is not the place for detailed discussions of motivations. Looking at the question from another angle, does it matter if we give the consecrated elements to people who are not Christian? Is doing so a failure of proclamation of the gospel, a compromise that slips into failing to hold a distinctly Christian identity? Does your understanding of Christian welcome mean that anyone who wants to should be allowed to the Lord's table? Or does your desire to be clear on the uniqueness of Christ mean that only certain people are allowed, after appropriate preparation?

Pause

- How would your church family welcome a Muslim asylum seeker into your church?
- How would you balance hospitality and proclamation to those who turn up at church unannounced?
- What do you think about the issue of those of other faiths wanting to receive Holy Communion?

Set-piece engagement

Sometimes a church will invite people of other faith communities to attend a particular service or event as a gesture of hospitality and welcome. One suburban church in Leicester has focused particularly on developing relationships with the Sikh community. This began with an invitation to Sikh friends to come to a tea party celebrating the Queen's ninetieth birthday and it developed from there. It has included a visit to a local gurdwara, an evening together discussing themes of light and darkness in Christianity and Sikhism and an invitation to Sikh friends to attend a Harvest Songs of Praise and shared supper in the church hall. Each event has built on and deepened the friendships that have been formed. The evening on darkness and light utilized the liturgical season of Advent in contrast with Sikh understandings of how Diwali is celebrated as a catalyst for conversations about what it means to celebrate light and goodness in each faith. The interaction included some very direct explanations from Christians of their understanding of Jesus as the Light of the world. The Harvest Songs of Praise did not include any formal exchange of views but a number of one-to-one informal conversations between members of the two faith communities. Each event placed a different emphasis on hospitality and proclamation. The tea party, for example, was solely about hospitality; the discussion evening on Diwali and Advent emphasized both, through an open welcome and also a clear explanation of Christian views; and the Harvest Songs of Praise was deliberately selected as a service to invite Sikh friends to because the element of proclamation was less stark than in other services.

There is an art to planning a service where you have deliberately invited people of other faiths to attend. The Harvest Songs of Praise where Sikhs were the main guests did not present any complex issues. The main issues, however, are as follows.

First is the choice of readings, which in a Christian service should be clearly Christian but not unnecessarily offensive. This is particularly relevant when inviting Jewish people to attend services, as many New Testament passages include polemic directed against a Jewish audience. I can vividly remember sitting in a service between two Jewish people who had come to observe a service of evening prayer, where one of the readings was 1 Corinthians 1.18–31 (which begins 'For the message of the cross is foolishness to those who are perishing ...'). I am not saying that such texts should not be read in church, but rather that if you choose to invite Jewish people to church, reading texts that they will hear as specifically rebuking them is not the way to build good relationships across faith communities. We should, of course, be clear in our proclamation of the gospel, but also be sensitive in our hospitality of those who are not Christian.

Personally, I am not in favour of including the sacred texts of other faiths as part of a church service. There have been a number of controversies around this, of which the reading of the Qur'an in Glasgow Cathedral is probably one of the better known.[7] Occasionally civic services in cathedrals become the exception that proves the rule, although if this happens the way in which the reading is introduced and engaged with during the rest of the service requires very careful thought. Personally, the only scenario in which I would actively seek to facilitate the reading of texts of other faiths is in the context of a vigil after a local or national tragedy (a topic I will return to below). I am very much in favour of being hospitable in how we organize and run a church service, but good hospitality does not require us to abandon our identity. A church service is a context of proclamation of Christianity, and people choose to enter into it or not of their own free will. Many of my friends of other faith communities tell me that they think Christians are sometimes too reticent to proclaim what they believe, arguing that proclamation can be done in a way that is not coercive or pushy, but simply confident in the identity we have chosen.

Second is the selection of hymns, which raises similar issues. Some hymns present a theological perspective that may be too exclusivist for certain occasions; conversely there are those whose generic reference to God or lack of any mention of the divine means that people of all faiths or none will quite happily sing them. Again, there is a need to be sufficiently and clearly Christian without being unnecessarily offensive. If Jewish people are to be present, the issue of supersessionism is of particular relevance. Thus, for example, hymns that use the term 'Jehovah' are problematic because this is a corruption of the divine name which Jews do not pronounce.

Third, there is the question of whether or not to celebrate the Eucharist. This point was referenced above but I mention it again simply to indicate that it is a choice that must be made. The crucial thing is to ensure that the invitation is clear, with expectations of how to respond (receive the elements, receive a blessing, stay in your seat) being set out, and then to treat everyone well, however they respond.

Sometimes, set-piece engagement in a church context might take the form of inviting an individual or group from another faith community to come and share something of their own faith. This is something that we often arrange at the St Philip's Centre. Our offer is of two main types of events, which we term 'Taste of Faith' and 'Festivals and Faith'. The former involves someone from a particular faith community giving a presentation about how they practise their faith, answering questions and sharing food from their faith and cultural background. The latter are comparative, following one of three themes: Advent and Diwali, Harvest and Eid, and Easter and Passover. I will illustrate by discussing past sessions on Easter and Passover and on understanding Buddhism.

The session on Easter and Passover consisted of a presentation from a Jewish colleague about how her family celebrate Passover, both at home and in the synagogue. We established clear parameters for the discussion, excluding the conflict in the Middle East, or current concerns about the rise of anti-Semitism in the UK. Through her explanation of Passover, the Christians present not only learnt how modern Jewish people celebrate this festival, but also began asking questions about their own Christian practice, including the extent to which faith is shared and is part of home life, the involvement of children in services and celebrations of significant festivals, and the extent to which Christians bother with the original languages of the Bible.

The session on Buddhism included reflection on Christian practices of contemplative prayer, as those who participated decided what, for them, were appropriate and inappropriate forms of Christian meditation.

We also agreed that there is not really such a thing as 'Buddhist food', although most Buddhists are vegetarian or vegan. So we shared snacks made by McVities, which is based in Leicester, as this food is as Buddhist as any! These events balance both hospitality and proclamation; welcoming guests from other faith communities and also sharing what we believe about the Christian faith.

Pause

- What types of set-piece engagement would suit your church context?
- How would you balance hospitality and proclamation in these events?

Church-led social action

Many churches engage in a wide variety of social action projects, and in some areas this can lead to significant interaction and engagement with people from other faith communities, either as service users or as volunteers. Typical projects would include classes teaching English as a foreign language, food banks, debt counselling services, and work supporting the homeless, bereaved or otherwise vulnerable. One challenge for Christians is to ensure that they do not fall into the trap of behaving in a paternalistic way, 'doing to' rather than 'being with' and working alongside. This is, perhaps, a particular challenge for some Anglican churches, which although they may feel under-resourced are, in comparison with many other faith community groups, much better resourced and equipped to make a significant difference.

For church-led social action to be a form of discipleship, then it must be an outworking of faith in Jesus Christ. One passage that Christians would make recourse to in examining their motivations would be the parable of the sheep and the goats in Matthew 25.31–46. While some find this passage challenging because it implies that actions are crucial to salvation, many read it in the light of the discussions in James, especially chapter 2, where he talks about the interplay between faith and works, arguing that actions are a visible sign of internal faith. If we love and care for all people, regardless of their faith background, then we can serve them all equally, again regardless of their faith background.

This brings us to the question of motivation and intended outcomes. Take classes in English as a foreign language, which can be taught in a variety of ways, with a variety of motivations and expected outcomes. Thus, for example, Tim Chester and Steve Timmis have produced a short evangelistic course, *The World We All Want*, which is deliberately written in accessible English. The idea is that people meet for conversational English classes that also share the Christian story with them and invite them to become part of it.[8] The charity Friends International works in partnership with local churches to set up informal English conversation groups for international students.[9] These are often known as world cafés or global cafés. The format will vary but often the expectation is that the friendships made at the café will make it easy to invite participants to attend church or evangelistic courses such as Christianity Explored or Alpha. Other classes will be similar to those offered at local further education colleges, with no overt or implicit Christian focus. The distinction is often that churches charge less (if anything) for the courses they offer, and so may not offer any accreditation to attendees. There is not a right or wrong way of running this type of course. But it is important for organizers to be clear as to their own motivations and expectations. Do we want people to come and get better at English and that is all? Or do we want them to come and investigate the claims of Jesus Christ for themselves and make a decision to follow him (or not)? Both are fine, but in a British context at least it would seem lacking in both integrity and faithfulness to Jesus to publicly say the former while secretly expecting the latter.

The question really concerns what you think constitutes acceptable behaviour for a host. The people attending the English classes come as guests of the Church. Perhaps the easiest way of deciding what we are comfortable with is to apply Jesus' teaching of treating others as we would want to be treated if the situation were reversed (Matthew 7.12). This can apply equally to any other social action projects, whether it is offering a meal to the homeless, providing advice about debt or running an after-school club or school holiday hunger project. If I view the question via the two lenses that shape this chapter, what is the appropriate balance of hospitality and proclamation? Must all activities of the Church have an overt element of proclamation, or is it acceptable for some to simply show hospitality with no expectation that those served develop any interest in the claims of Christ? Elmer Thiessen offers a full discussion of the ethics of evangelism, developing a list of 15 criteria for distinguishing ethical and unethical proselytizing. These are: acting to protect the dignity and worth of those proselytized; expressing care for whole person, including physical, social, economic, intellectual, emotional and spiritual needs; avoiding any form of physical force; avoiding any psychological coercion; avoiding any exploitation of power imbalances; not offering any forms of inducement; engaging positively with human reason; always being truthful, avoiding hidden agendas, deception or lying; acting with humility; holding different beliefs with love and respect; acting primarily out of a love for humanity and a love for and obedience to God; respecting the communal identity of those proselytized; displaying cultural sensitivity; seeing results as a by-product not the main goal; and following the golden rule, which includes recognizing that the other also has the right to proselytize (2011, 234–7).

Pause

- How do you balance hospitality and proclamation in the context of the social action your church engages in?
- How do you love Jesus in this context and what does it mean to share his love with others in both word and action?

Schools

Many schools are places of interfaith encounter. While some parents choose to send their children to a faith school that reflects their own belief tradition, others through either choice or necessity will send their children to schools that have no faith ethos or schools where the faith ethos is different from their own. I will discuss three types of interaction: between parents; between pupils; and the particular case of church schools.

Parents

The most obvious topic of conversation for parents at the school gate is school life: what the homework topic is, what pupils are expected to bring for a school trip and so forth. Sometimes conversations will move to a deeper level, and parents will share more personal experiences, building close friendships across faith boundaries. Issues of hospitality and proclamation are as relevant here as in any other context; and all parents will find an appropriate balance that works for them. It is also important to recognize that children pick up all sorts of unspoken or casually expressed attitudes; how we talk at home about other faith communities, including world events that impact on them, will affect how our children engage with people of other faiths in a school context.

Pupils

As pupils grow up they begin to develop a sense of self, which necessarily includes making decisions about religious worldviews. It is commonplace to note that many young people identify as having no religion,[10] but it is also the case that often children grow up adhering to the faith of their family. Schools can become places of both interfaith and intra-faith conflict. Sometimes historic tensions, for example those that exist between different faith communities in the Indian subcontinent, surface in school life. Thus, if Sikhs have grievances over how they are treated in India, this may impact on relations with Hindus in England. Similarly, if Christians have relatives in Pakistan who are suffering for their faith, then their ability to relate to Pakistani-heritage Muslim peers can be compromised.

Sometimes there is potential for intra-religious tension. Muslim pupils may disagree as to the necessity of fasting or performing the relevant daily prayers during the school day. Jewish pupils may have different understandings of how to implement dietary laws in daily life. Christians may disagree over whether it is appropriate to share faith in a classroom context. These questions revolve around the tension between personal choice and peer pressure, around what constitutes socially acceptable norms of behaviour in a school environment. Pupils thus have to work out for themselves what is the appropriate balance of hospitality, service and proclamation for their school context. This is particularly difficult for those who are still forming their own identity, not least because they are more guest than host in the school environment.

Church schools

When writing about church schools I do so from my experience in Church of England foundation institutions. The particular challenge for these types of schools consists in finding the balance between encouraging Christian discipleship and welcoming, caring for and supporting those who are not Christian (Wilson 2013). This challenge is not, of course, unique to settings where many of those present are members of another faith community. But it is clear in this setting. One striking example is St Luke's Church of England Primary School in Bury in Manchester Diocese, which has a Jewish head teacher and well over 90 per cent of the pupils are Muslims.[11] There are, in fact, many schools of this type. I have written elsewhere about my experiences in one of them (Wilson 2015b).

Hospitality is a common theme for church schools where there is a significant presence of people of other faith communities. Much of the biblical reflection in Chapter 3 is relevant here but must be developed to the particularity of a school context (Wilson 2014). One area that merits particular reflection is the nature of the power dynamics. If the governing body of a school is solely Christian but the pupil (and staff) profile is largely that of other faith communities, or no faith, then there is a danger of imposition of Christianity by force, which raises an interesting point of theological reflection: can people be coerced into adopting Christianity?

If Christians are called to model their lives on Jesus, who emptied himself in humble obedience to his Father (Philippians 2.5–11), refusing to call on the legions of angels that could have prevented his arrest and trial (Matthew 26.53), then what place do Christians have insisting that pupils must be Christian in order to be part of a particular school community? That is to say, when does confident proclamation of Christian faith cross the line and become coercive or even spiritually abusive?

While it is important to avoid being overly pushy in proclaiming faith, there is also a converse risk of lacking any confidence in the truth of Christianity and avoiding proclaiming it to those of other faiths and beliefs. A colleague who was a vicar in a rural area told me that when a Muslim family joined a local Church of England school, he had agreed with the head teacher that the Muslim pupils should be excluded from the collective worship he took, in case they were offended. One of my PhD supervisors once told me of his experience as a head in a Catholic secondary school. He asked some of the pupils in years 12 and 13 (that is, those aged 16 to 18) to talk to the school senior management about how they received the Catholicism of the school. The pupils were uncompromising in their assessment: the staff were afraid. There was a fear of causing offence in speaking of Christianity, to the point that the staff were compromising their beliefs rather than speaking clearly about them. The pupils suggested that this fear was ill-founded. They were sure enough in their own identity that they were not concerned about how the school presented Christian faith. That is to say, while the staff were worried that their presentation of Christianity might coerce someone to embrace the faith unwittingly, the pupils were sure that this would not take place. My own fieldwork in an Anglican primary school supports this idea. Pupils who are secure in their own identity as Muslims were not persuaded to become Christians as a result of attending a Church of England primary school, but deployed a variety of strategies of confrontational and non-confrontational passive and active resistance in response (Wilson 2015b, 101–214).

This should not be a cause of concern. Staff and governors should be happy to share their Christian faith but also be interested in the spiritual development of all pupils. The primary purpose of a school is education, and therefore the primary aim of a church school should be education in a Christian context. There have been many efforts at developing a particularly Christian pedagogy for a range of educational contexts. Within Anglican schools, the approach known as *What if ...* learning has been especially popular, as has the argument of John Cox that Christian schools should be about more than just 'caring and sharing' (Cooling and Cooling 2013; Cox 2011). Church schools must work out how to establish a clear Christian identity, a proclamation of their Christian foundation not simply in espoused ethos but in the operant ethos that includes ensuring that the toilets are clean, pupils are warm and well fed and parents know that their children are suitably provided for. This Christian identity includes being hospitable, serving those who come to the school in need, while ensuring that everyone who attends is enabled to learn and grow, achieving the best possible educational outcomes.

Pause

- What makes a school distinctively Christian? Does this change if the school has a significant proportion of people of other faiths present?
- What role do Christian parents have in the life of a local school?
- What role do Christian pupils have? What can they contribute?

Other places of worship

It is easy for Christians to fall into a trap of presuming that they are the hosts and people of other faiths are the guests. While this may have been partially true 50 years ago, it is no longer an accurate reflection of contemporary British society. Of course, there are still many people newly arrived in the UK who are from a faith background other than Christianity. But it is also true that many people of other faith communities were born in the UK, to parents who were also born in the UK, and we visit their places of worship as guests. (It is equally true that many Christians are new arrivals to the UK, but that point is not relevant to this discussion.) There are at least three different types of interfaith engagement Christians might participate in in the places of worship of other faith communities: open days; festivals; and engagement in times of tension.

Open days

The places of worship of other faith communities often hold regular open days as a means of establishing strong relationships with their neighbourhood. The only nationally organized initiative I am aware of in the UK is 'Visit My Mosque Day', which is an annual event.[12] The focus is, as the name suggests, on encouraging non-Muslims to enter their local mosque, perhaps for the first time. Normally there are talks explaining Islam for beginners, exhibitions of the history of Islam and tours of the mosque in question, and often activities associated with Islam such as calligraphy, or Muslim majority contexts such as henna tattooing. There can be attractions you might find anywhere, such as a bouncy castle and free food. Some also focus on raising awareness of anti-Muslim hatred and the lived experience of British Muslims. The overall aims of the Visit My Mosque initiative are myth busting and relationship building. These are aims that Christians can support.

Personally, I approach Visit My Mosque Day primarily as an opportunity to build relationships. I meet Muslims for the first time, and show my long-standing Muslim friends that I am interested in them and their initiatives. The hospitality is normally excellent, including some very tasty food. I have many questions about Islam, and sometimes the conversations during Visit My Mosque Day are the right time to raise them. But often they are not. I have listened to many presentations of the basics of Islam and normally learn something, especially about how Muslims see Christians, as the presentation is often tailored to make what my Muslim guide sees as points of connection between our two faith communities. Learning how you are perceived is of great value to the Christian disciple. You might, for example, be surprised to discover that most Muslims presume that prayers are the sole activity in a church, or that every Christian wants to visit Jerusalem as a religious obligation in the way that Muslims are religiously obliged to visit Mecca once during their lifetime. Visiting a place of worship open day allows a Christian to learn about the faith community in question and build relationships with them; learn how Christians are perceived by that community; reflect on how Christians, as a minority in a society increasingly indifferent to or intolerant of religious faith might relate to the wider community; and in the case of marginalized or ostracized communities, act as a prophetic witness to God's love for all people.

Sometimes a single community may organize an open day, perhaps for their own internal purposes. Often this is linked to fundraising efforts, especially if the community is seeking (or in receipt of) funding from the

Heritage Lottery Fund or other major funder. I am very happy to support such initiatives by attending, but I normally do not contribute financially to the appeal. I have some fairly obvious criteria that I use to check I am happy to participate. First, is this a faith community I am content to engage with? This includes reassuring myself that they do not support anything that I cannot, in all good conscience, support. Second, what is their charitable status? Third, how confident am I that proper procedures are being followed in relation to handling donations? Fourth, what exactly are they raising money for? Fifth, I find out more about the event itself. Who will be present? What are they expected to do? Will I be asked to engage in a public act of worship that compromises my Christian faith? Sixth, what are the long-term goals of the organization in relation to the project? This is especially relevant when a community promises that their building will be available for usage by the wider community. How confident am I that there is a reality behind these promises? Sometimes groups make all sorts of promises in pursuit of funding or planning permission, some of which they have no intention of keeping. You can get a sense of what is likely to happen by the quality of engagement with the neighbourhood. And if you develop good relationships with those in senior positions in the organization, you have the opportunity to hold them to account if they stray from their promises.

I enjoy living in a procedurally pluralist society, that is, one where different faith and belief perspectives have the right to present their view of the world and flourish side by side. This type of society is good for Christians; it gives us the opportunity to share our faith, to grow personally as disciples of Jesus and encourage others to do the same, and to engage in loving service of our neighbours. Part of the health of a procedurally pluralist society is that other faith groups also flourish; hence I am happy to offer limited and thought-through support to their projects and initiatives, much as I would hope they would do to any I am involved with. As Kaemingk argues, part of being a Christian who favours a pluralist society is arguing for the rights of other faith communities to have their fair stake within that society. Kaemingk's case is based on a conviction that ultimately Christ is in sovereign control, but this must not be confused with notions of a Christian society, as it is Christ, not the Christian, who is in charge (2018, 165–259).

Festivals and acts of worship

The festivals of other faith communities can present a different challenge. What should a Christian do if invited to participate? What counts as being a good guest and what is participation in heresy? There are no clear, hard-and-fast rules, but in what follows I offer a few reflections.

Regarding Jewish festivals and synagogue worship, I often take small groups to visit one of our local synagogues for a Shabbat service. Participants find this moving, and often feel that because of the historic proximity of the two faith communities they are able to participate in worship. Christians should be alert to issues of supersessionism, that is, of presuming that Judaism is now redundant because of the advent of Christ. Sometimes individuals are also invited to Pesach (Passover) for a Seder meal. I am happy to participate fully in a Seder meal, as although I would express it slightly differently the Exodus story is one that I own as part of my discipleship. I must be careful not to abuse the hospitality I am offered, but this is a story I also celebrate.

When engaging with Muslim communities, if I take visitors to a mosque we tend to sit at the back and observe prayers rather than participate. The same would be true when I am invited to an iftar, the breaking of the fast at the end of the day during the month of Ramadan. I am very happy to eat with people and share fellowship with them in this way, but since I am not a Muslim I do not fast because they are fasting. If I do fast, it is an act of Christian discipleship, not a way of 'playing at being a Muslim'. I find this an important distinction to make. Ethnographers sometimes engage in what they term 'participant observation', that is, taking part in the activities of the group they are observing as a way of immersing themselves in the experience and so learning about it at a deeper level. This is a well-established academic practice and results in deep learning, but it is not the same as becoming a member of the community and participating as an insider. Even if I fast for the day during Ramadan, I am doing so as a Christian not as a Muslim. Since I want to maintain a distinction between those two faiths, I avoid any unnecessary blurring of the boundaries between us as to do so would simply generate confusion.

Not everyone shares this conviction. Ray Gaston has written about his experience as a parish priest in Leeds. Initially he fasted on his own for one day during Ramadan, then for a week, and then for the whole month. During his fourth year of engaging in this way, he not only fasted for the whole of Ramadan, he also read the Qur'an in English. He also started attending Jummah (Friday midday) prayers at a local mosque, and then more of the times of prayer, eventually even joining the line of worshippers praying. He reasons that he could not enter a building where 'hundreds are praying to the God of Abraham and not join in' (2017, 47), although he notes that after he left Leeds he no longer felt the 'pull to participate' in prayers at a mosque and has since stopped doing so (2017, 48).

I would emphasize the distinction between going to an iftar and organizing one, and between a set-piece iftar and informal participation. While I am happy to attend an iftar, I would be cautious about organizing one, primarily because of the high potential for confusion and misunderstanding. An iftar organized in Southwark Cathedral in 2018 was seen by some as a compromise that prioritized hospitality at the expense of proclamation, although the cathedral authorities were clear that their intentions were of hospitality tempered with appropriate proclamation, and others argued that their actions were entirely appropriate.[13] Sometimes Christians have organized iftars with no adverse effects, but the potential for upset remains. I find it helpful to consider the situation from a different angle: what would you make of Muslims organizing a Lent lunch and expecting you to come?

I have found that informal participation in an iftar can be more valuable than going to a set-piece one. The latter is invariably formal, often primarily dominated by guests who are not themselves Muslim. It is as much a civic occasion as a religious one. These can be great opportunities for networking and building wider relationships, as well as a chance to show the wider world that Christians and Muslims can be friends. But I have found sitting on the floor in a mosque as the only non-Muslim present while everyone breaks their fast to be a much more authentic experience of how Ramadan is lived out by British Muslims. It really depends what your aim is: individual friendship held in tension with participation in civic society. The context will also help you balance your role as a guest with a desire for proclamation of the Christian faith; what might you say if you were invited to speak at an iftar?

The same general principles apply to engagement with events put on by Sikh, Hindu and Buddhist communities. I have included these as a single group mainly because Christians are less likely to be engaged with these smaller communities. In essence, the question you need to ask yourself is what you are comfortable doing as a guest of another faith community. This includes whether you are happy to eat food that may have been offered to a deity, what ritual actions you are prepared to perform, and what you might say if given an opportunity to speak as an honoured guest of the community you are visiting. This applies equally to any other faith community: the Baha'i, the Pagan community and so forth. Forewarned is forearmed; if you receive an invitation it is best to enquire as to exactly what you might be expected to do and engage in conversation with your host as to what you feel comfortable doing.

Times of tension

It is important for Christians to demonstrate solidarity with other faith communities when they are under pressure, either because of local tensions or because of national or international incidents.

When I was a parish priest in Gloucester there was an attempt to fire-bomb one of the local mosques in the parish. I found out about it at around 6.45 a.m. when I went to buy a newspaper from my local Muslim news-agent. He had learnt about it on a social media group; it was clear that the local Muslim community knew all about it, and were feeling afraid. The incident itself was not actually that serious: two men, who did not live in the area, had attempted to set fire to the mosque. They caused only minimal damage as the fire burned for just a few minutes on the concrete steps of the building.[14] But the point was not about the risk of damage, it was about the feeling of the community. I spent several hours that day (and in subsequent days) in or near the mosque, talking to people as a visible sign that I, as a Christian minister, supported them and would speak up with them. Many others can tell similar stories of working together in solidarity in the face of local opposition; Ray Gaston discusses Christian responses to the English Defence League in some detail (2017, 90–112).

The situation is slightly different in times of national and international tension. What position should Christians take over the situation in Israel-Palestine, for example? My view is that it is not my place to try to solve this conflict, but there are two positive types of action I can take. First, I can encourage those of different perspectives to speak to each other, to understand the many stories and experiences and competing truths that are present in the region. Second, I can encourage people in the UK to work together despite their differences. We may have different views as to what should happen in the region. But we should not let that get in the way of working together for the good of the area in which we live. Where possible it is therefore appropriate to release joint statements of solidarity and unity, organize vigils in which people can together make a stand for peace and engage in social media and other campaigns for the good of all.

Sometimes Christians may take the lead in organizing these actions; at other times they may respond to and join in with the good ideas that others have. In 2016, in the wake of the increase in reported hate crime after the European referendum, a campaign on the theme 'love thy neighbour' was run in Birmingham. Although the phrase sounds Christian, the original stimulus for the campaign actually came from a member of Birmingham's Humanist Association, who worked with Christians in Birmingham in what soon became a wide-reaching campaign supported by different faith groups, civic leaders and people from business and the arts (Smith 2018, 83). My experience of organizing vigils in the aftermath of national and international terrorist incidents is that there is a greater public buy-in if it takes place in an outdoor public venue rather than inside a church building. This is a learning point for Anglican Christians in particular: although we may think that a cathedral is a building for all, not everyone sees it that way, and the likelihood of participation in what is planned as a public solidarity event is much higher if the venue is a neutral one, such as the town hall square or similar public space. I will return to the issue of vigils below.

Pause

- How would you balance being a guest and being clear about your Christian faith when you visit the place of worship of another faith community?
- What faith communities near you could you visit? How could you support them?

Home

If you develop strong friendships with people from other faith communities then it is natural that you will visit each other's houses. Many people in other faith communities come from a culture that prizes hospitality, and they will make great efforts to ensure that you are welcomed and cared for if you visit them in their home. There are at least three areas of consideration when inviting people into your house: food; pets; and expectations of gender roles.

Regarding food, the simplest thing to do is to ask what food your guests can eat. Different religions have different stipulations about food, but more importantly for this context, different people have different attitudes towards those stipulations. In what follows I outline some basics in relation to food, but be aware that people live out their faith in different ways, and so a personal enquiry is far more useful than simply following a list.

Within Judaism, the laws of kashrut stipulate that meat and milk products should be prepared and served separately; orthodox Jewish people therefore have two sets of utensils, and never eat food that mixes meat and dairy products. If a kitchen is not kosher, an orthodox Jew would not eat food prepared there, so do not be offended if a Jewish friend politely declines an invitation to a meal. Within Islam, there are strict rules about ritual slaughter of animals, and as in Judaism some foods are forbidden. Some Jews and Muslims opt to become strict vegetarians when eating in public settings, as that becomes the simplest solution to adhering to dietary laws and being a guest whose dietary requirements are not too onerous.

Within the dharmic faiths, vegetarianism is the norm for those who are active in their religious observance, but there are degrees of vegetarianism and veganism. Some Hindus, for example, will not eat onions, garlic, eggs or mushrooms. Some will only drink organic milk. Many will avoid alcohol or caffeine. But other Hindus will eat most foods, including some meat, but not beef because they regard cows as sacred animals. The same can be said of Sikhs, Jains and Buddhists; vegetarian or vegan food is the norm, but it is best to enquire of any particular restrictions. Most of all, be aware of the distinction between doctrinal and lived religion; every faith has teachings that not everyone who self-identifies as a follower of that faith actually follows.

Regarding pets, this is more of a cultural than a strictly religious issue. Many cultures around the world regard the concept of keeping animals as a pet to be an unnecessary indulgence. Working animals may be kept: a dog as a guard, a cat to catch rodents and so forth. Some animals, notably dogs, are regarded as unclean in some cultures and so your visitors may therefore not want to be near a pet. Again, this will vary greatly from person to person. Within a home context it is relatively easy to manage, as a simply enquiry will provide guidance. There are certain situations where it does get more complicated, especially if someone with an assistance dog wants to attend the place of worship of another faith community, as there is a legal obligation to allow the dog to enter.

Finally, expectations regarding gender roles are also as much cultural as they are religious. The socially conservative elements of many religious traditions insist on the separation of men and women in social settings, including in the home. I have experienced this in public settings within Christianity, Judaism, Islam, Hinduism and Sikhism, but my experience in a home context is much more limited. It is certainly true that many Muslim households maintain a distinction along gender lines. People may therefore be cautious about visiting your home, unsure if the protocols they regard as normal will apply in your house. As with everything mentioned in this section, the simplest solution is to ask. If you have a good friendship, then it will only be strengthened by honest and respectful enquiry into how your friend sees the world.

Christians have to decide on the extent to which they are prepared to adapt their own behaviour for the sake of their friends. Sections of the apostle Paul's letters provide interesting stimulus for thought in this area. A particularly fruitful section for reflection is Paul's discussion in 1 Corinthians 8.1 to 11.1, where he talks about his willingness to compromise his eating habits and become like those he seeks to relate to in order to win them for Christ. Gordon Fee suggests that in these chapters Paul is arguing against eating food as part of a cultic meal in a temple, but allows food that has been offered to an idol and then sold in a market to be eaten in a private home, so long as this does not trouble the conscience of anyone present (1987, 357–63). Anthony Thiselton concurs, arguing that Paul's underlying theology of unity and ordered differentiation of the body, that is the Church, applies just as much to these chapters as elsewhere in 1 Corinthians (2000, 607). Ben Witherington adds that for Paul, 'the essence of Christian theology is love, not knowledge' (1995, 196), which guides his response to this complex problem.

If you want to think further about how to practise hospitality, service and proclamation in your own home, then get a copy of *Simply Eat: Everyday Stories of Friendship, Food and Faith* published by Instant Apostle. It contains 47 different reflections from Christians on how they have shared friendship, food and faith. The book is divided into five main sections: faith-filled memories; welcoming the outsider; nourishing community; sharing living bread; and tasting and seeing. There are many recipes for you to try and encouragement for even the most inexperienced or novice cook to give it a go. Not all the reflections are specifically about engaging with those of other faiths, but there is much food for thought, and plenty of ideas for tasty food to share.

Pause
- Could you welcome people of other faiths into your home?
- How would you resolve the issues related to food, pets and expectations of gender roles?

The public square

The final section of this chapter considers Christian participation in the public square. Christians are slowly learning the lesson that we are no longer a dominant voice in the public square; if anything, we are a marginal one that is sometimes out of step with the expectations of the majority. But Christians have been a significant presence in some local and national campaign movements. Ray Gaston discusses this in some detail, referring to issues including the 'war on terror' (2017, 65–70). Richard Sudworth explores the history of engagement between (Anglican) Christians and Muslims in the public square, noting the particular challenge that the international context sets for any engagement, since globally far more Christians experience persecution at Muslim hands than vice versa (2017, 72). The situation in Israel-Palestine is particularly complex in this regard. Sudworth reflects on the importance of the 'other' remaining other, and therefore always somehow strange and distant, suggesting that Christian engagement in the public square should be rooted in a confident self-identity that is open to the mystery and challenge of relating to those who are very different from ourselves.

The community-organizing charity Citizens UK is concerned with bringing faith groups together. While not country-wide, in the cities where they are present it is common to find Christian groups participating in conjunction with groups from various faith backgrounds as well as from other sectors of society. The charity One Roof Leicester, discussed in Chapter 5 below, is a local example of how different groups work together in response to tragedies. Many have noted that both Christians and Muslims were at the forefront of responses to the Grenfell Tower fire, working together to respond to the needs of others regardless of their faith background.

Finally, a word about vigils. I was involved in the organization of a number of vigils in 2017, in response to a range of incidents that included the Manchester Arena bombing, the Westminster and London Bridge attacks, the Grenfell Tower fire and the attack on worshippers outside Finsbury Park mosque. All the vigils took place in Leicester, that is, not in the primary location of the tragedy being marked, and this has an impact on the style and shape of the event as numbers attending are invariably smaller. I do not have direct experience of organizing a large public vigil at or close to the site of a tragedy, but nevertheless, I believe the following principles are worth bearing in mind.

Vigils are always organized at very short notice; to be meaningful they tend to take place within 48 hours of the event, or perhaps even sooner.

There is a lot to organize, and so preparation is important. Having strong relationships with people across faith and other community boundaries enables you to quickly bring together a small planning group to decide what to do and where. Maintaining good relations across communities is crucial in times of tension. Yet when people are feeling threatened and under pressure it can be difficult to reach out or engage with new people. This is one of the reasons why it is important to work hard at maintaining relationships with a range of communities, as it will stand you in good stead when things get difficult.

Different issues will require quite different responses. When the MP Jo Cox was murdered the whole community rallied to show their support and solidarity (Cox 2017). But the issue may be one that divides a community, and then it can be difficult to plan any form of public act of solidarity. To give an example from Leicester, a planning application from a Muslim community group to turn a light industrial unit into a nursery with prayer facilities became very controversial among local residents, especially those within the Hindu community.[15] The nature of the tension meant that it would have been inappropriate to organize any form of public show of unity; rather the work had to be done behind the scenes, encouraging people to maintain good communication and understand the different perspectives of those involved.

Times of national tragedy normally bring people together to show support. My experience of helping organize such vigils suggests that the following are all important. First, act quickly, aiming for the event to take place within 48 hours. Separate, formal services or acts of commemoration that can take place several weeks later, or on a one-year anniversary and so forth are important, but if there is tension as a result of what has happened, this must be dealt with quickly, with a public show of solidarity. Second, be as broad as you can be in who you involve. I have a decision tree and list of contacts on file so that I can quickly contact a wide range of stakeholders, including the City and County Council, the police, leaders of a variety of faith communities and civil society groups, as well as local media outlets. If you are able to gather a small group together this helps with planning and ensuring there is wider buy-in. People will normally make time in their schedules to attend such meetings, but it is important to ensure that there is one coordinated response rather than three or four rival activities happening at the same time.

Third, have a plan, a compere and a PA system. You do not need to produce a running order for everyone to see, but those involved need to know what is happening when. There should be a sense of order and control; part of the purpose of a vigil or similar gathering is to bring order back in the face of the chaos of whatever tragedy you are responding to. The compere needs to be someone who has sufficient experience and authority to keep things calm and managed. It might be a local religious leader, a local civic leader, or someone from a local civic society organization. The circumstances will probably suggest an obvious candidate. To give three examples from my experience in Leicester, the vigil that marked the Pulse nightclub shooting in Orlando, Florida was led by the LGBT Centre; the Manchester Arena bombing vigil was led by a local vicar; and the Grenfell Tower memorial was led by the chair of the Leicester Council of Faiths.

Fourth, ensure that whatever you do is short, simple and accessible. My experience suggests that outdoor public places get a bigger response, but some may prefer to use a local community building or place of worship. It is good to have two or three people speak for a few minutes: a local civic leader, a member of one or two faith communities, especially a member of any community that has been particularly impacted by whatever has taken place. These speeches need to be short; people have not come to listen to long talks. Someone singing or leading people in song can be helpful, although you have to be careful about the songs you pick. Asking people to stand in silence for a few minutes is an accepted way of showing respect and mourning, but sometimes the silence can be too long. I once attended a vigil where the silence lasted 30 minutes, which was too long for people to maintain focus. A variety of symbolic actions can be offered: lighting candles can be popular, perhaps using electronic ones outside as tealights are easily blown out. Using chalk to draw on the ground is quite effective. After the Manchester Arena bombing in 2017, we encouraged people who came to the vigil in Leicester to contribute to a drawing in front of the Town Hall that read 'Leicester loves Manchester'. The letters were soon coloured in and other messages of support were written around it. The obvious advantage of chalk is that it can easily be washed away a few days later (or when it next rains). Sometimes people may want to come and lay flowers; if this is offered, it is important to liaise with the local council about the best place to do this, and how the clear-up will be managed afterwards.

Times of tension are times to serve, not to proclaim. Depending on the nature of the issue, you may find yourself as host or guest, or that distinction may become irrelevant. The main aim should be to demonstrate unconditional love for those who need it, and condemnation of those who spread hatred and violence.

Pause

- What opportunities do you have for engaging with people of other faiths in the public square?
- What role might you have in organizing a vigil in response to a local or national tragedy? Do you have the resources you need in place to do this well?

Conclusion

There are many different places in which Christians engage with people of other faiths. This chapter has considered five broad categories: church, school, other places of worship, the home, and the public square. There are issues that are of particular relevance to the context; the nature of a relationship within a school setting is different from sharing a cup of tea with your neighbour or campaigning together for the living wage. But wherever you meet people of other faiths some basic considerations remain relevant: Christians are called to love their neighbours as God loves them, wherever and whenever they meet.

Notes

1 For further detail, see www.marrakeshdeclaration.org/index.html (accessed 19 June 2018).

2 http://presenceandengagement.org.uk/sites/default/files/P%26E%20Evangelism%20and%20Witness%20Report.pdf (accessed 20 June 2018).

3 www.liverpoolcathedral.org.uk/650/section.aspx/44/sepas_service (accessed 21 June 2018).

4 www.stocktonparishchurch.org.uk/sunday-services/

5 www.ststephenswithstpauls.org.uk/

6 www.sanctusstmarks.co.uk/

7 The incident caused much internet chatter. See www.bbc.co.uk/news/uk-scotland-glasgow-west-38591559 for a summary report. See https://ashenden.org/tag/glasgow-cathedral/ and http://archbishopcranmer.com/quran-eucharist-provost-glasgow-cathedral-christian-revelation/ for examples of negative responses.

8 https://timchester.wordpress.com/2014/05/23/the-world-we-all-want/

9 https://friendsinternational.uk

10 See, for example, the British Social Attitudes survey for 2017, which found that 53 per cent of the population as a whole has no religion, rising to 71 per cent for those aged 18 to 24 (www.natcen.ac.uk/news-media/press-releases/2017/september/british-social-attitudes-record-number-of-brits-with-no-religion/).

11 See www.theguardian.com/education/2015/oct/11/primary-school-headteacher-faith-gaps-melanie-michael

12 See www.visitmymosque.org/

13 See www.psephizo.com/life-ministry/should-christians-share-in-muslim-iftar-meals/ for a negative assessment, and http://archbishopcranmer.com/iftar-southwark-cathedral-queen-jesus/ for an argument that what happened in Southwark would be exactly what Jesus might have done.

14 www.dailymail.co.uk/news/article-2511434/Moment-anti-Muslim-extremists-petrol-bomb-Gloucester-mosque-revenge-Lee-Rigby-killing.html

15 www.leicestermercury.co.uk/news/leicester-news/plan-muslim-education-centre-prayer-1148416

5

How can interfaith engagement take place?

This chapter presents five case studies of how interfaith engagement can take place. They examine personal friendships between Christians and people of other faiths; organized church or small group engagement with other faith communities; bilateral groups, focused on the Council of Christians and Jews, the Christian Muslim Forum and the Hindu-Christian Forum; reading of sacred texts, within both an Abrahamic and a dharmic faith context; and social action, utilizing the example of One Roof Leicester, which runs a multifaith winter night shelter.

Personal friendships

This section discusses personal friendships across faith communities under four themes: vicarious friendship; difficult questions; personal challenges; and living as neighbours.

Vicarious actions are those done on behalf of another person; the sociologist Grace Davie has popularized the concept of 'vicarious religion', arguing that many people in Britain today 'outsource' their Christian faith to a representative figurehead (Davie 2007). I have written on the idea of a Christian minister as performing a vicarious function in relation to a Christian school (Wilson 2015b, 88–98). It is also the case that interfaith friendships can have a vicarious quality. One illustration of this came in a conversation between the newly appointed Bishop of Loughborough and a gathering of people in different faith communities in Loughborough. We were discussing the challenge of engaging our whole community in interfaith work. One church representative explained that she had been told by members of the congregation she was part of that they did not need to do interfaith work because they had her to do it for them. Those in conversation with her agreed; this is not an issue that is particular to the Christian community. The reality is that those Sikhs, Hindus, Muslims,

Jews and others who engage in interfaith work are often viewed with suspicion by some within their own communities, while others, as is the case in many churches, are simply told something along the lines of 'We're glad you're doing this, it means we do not have to!'

If I co-host an interfaith gathering with a friend from a different faith community, the nature of the event is shaped by our friendship. The fact that we are at ease with each other, prepared and willing to have difficult conversations and challenge each other in a respectful but honest way, gives others permission to do the same. (Kendall and Rosen 2006 and LeDonne and Behrendt 2017 are written forms of this same concept.) There is some logical sense to the concept of vicarious friendship shaping interfaith relations. People face a variety of pressures on their time, and it is not possible for everyone to do everything. Interfaith relationships take time to develop and require trust in order to encourage vulnerability, so it makes sense to leave the work to someone who has the time and energy to put into it. But if this is all that happens, then there is also an element of failure to prioritize something that is important and valuable. Not everyone can be friends with everyone, but everyone can be friends with someone from another faith community.

Personal friendships are often the best place to have in-depth conversations and ask difficult questions about other faith communities. When people are engaged in formal dialogue, they often do so in a representative capacity and feel constrained to defend the official position of the faith community they are part of, even if they personally have some questions about that understanding. In 2017 the St Philip's Centre conducted a small-scale research project into attitudes towards LGBT people across faith communities, working in partnership with Trade Sexual Health, a LGBT sexual health charity.[1] Part of my role was to have one-to-one conversations with people in different faith communities asking them what they thought about the issues. For some, the condition of anonymity allowed them to explore their own understanding, often recognizing that while there were prohibitions within their faith community about LGBT relations, they did not personally agree with all the prohibitions that were the official teaching of their community. Similarly, when we discuss complex political questions, such as the situation in Israel-Palestine, or the Indian subcontinent, personal friendships can be safe places to explore the issues and begin to develop a nuanced position and understanding of the complexity of the topic under scrutiny.

Interfaith friendships are just like any other friendship. There is no need to regard them as a particularly special category that must be treated differently. To give a personal example, when my daughter was three she had difficulty forming some of her sounds. A Jewish friend of mine is a retired speech therapist, and we asked her round for a meal and talk with our daughter. Like any friend coming for a meal, we checked that what we were going to serve would be something she could eat. When she came she talked with our daughter, gave us a few hints and made some suggestions to her about how to pronounce certain sounds. The fact that our visitor was Jewish was not particularly relevant; in fact, it meant that the next time my daughter accompanied me to an interfaith event, she had a friend she recognized, someone she could go and talk to, proudly demonstrating that she had mastered the sounds she had been helped with.

The logical extension of this idea is that we must learn to live as neighbours, regardless of the faith background we come from. This is not without its challenges. It can be particularly difficult to build relationships with people who are religiously and socially conservative. This affects many different faith communities, but the most visible is the Muslim community. If a Muslim neighbour chooses to wear the niqab in public then you may never know what she looks like, and for many British people, used to face-to-face conversation, this can be a struggle, although as a Muslim friend pointed out to me, those same people would be very happy having an in-depth conversation on the telephone with a person whose face they could not see. Similarly, those communities who believe that men and women who are not related by blood or by marriage should not talk together can be great neighbours, but you may not get to know them as well as you may your other neighbours. But you may also find them very generous; I know many people who speak fondly of their Muslim neighbours bringing round presents at Eid or Christmas. Choosing to live as good neighbours is something any of us can do, regardless of the depth of our knowledge of the faith of our neighbour. Faith may or may not be a topic of focused conversation, but developing a friendship certainly is.

Personal friendships can be a very appropriate context for proclaiming one's faith, but arguably we have to do the hard work of offering hospitality and service first in order to gain the right to be heard. That is not to understand the three as being in some kind of linear progression, nor to argue that we should manipulate people into a place where we can pressure them into becoming Christian. Rather, it is to argue that proclamation of Jesus Christ as saviour is much more likely to be heard as good news in the context of a relationship where your conversation partner is a friend, someone who knows from her own experience that you care for her as a person, and that you will go on caring for her, regardless of how she responds to the message you share.

> **Pause**
>
> What friendships do you have with those in other faith communities?

Church engagement with other faith communities

Even in a congregation that has a particular passion and focus on building relationship with other faith communities, it is unlikely that the majority of the congregation will play a regular part in ongoing engagement with another faith community. Occasionally the St Philip's Centre organizes pulpit swaps, whereby a leader of another faith community is invited to share something of their perspective with the congregation while the minister does the same with that community. These invariably happen during National Interfaith Week, which is held annually in November.

In 2017, for example, Leicester's Bishop Street Methodist Church engaged in a pulpit swap with the ISKCON centre. The two places of worship are within 200 metres of each other, so this was very much a neighbourly visit. In the morning, the president of ISKCON Leicester visited Bishop Street Methodist, engaging in conversation with the minister over his understanding of the lectionary readings for that day. In the afternoon, she came to the ISKCON centre, and they had a conversation about some key verses of the Bhagavad Gita, the main scripture for ISKCON. In 2016, we organized an exchange between Leicester's Progressive Jewish Congregation and St Guthlac's Anglican Church. The vicar spoke at the Saturday morning Shabbat service, and the rabbi at the Sunday morning Eucharist. On that occasion, more members of the respective congregations attended the other place of worship. The fact that the Sunday was Christ the King meant that the rabbi had some particularly challenging texts to respond to, which he did with good grace and humour, as well as an appropriately robust challenge to the congregation to examine their attitudes towards Jewish people.

As well as this type of one-off engagement, there is also a place for more long-term relationships (which we hope will result from pulpit swaps, although that is not always the case). The Christian Muslim Forum organizes church-mosque twinning initiatives, notably in Southwark and Bradford, a topic I will return to in the next section.

In my experience, there are invariably one or two individuals who have a particular passion for interfaith engagement, and they encourage others to join in. They may themselves live in a very diverse context, but they may not; several of our most committed Christian interfaith activists at the St Philip's Centre are members of rural congregations throughout Leicestershire. They see their role as encouraging other people to engage, recognizing that although they may not live in a context where there are people of other faiths, it is important nevertheless to be aware of the issues and establish friendships wherever possible. In what follows I briefly outline the engagement undertaken by two different church communities, one with Muslims and the other a broader, more general engagement. (There is also an example of a church engaging with the Sikh community in Chapter 4.)

The church that has engaged particularly with the Muslim community first began their interfaith activities with a 'Taste of Faith' session on Buddhism (more details of these engagements are in Chapter 4). Having been enthused by the session on Buddhism the congregation asked for another on Islam, which they enjoyed so much that they asked if the presenter would return for further in-depth conversation. Having explored the basics of Islam, they then had more detailed discussions about the understandings of Jesus' crucifixion and the significance of Mary in Islam and Christianity, and they visited a local mosque to learn about how Islam is practised in daily life. As white British people who live in a white-majority context this was their first chance to engage with a faith other than their own.

A different church decided that they wanted to engage in a broad sweep across the different faith communities, in order to develop their understanding of the diverse communities that live around their church. Their interest was sparked as a result of undertaking a process called 'Partnership for Missional Church' which helped them articulate their disconnection from their neighbourhood. PMC is an initiative of the Church Mission Society, and is a three-year journey of listening, experimenting and engaging in contextually appropriate missional outreach in a local community.[2] This particular church community recognized that the demographics of their neighbourhood had changed considerably over the past few decades and they no longer understood the worldview of all their neighbours. Having recognized their need to understand more in order to build relationships of trust and cooperation, the core group of 'Mission Vision Enablers' agreed to meet several times a year to learn about other faith communities with a view to strengthening relationships with those communities. So far, we have helped them meet a Muslim, a Jew, a Sikh and a Buddhist, and they have requested a meeting with a Hindu as their next engagement. But they have not simply engaged in personal learning; they have also worked hard at intentional outreach, hosting an annual spring festival since 2015. Initially this was entirely the initiative of the church community, but now they partner with members of other faith communities in organizing activities throughout the day. To give one example, the local Sikh faith school attended the 2018 fair, with children singing and playing traditional Sikh music. This focus on cooperation has enabled the church community to remain at the heart of the wider community, a position they were in danger of losing because of a decline in numbers and an increasingly inward focus.

As these examples have shown, the circumstances will shape the type of engagement a particular congregation favours. Some may look for a deep relationship, perhaps building a strong partnership with one faith community or place of worship. Others are looking for breadth, getting a broader understanding of the diversity of people in the area. These examples primarily concern building relationships of trust and cooperation over time, which are important for helping forge a cohesive and coherent society. There is also space for outreach activities; churches may have a particular focus on helping people learn English, on caring for asylum seekers or on overtly evangelistic activities. This may include running book tables in the city centre at the weekend, knocking on doors in their local community offering copies of the *Jesus* film on DVD,[3] or holding evangelistic events designed primarily for those of other faith backgrounds. As noted in Chapter 4, arguably the biggest area of conversion growth from other faith backgrounds has been among those of Persian heritage seeking asylum in the UK. There has also been considerable growth among other refugee communities, and modest conversion growth from those who were born and brought up in the UK.

Organizations such as the Mahabba Network and South Asian Concern are particularly active in evangelistic engagement with other faith communities. The Mahabba Network describe their work as have three aspects: prayer for Muslim communities; increasing understanding of Muslim communities; and equipping Christians to share Jesus with Muslims in a local setting.[4] Their website states that they have over 50 local groups, which tend to meet monthly to pray and share information together. They are a loosely affiliated organization whose primary emphasis is on local activity, encouraging Christians to show their love for Jesus to their Muslim friends by what they say and do. A typical example of their work is *LoveFast*, an annual initiative during Ramadan where Christians sign up to receive a daily email giving them information about Muslims, prompts for prayer and suggested ways of showing love to Muslim friends and neighbours. The Mahabba Network promotes a trio of courses: *Friendship First, Joining the Family* and *Come Follow Me*.[5] These all build on each other: the first is designed to give Christians confidence in sharing faith with their Muslim neighbours and colleagues; the second discusses how to welcome converts from a Muslim background into a Christian community; and the third is a discipleship course for those who have become Christians from a Muslim background.

South Asian Concern focuses on equipping Christians to engage missionally and evangelistically with those of South Asian heritage who are not Muslim, that is to say, primarily focusing on Sikh and Hindu communities.[6] They partner closely with Interserve, a Christian mission agency concerned primarily with work in the Arab and Muslim world.[7] Between them, SAC and Interserve offer courses, such as *Jesus through Asian eyes*, which focus on understanding and engaging with people of other faiths and visiting speakers who will unpack these issues in greater depth.

As well as these national organizations there are many locally based groups, either within a single church or a collaboration across different churches, of like-minded Christians who meet together to pray and share Jesus with those of other faith communities. Since their activities can be regarded with suspicion or hostility, such groups tend to be quite private and adverse to much publicity. This highlights the tension between proclamation, service and hospitality in church engagement with other faith communities. While it can be quite popular with the wider community when it practises hospitality or service, a church community can receive criticism if they are active in proclamation, especially across faith boundaries. Members of other faith communities are often particularly sensitive about Christian outreach, seeing it as a hangover from the colonial era, worrying that conversion would mean someone abandoning their family and culture as well as their faith (since all three are closely interlinked). Any form of proclamatory work must therefore be conducted with great sensitivity and care, a point I return to in the discussion of the Christian Muslim Forum below.

Churches are by their nature places of proclamation, hospitality and service; different traditions will place their emphasis in accordance with their theological perspectives. It is not my place to tell you or your congregation where and how to position yourselves, but I encourage everyone to think through the issues carefully. A church that fails to proclaim Jesus Christ fails, I would argue, to retain its identity as a Christian place of worship. Equally a church that no longer serves its wider community in a sacrificial way, that does not offer hospitality to the marginalized, the broken, the lost, fails its calling to be the body of Christ. The precise nature of how this tension works out will vary from local context to local context. But at the very least, elements of all three, hospitality, service and proclamation, should be present in how you engage with other faith communities in your area.

Pause

How would you balance hospitality, service and proclamation in the way your church engages with those in other faith communities?

Bilateral groups

This section discusses three established national bilateral groups: the Council of Christians and Jews, the Christian Muslim Forum, and, more briefly, the Hindu-Christian Forum. Participation in a bilateral group raises particular issues about the balance of hospitality, service and proclamation. The nature of the engagement means that proclamation becomes less appropriate; if people are meeting to work together on a social justice issue or to receive the hospitality of one community then they do not expect to be on the receiving end of a proselytizing drive. But that does not mean that we should shy away from difficult conversations or not be prepared to explain our faith perspective. I would suggest that it primarily means responding to questions rather than speaking without being asked.

The Council of Christians and Jews

In 1942 the Archbishop of Canterbury, William Temple, together with the Chief Rabbi, Joseph H. Hertz, and other Jewish and Christian leaders, established the Council of Christians and Jews. This was a time of growing awareness of increasing anti-Semitism in the UK as well as of the Holocaust taking place on continental Europe. CCJ now operates both as a national, London-based forum and also through its branch network as a local forum where Jews and Christians can meet, build relationships and understand each other better.

In October 2017, CCJ celebrated 75 years of operation, under the theme 'How good it is to dwell together'. This extract from the CCJ website explains further:

> This quote, derived loosely from Psalm 133 which states 'behold how good and how pleasant it is that brothers dwell together', was a natural

starting point when considering how we wanted to frame celebrations for CCJ's 75th anniversary.

For three quarters of a century, CCJ has been a leading player in interfaith engagement. It has provided an open tent for people to come together, share ideas, learn about one another and build a stronger, more tolerant society.

Dwelling together does not require assimilation, conversion or complete cohesion. Rather it demands the opposite – that we are able to live together despite our differences, open to conversation and invigorated by each other's differing experiences and practices. It provides space to celebrate our similarities and the values that we share, while acknowledging that diversity is what makes dwelling together so rewarding, so valuable, so pleasant, so good.

As we reflect on 75 years of transforming relations between Christians and Jews, we reaffirm our commitment to these values and once again invite everyone, of all faiths and none, into our open tent to strengthen our communities through education, dialogue and social action.[8]

The three priorities of social action, dialogue and education shape the variety of activities that CCJ carries out, both locally and nationally. The education strand covers three areas: anti-Semitism, Holocaust education and education in relation to Israel-Palestine. The first is a broad-reaching effort, under the umbrella slogan #stillanissue, and is also a social action initiative. Education about the Holocaust includes an annual study tour to Yad VaShem, the Holocaust Education Institute in Jerusalem, open to Christian leaders and Parliamentarians, as well as cooperation with the UK's Holocaust Memorial Day (HMD). CCJ produces liturgical resources for Christian clergy to use at the time of HMD,[9] and has a strong relationship with the National Holocaust Centre, which was founded by a Methodist family and is a leading centre nationally and internationally on holocaust and genocide education.[10]

CCJ also encourages dialogue between Jewish people and Christians. There are three broad strands to this work. First are the local branches. According to the CCJ website, there are 21 branches outside of London and ten branches in London.[11] The Jewish community is not spread evenly across the UK, and as such the nature of the branch is very different depending on geographical locality. Branches organize a wide variety of events and have a varying frequency of meetings, but at their heart their aim is to encourage open and honest conversations. Topics range from a conversation with an Ahmadi Muslim, perspectives on the Holy Land, joint study of the prophet Elijah, discussion of the use of psalms in

Christian and Jewish worship, and garden parties and other social events.

The second area of CCJ's dialogue work concentrates on university campuses. This includes a training scheme for student leaders from both the Jewish and Christian communities, which for the 2018/19 academic year ran in nine universities (Birmingham, Bristol, Cambridge, Cardiff, Durham, Edinburgh, Leeds, Oxford and Sussex).[12] There are other leadership events and a broad encouragement of interfaith activity. Dialogue also takes place at a national level, through conferences and discussion forums. There is an obvious overlap with the education work here, as one of the particular topics for discussion is the variety of views held on Israel-Palestine; a second is how to respond to issues of anti-Semitism. CCJ has also recently formed a Rabbi-Clergy network, to encourage theological discussion and joint action by the two communities.[13]

Social action, the third area of CCJ's work, builds on the previous two, as those who have learnt more about each other and dialogued together are now better able to work together pursuing common goals. The CCJ website lists three particular social action issues: anti-Semitism, the situation of Christians in the Middle East, and modern slavery. Modern slavery is the theme for CCJ's 'freedom Seder', an annual initiative during Pesach (Passover), highlighting the fact that slavery is as much an issue in the world today as it was for Jewish people when Moses led them out of Egypt. In partnership with the Clewer Initiative, an Anglican charity raising awareness of slavery, CCJ recently launched a Safe Car Wash app, which enables users to raise awareness and potentially spot the signs of forced labour at a hand car wash.[14]

Although CCJ's work is formally split into three strands, it is clear that there is considerable overlap between them. There are a number of challenges for Christians who want to engage with the Council of Christians and Jews. The first is a very practical one, as the likelihood of your being able to do so varies greatly depending on where you live. Although Jewish people live and work all over the UK, there are particularly high concentrations living together in areas of Manchester, north London and Leeds. If you live in one of these areas, the nature and scope of your interaction will be very different from, say, those who live in Liverpool or Leicester, which both have CCJ branches, or Derby or Swindon, which do not. There are therefore complex issues of the power dynamics of numbers, resources and so forth that must be thought through carefully. A second challenge is that Christians need to come to terms with their own history. Whether we like it or not, over the centuries a lot of anti-Semitic activity was sanctioned or even actively encouraged by Christian clergy. An appreciation of history is vital for building good relationships. In addition, Christians have to think through their theological understanding of the covenant between God and the Jewish people.

Theological disagreement lies at the heart of the difficulty in establishing good relationships between Christians and Jews. There are several notoriously difficult texts to interpret, of which Matthew 27.25 and John 8.44 are probably the most challenging. In the former, the people respond to Pilate's claim of innocence in relation to Jesus' blood by shouting 'his blood is on us and on our children'. This statement in Matthew's Gospel is the theological foundation for the charge of deicide, that it was 'the Jews' who killed Jesus, and has been the justification for pogroms and violence against Jews for centuries. In John 8, Jesus is in dispute with 'the Jews' and in 8.44 he tells them that because they do not recognize him as the Messiah they are of their father, the devil. This verse taken out of context has been used to justify the blanket condemnation of all Jewish people as of diabolical origin; it was, for example, deployed regularly in Nazi propaganda aimed at children. It is beyond the scope of this brief introduction to CCJ to discuss these and other problem texts in any detail. But any Christian who wants to build relationships with the Jewish community must be aware of them and the interpretative challenges they pose (for a Jewish response, see Levine 2006). As noted in Chapter 3, Paul's discussion of the relationship between the new Christian community and the existing Jewish community in Romans 9—11 also requires serious study as Christians develop their theological understanding of the covenant they believe God has with Israel.

The Christian Muslim Forum

The Christian Muslim Forum (CMF) was established in 2006 by Rowan Williams, then Archbishop of Canterbury, to bring together Muslims and Christians of various theological perspectives and traditions from across Britain, to discuss issues of mutual concern and to forge better relationships between the two faiths. I will cover three areas: reports that CMF have produced; church-mosque twinning initiatives; and guidelines for ethical witness.

In the summer of 2016, CMF set up a small working group to meet together regularly for dialogue and joint working. The aim of this group is explained as not to agree on everything, but to provide a space where differences could be shared and a public CMF position developed (CMF 2017a, 3). In 2017, CMF published two reports, one on religious supplementary schools and the other on the Casey Review, which were the result of this group's activity. Both were reactive documents, responding to government policy debates and plans.

The brief report *Religious Supplementary Schools* (CMF 2017a) was written in response to a call for evidence, in November 2015, in which the government asked for views on religious supplementary schools. Many concerns were raised in the national press and in parliament, in particular as to whether this would result in inspections of Christian Sunday schools.[15] Muslim communities were particularly worried, as they saw the proposals as a thinly veiled attempt to regulate and control madrassahs (Mogra 2018). *Religious Supplementary Schools* tackles the main issues of the debate. First, religious supplementary schools are important to minority faith and ethnic communities because they are the primary means of transmitting the culture and identity of the social group. This is equally true of an African Caribbean church as it is of a Sri Lankan mosque. Second, there are issues with provision; budgets are low (or non-existent), many teachers are volunteers or very poorly paid, and not trained in modern pedagogy or safeguarding, and so religious supplementary schools are often a poor second to mainstream education. There are issues in relation to safeguarding, security and combating extremism, but the CMF report questions whether the government approach will actually tackle the issues properly, or simply impose unworkable attempted solutions. Third, *Religious Supplementary Schools* questions government intentions to regulate the private religious affairs of British citizens, asking, for example, whether a Christian supplementary school would be free to teach creationism, or whether there would be state-sponsored theological monitoring. Fourth, the report questions whether madrassahs are being unfairly and disproportionately targeted. Finally, the issue of resourcing is raised, calling for the government to support efforts to improve the pedagogic skills of teachers.

Since the report was published in 2017, the Department for Education has released a document in response to their original consultation. They have decided not to pursue the model proposed in the call for evidence, but instead encourage local authorities to use existing powers to intervene in areas of concern and through that discover if there are gaps in existing legislation that could be addressed in the future. Their report also promises a consultation on a voluntary code of practice for religious supplementary schools as well as guidance for parents to make informed choices about which setting to choose (HM Government 2018, 19).

The report *Integration and Opportunity* (CMF 2017b) was written in response to the Casey Review, which was published in December 2016. The review looked at social integration in the UK, specifically 'not just about how well we get on with each other but how well we all do compared to each other' (Casey 2016, 5). It made a number of critical observations about the actions of local government and public institutions that have, in Casey's view, been overly liberal and accommodating of practices that are in fact detrimental to social integration. The review is especially concerned about the safety of children and the growth of socially conservative and isolationist religious groups. It made four sets of top-line recommendations: to build the resilience of local communities where the greatest challenges exist; to improve the integration of communities and establish a set of common values those communities could unite around; to reduce economic exclusion, inequality and segregation; and to increase standards of integrity and leadership in public office (Casey 2016, 17–18).

Integration and Opportunity is a series of short reflections on topics related to the Casey Review. It first discusses the reality of interfaith engagement between Christians and Muslims, recognizing that a contextual understanding is vital, and also that not everyone is interested in or enthusiastic about interfaith work. Second it argues that there is a disproportionate focus on Muslims in the Casey Review, and in government policy on integration generally. There is, however, no clear CMF stance on this issue, with a variety of perspectives presented in the report as to the role of religious authorities in enabling communities to feel more part of wider British society. Third, the question of integration is recognized as a vexed one, asking who will be doing the integrating and what compromises they are expected to make. Fourth, the experiences of Muslim women are explored in terms of both experiencing discrimination within their own communities and being disproportionately targeted in anti-Muslim hate incidents. Fifth, regarding the place of Christian communities *Integration and Opportunity* argues that the complex picture of Christianity in Britain today is not drawn out in the Casey Review, not least in the status of black Christians. Sixth, the issue of extremism is discussed, arguing that we must avoid conflating sincere faith with extremism. Finally, while noting that the Casey Review said little that was new, it is to be valued for keeping the issue live. CMF advocates continuing to have difficult conversations about how we can learn to live well together.

These two reports are illustrative of how Christians can work together with another faith community both to strengthen a campaign for a Christian cause and also to demonstrate love for those who are not Christian. Returning to the issue of religious supplementary schools, neither Christian nor Muslim communities would be comfortable with state-sponsored theological regulation of private religious activities that were well within the bounds of the law. Campaigning together on this issue is likely to be more effective. And while Christians may not experience anti-Muslim hatred, they would want to campaign for better protection for those who do, as a sign of their love for their Muslim neighbours.

The second initiative of the Christian Muslim Forum discussed here is the church-mosque twinning project. Details of this work in south London can be found in a report on the CMF website, from which much of what follows is drawn.[16] The project was funded by the Near Neighbours initiative and stemmed from a recognition that although the diverse communities of south London had good relationships, there was a gap at the institutional level. The project leader, Siriol Davies, who is interfaith adviser to the Anglican Diocese of Southwark, oversaw the project, which resulted in nine twinning relationships being formed. Each partnership is contextually shaped, and overall a range of Christian and Muslim theological perspectives are represented. Further details of each partnership can be found in the CMF website report. The primary aim of the project is relationship: people coming to know their community and each other better. One of the key lessons learnt in this first phase was that the process must be kept simple, to enable time-poor, pressured leaders to have the capacity to enable the project to thrive. Furthermore, women must be involved from the first stages, which can be a challenge where women are not in formal positions of leadership. But with perseverance, progress can be made.

Since the publication of this first report, the church-mosque twinning project has also worked in Bradford, establishing similar relationships as in south London. The principle of building a close relationship with a neighbouring faith community is one that any Christian community could enact in their own local area. My experience suggests that it would probably be an established Christian church that would be more likely to make the first move, but this is not exclusively true. The Dialogue Society, for example, is a Turkish Muslim group who are very keen to build partnerships outside of their own ethnic and religious network.[17] The primary aim of such relationships is the flourishing of the local community, which may be understood at a very geographically constrained level, such as an Anglican parish or a city council ward, or it may be town or city wide, depending on the ethnic and religious make-up of the area.

The third area of CMF's work I discuss are the guidelines for ethical witness, which are the most downloaded resource from the CMF website.[18] The guidelines make ten statements, which provide a sound basis for engagement across faith communities. The first recognizes that faith is proclaimed not just verbally but can also be embodied by actions and attitudes. The second acknowledges that conversion is a divine prerogative not a human one. Third, faith sharing cannot be coercive, a principle that is of critical importance when working with children, young people and vulnerable adults. Fourth, provision of services and support to those in crisis must not become a pretext for persuading someone to convert. Fifth, no attempt should be made to offer any form of financial or material inducement to change faith. The sixth principle is one of respect, agreeing to speak of one's own faith without speaking negatively of any other faith. Seventh is the principle of honesty, agreeing to speak about all aspects of one's faith, even if that is complex, controversial or discomforting. The eighth principle expands the notion of honesty to include motivations for action and warning if events will include faith sharing. The ninth and tenth principles concern what to do if someone joins or leaves your faith community. While we may be glad when someone joins us from another faith community, we must also recognize the pain of those who have been left. Conversely, while we may be sad if someone leaves our faith community, we must respect their right to make that choice and let them leave.

From a Christian perspective, these ten statements can be seen as an outworking of Jesus' command to us to love our neighbours as ourselves. They expand upon the concept of love for those who are different from us; after all, the parable of the good Samaritan teaches us that 'neighbour' includes 'enemy' and so Christians have no excuse for not demonstrating sacrificial love for those whose theological perspective they do not share. Ethical proclamation is possible, but requires considerable self-awareness and careful examination of the purpose and intended outcome of any given activity.

The Hindu-Christian Forum

The Hindu-Christian Forum (HCF) was established in 2002. Although attempts have been made to establish a body of similar stature and activity to CCJ and CMF, these efforts have not yet borne fruit. The organization received a government grant to fund the Oxford Centre for Hindu Studies to produce a report, *Bridges and Barriers to Hindu-Christian Relations* (Frazier 2011). The report suggests that the main bridges were genuine personal relationships that existed, either between individuals or as part of an organized activity, whether that was through shared activism, working together to improve the local community or in-depth encounters from living and working side by side. Issues of education and ignorance are raised, suggesting that Christian 'host' cultures are ignorant of Hinduism, especially the spiritual side, and Hindus feel under-resourced to explain themselves. The converse was also true. Questions of religious truth, tolerance and exclusivism were raised, with the emphasis being on relational discussion of complex issues (2011, 21–4). The issue of perceived Christian colonialism and exclusivism is one significant barrier to positive interaction, but the main challenge is the fact that HCF is not very active.

The group has produced a code of conduct that is similar in ethos and outlook to the CMF guidelines for ethical witness,[19] but the reality is that the group has had only one or two formal meetings since 2015. Wingate (2014, 164–79) details the ups and downs of the history of the group, but its failure to flourish indicates that where there is no trust between the two parties, any bilateral arrangement will flounder.

Pause

Are there bilateral groups in your area that you can engage with?

Reading together

One process that is often used in interfaith engagement is some form of reading of sacred texts. In my experience, there are two main benefits to this process. First, you learn about the text under discussion and how it is interpreted by those who regard it as sacred and normative for their faith. There is a lot of value in interpretation with the help of followers; think of some of the obscure and complex passages in the New Testament, such as Jesus cursing a fig tree (Mark 11.12–14, 20–25). What would a Sikh or Buddhist make of that? Second, you learn about the person you are in conversation with. For me this is the most valuable part of the process; as people talk about a text that is important to them, which shapes their worldview, informs their value judgements and guides their daily life, I come to know more about them as a person. In this section, I first of all introduce three established forms of reading together: the process known as Scriptural Reasoning; and two bilateral reading groups for Christians and Muslims, namely Prophets' Stories and the Holy Book Club. I then discuss the 'Texts Together' reading group at the St Philip's Centre, before explaining the bilateral Hindu-Christian text reading project I have helped organize. The intention is to illustrate the two points made above, that is, the value of reading together both for understanding texts and for building relationships.

Scriptural Reasoning, Prophets' Stories and the Holy Book Club

The most widely known form of reading together is that described as Scriptural Reasoning, as pioneered by Cambridge Inter-faith and the Rose Castle Foundation.[20] This method is primarily focused on engagement between the three Abrahamic faiths of Judaism, Christianity and Islam, following a carefully defined and rigorously applied format, aimed at ensuring equal access and engagement with each text.

Scriptural Reasoning follows a four-stage process. First, a theme is identified. Second, each faith community selects a text from their scriptures that speaks to that theme. Invariably these 'text bundles' are produced containing both the original language and also an English translation. Third, when the group convenes they agree who will facilitate, and an equal portion of the available time is allocated to each text, to be discussed in turn. Fourth, normally each text is introduced briefly by a member of that faith community, and then the facilitator guides a discussion of wondering and questioning, asking each participant what struck them from the passage and allowing any questions of clarification and understanding to emerge.[21] The process is open-ended and all views are given equal weight in the discussion.

A number of bilateral exchanges exist, especially between Christians and Muslims. Two examples, Prophets' Stories and the Holy Book Club, are discussed in a Grove Booklet, *Storying Christian and Muslim Faith Together*. The authors, Jan Pike and Georgina Jardim, share their experiences as Christians who have engaged with Muslims and how they established their respective reading groups. They reflect on the theme of hospitality and how reading together enabled participants to build deeper, more personal relationships with one another. One important reflection concerns power dynamics; this is especially true if the Muslims taking part are recently arrived in the UK, do not speak English as a first language and have received relatively little formal education (2018, 23). The focus of both groups is primarily on stories or figures held in common across the two faiths, with the Queen of Sheba, Esther and Abraham all given as examples. An appendix lists eight guidelines for the Holy Book Club: stick to the texts; feel invited to explore others' texts and invite them to explore yours; listen carefully and charitably, giving time and space; be honest; avoid generalizations, speaking in the first person; be present; be respectful when handling the texts; and use original languages to open up the conversation, not close it down (2018, 27). These guidelines illustrate the twin aims I noted above, of understanding texts and building relationship.

Texts Together

Texts Together is a series of meetings based on the concept of Scriptural Reasoning but with a more relaxed view of what is an admissible text and a broader understanding of which faith communities might take part. Texts Together sessions have a thematic focus, but welcome contributions from a wide range of faith and belief perspectives, including Baha'i, Mormon, Jewish, Christian, Muslim, Sikh and Hindu views. The format is similar to that outlined above, but the texts brought vary considerably. Different religious traditions have very different understandings of the nature and importance of the written word, from the Sikh understanding of the Guru Granth Sahib as a living guru to those within other faith traditions who see texts as useful but no more than human reflections on the divine. The Buddhist understanding of written texts is particularly illustrative of this latter view. This means that people bring different texts with them, some preferring hymns, poems or prayers to the authorized text of their own faith community.

My aim in facilitating these meetings is primarily to build relationships; I am less interested in acquiring academic knowledge than I am in developing my understanding of the people with whom I am in conversation. A discussion of texts that have significant personal meaning is a valuable way to understand the worldview and perspective of your friends from other faith communities. To give an example, one meeting discussed the understanding of refugees in the different faiths represented. We heard from Christian, Jewish, Baha'i and Muslim participants, who read from their own texts and shared their views with each other. On other occasions, I have used the concept of reading texts together as a way of introducing people to each other, inviting Sikh, Hindu, Christian, Muslim and Jewish participants to each bring an extract from their sacred texts or a poem or a prayer that has significance for them. The focus here is much more personal than the formal one of Scriptural Reasoning; the offerings are correspondingly quite eclectic and as facilitator you have to be careful to ensure that everyone is treated equally regardless of the text they bring with them. This raises the issue of providing appropriate hospitality, as well as being a well-mannered guest when engaging with the texts of other faiths. It is also an opportunity for proclamation, understood in the sense of giving an accurate and clear account of what Christians believe.

A Vaishnav-Anglican dialogue project

One initiative of the St Philip's Centre is a dialogue project coordinated with the Oxford Centre for Hindu Studies. It grew out of a recognition that there was considerable work to be done in building stronger relationships between the Christian and Hindu communities in the UK. In choosing how to approach building this type of relationship, we decided that we had two foundational premises that we wished to follow. First, we had to be clear who was talking to whom. The labels 'Hindu' and 'Christian' are both very broad, encompassing a wide range of theological perspectives. Our aim was a narrower focus, a conversation between Vaishnav Hindus and Anglican Christians. This is not because we object to a wider conversation, but simply because it is helpful to have some parameters for selecting dialogue partners and some limitations of the breadth of theological views likely to be present. Second, we decided to begin talking about theology and see where that took us in terms of developing relationships of trust that would then enable other conversations to take place.

We began by reading and discussing *Hindu and Christian in Vrindaban*, by a Catholic scholar, Klaus Klostermaier. This enabled us to establish some parameters for our discussion. We then had a series of theological discussions, in which two members of the group, one Vaishnav, the other Anglican, presented their thoughts on topics such as the nature of the self and the nature of God. In the third phase of our discussions we moved on to comparing specific texts from the Bhagavad Gita and the New Testament on topics including 'divine descent', 'offering food' and 'life after death'. In what follows I give short summaries of our discussions on the self, on the nature of God, and on texts discussing attitudes to food.

The self in Vaishnav and Anglican perspectives

Our discussion of the self in Vaishnav and Anglican perspectives revealed that while there is much that the two views had in common, there were some notable differences that are worth further consideration. In particular, our understanding of the nature of eternal existence varied greatly. In the Anglican understanding, human beings are created in the image of God. Human beings have greater intrinsic worth because they bear the image of God; while everything created is precious because it is made by God, Christians do not see the 'divine spark' in all creation in the way that Hindus do. Christians understand people as existing eternally once they have been created by God, but there is a beginning to existence. This contrasts with the timeless notion of spiritual existence postulated by

Hindus. Physical continuity also differs. The mainstream Christian view, of the physical resurrection of a body that is in recognizable continuity with the previous pre-mortem body, is not shared with the Hindu notion of reincarnation. Even the experience of *moksha* (liberation) within Hinduism has a different basis, as that liberation includes release from any form of physical existence. The Christian hope for a renewed and restored, perfected creation is very different.

Reflections on the nature of God

The discussion of the nature of God revealed points of contact and of disagreement. From a Hindu perspective, the idea of the Trinity, that of complexity and unity within God, is perfectly comprehensible. Speaking very broadly, Hinduism does not expect there to be a single true or correct understanding of the nature of God, and so the notion of debate and discussion on how God is to be understood is comfortable. There are details of the answers that Christians come to which Hindus would probably not naturally land at, but the fundamental stumbling block that occurs in, for example, Christian-Muslim dialogue is not present.

One notable difference between Christian and Hindu perspectives would be the broad Hindu understanding that God is invested in everything to some degree. That is to say, there is a divine spark present in everything; not just in every human being, or even every living thing, but in everything. This is functionally quite distinct from a Christian understanding of complexity within the Godhead. Those Christians who adopt a panentheistic perspective might well find more that is familiar here, but conventional Christian teaching, of a distinct creator, separate from and in no way dependent on creation, and of creation contingent on but not actually part of God, does not relate to this understanding.

The new food laws of our secular age: reading sacred texts on food and drink

This discussion group focused on the theme of food and drink, using Bhagavad Gita 17.5–10 and Mark 7.17–23. The passage in the Gita focuses on how the three *gunas* (or qualities, namely *sattvic* (goodness), *rajas* (passion) and *tamas* (ignorance)) are related to foods. The text argues that you are driven by the nature that you have. In turn, your nature is affected by the foods you eat, so, for example, foods that drive the *raja* (passionate) nature are described as bitter, pungent and burning. One of the main questions discussed was the extent to which Vaishnav Hindus see the *gunas* as needing to be balanced. While the *sattvic* (goodness) nature is ideal for the spiritual life, it is still important that the three *gunas* are balanced, because too much *sattva* could lead to a smug complacency. Another discussion was around the extent to which *rajas* and *tamas* are to be viewed as negative. A good example was that passion is not a bad thing, but too much of it can lead to a person being driven by their ego, hence the need for balance. Another example given is that antibiotics are regarded as *tamasic*, yet are obviously beneficial to health. When the Christian text was discussed, many topics were brought up, including why some foods were (and still are) prohibited. Was this because, for example, pigs were sacred in the ancient world or because if you prohibit certain foods, then if someone eats them they are reminded of God?

The initial discussion of the texts moved on to exploring the idea of 'new food laws'. The issue of what we do or do not put into our bodies is still very relevant, even in our supposedly secular age. This linked with the concept of body image, as the new food laws of our age are driven by the desire for attaining the perfect body image. In the Gospel of Mark, Jesus is seen to be commenting on the desire for attaining spiritual perfection, challenging ways that missed the mark. The extract from the Bhagavad Gita strongly links physical, mental and emotional well-being to that which goes into one's body; the *gunas* must be balanced in the food one eats, in order to balance one's nature and to strive for a life of spiritual richness. Thus, once the two texts were probed more deeply, it became clear that there were underlying connections, especially in relation to the topic of attitude and approach to both religious activity and everyday life. How we approach something as prosaic as the food we eat is a strong indicator of our spiritual condition. While the Gita and New Testament may analyse the issue differently, they both share that basic premise.

Relationship and understanding

One great advantage of reading sacred texts together is that it gives structure and shape to interfaith meetings. There is a tendency for people only to be interested in meeting those of other faith communities at times of crisis: in the immediate aftermath of a disaster, for example. When things are quiet, other concerns become more pressing. Reading together allows a group to establish a pattern of activity, to build an understanding of what they all believe and to nurture friendships. Not everyone welcomes this approach; it is arguably more an Abrahamic practice, as those faith traditions place more emphasis on reading than the Dharmic faiths. Some may also be concerned that this is just a form of covert evangelism, an opportunity to encourage people to read Christian scriptures in the hope they might convert. Discussing this issue at the outset is important for establishing the identity of the group.

Many would see reading together primarily as an opportunity to display Christian hospitality (Pike and Jardim 2018, 10–13). Depending on the context and make-up of the group, it provides the opportunity to be both guest and host. I have, for example, participated in Scriptural Reasoning as the only Christian in a group of very sympathetic and engaged Muslims. Discussing the parable of the sheep and the goats (Matthew 25.31–46) with this audience made for a very stimulating afternoon. Reading texts together is therefore also an opportunity for proclamation. Careful attention to language is important here; phrases such as 'As a Christian, for me this text says …' can be used to introduce a clear expression of Christian faith, even from an exclusivist standpoint, in a manner that opens up conversation and allows people to be honest in sharing their own views. I have discussed a conservative Christian understanding of John 14.6, for example, with Hindu friends on more than one occasion. If proclamation occurs in the context of relationship, then it is better to be honest than to conceal one's views.

Finally, reading texts together helps Christians see the New Testament in a different light, making the familiar strange and new. Two examples will illustrate. First, Chapter 3 discussed the potential offence that Jewish people might find in the parable of the good Samaritan (Luke 10.25–37). Arguably this response was also that of Jesus' first audience, an insight that was reinforced for me as I discussed the text with Jewish friends. Second, Hindu understandings of John 14.6 as teaching the necessarily exclusivity of a relationship between guru and disciple made me reflect on how I understand my relationship with Jesus and who else that applies to. Reading texts is rewarding and enables growth in both friendships and understanding.

Pause

Who could you engage in reading sacred texts together with?

Social action

In this final area of discussion of interfaith engagement, I will use the example of One Roof, a Leicester-based charity that focuses on issues of homelessness.[22] The current chair of trustees is an Anglican pioneer priest and the director is a Muslim. The project began as a collaboration between an Anglican church, St James the Greater, and the Islamic Society of Britain, running a drop-in meal for the homeless called 'Saturday Stop-By'. The church provided the facilities, while the staff came from both the church and the ISB. They have both worked to raise funds for this particular work, which expanded to become the charity One Roof Leicester. In the winter 2016/17, ORL ran what was reported as the UK's first multifaith winter night shelter.[23] The shelter moved venue each night of the week, visiting Jewish, Christian, Hindu and Muslim premises, and acquired volunteers from those four faith communities, also joined by Sikhs and many others from no faith background. The night shelter ran again in 2017/18, and there are plans for it to continue.

ORL's other main activity is supporting the homeless and vulnerably housed to transition to more secure and stable accommodation. Here also the work cuts across faith boundaries, with Christians joining forces with people from many different faith communities in both funding the work and supporting in other ways where they can. The chair of trustees, a vicar, commented to me that she has far more robust conversations about faith with the Hindu, Muslim, Sikh and Jewish volunteers and staff at the project than she ever has in a church setting. For her this is one of the real benefits of the work. She sees it as a vital component of wider social cohesion, arguing that if we do not work out how we are going to live and work together in the future, we face some serious challenges for generations to come.

Ray Gaston discusses a different form of social action in his examination of Christian responses to the English Defence League. He presents three case studies of work conducted in Bradford, Luton and the borough of Tower Hamlets in London. He points out the importance of long-term relationships in the face of action designed to divide; the need for an inclusive mindset that sees people of other faiths as part of 'our' community; the centrality of women in combating hate, and so the need to ensure that they are included at all levels of decision-making; and the value of infrastructure and groups such as local councils of faiths (2017, 94–112).

These are just a few examples of the way in which Christians can become part of wider social action initiatives. Some will argue that it is important to keep the Christian ethos of any charitable work pure. I recognize this concern, but propose that intentionally cutting oneself off from partners diminishes the scale of what can be achieved. When I was a parish priest in Gloucester, one of the two churches I had responsibility for helped to put on a community fun day every summer. We were a vital part of the day, not least because our building was next door to the park in which it was held and so we provided both the nearest toilets and the wet-weather alternative venue. We did not have the resources, either financial or in personnel, to be able to put on an event of the scale and scope of the fun day. So we worked with a range of partners including the local police, the Muslim-run City Farm, as well as local shops and businesses to ensure that the whole community benefited.

If Christians are to be salt and light in the world, then we have to be identifiable and visible in the wider world. Those churches that have the resources might want to put on a community fun day themselves; I know of a number that do this, and do so very well. But I also know of many more that simply do not have the resources to work by themselves; they have to work in partnership in order to achieve the desired result. One church in Leicester is working with the Muslim-run pre-school that uses their facility during the week to raise money for the Toilet Twinning initiative.[24] By working together, they will raise more funds, and so ultimately a greater number of people will benefit from access to this most basic of necessities.

Social action is an expression of Christian service and an opportunity to practise Christian hospitality, or to be the guest of others. But it is important to recognize that it is also a context in which proclamation can and does take place. This proclamation is primarily relational, as one individual tells another what she believes. We must allow for the possibility that people will become more interested in Christianity as a result of the activities we engage in. My experience of running fun days in the local community, both in Gloucester and in Liverpool, was that invariably people started attending church as a result; this happened even if we were only simply present at a wider community event with the aim just to be of service to the community. If greater interest in Christianity is understood as a by-product rather than a main aim of social action, then this ought to remain uncontroversial.

Pause

What types of social action projects could you engage in? How would they involve people of all faiths and none?

Conclusion

Ultimately, interfaith engagement takes place however you want it to. Andrew Smith points out that as well as evangelism, dialogue and social action, an important area of interfaith engagement that Christians are called to is peacemaking. This is a lifelong discipline for those who want to be called children of God (Matthew 5.9) and can operate at all levels, from peace between neighbours to initiatives to tackle serious issues such as hate crime, or knife crime, and even international conflicts (2018, 79–88).

As this chapter has shown, any Christian can do interfaith work. If you are secure in your own faith, and willing to meet those who think differently from you, then it can be a great opportunity to learn and grow. As you do so, I would invite you to remain alert to the tension between service, proclamation and hospitality, as both guest and host. All are important elements of Christian faith, and no one element can be prioritized at the expense of the others. Each context requires a different emphasis and it is up to Christians, individually and collectively, to discern together exactly how the Holy Spirit is leading them at any given time.

Notes

1 Details of the project, including a link to download the report are at www.tradesexualhealth.com/support/SGIB-Leicester.html

2 See https://churchmissionsociety.org/partnership-missional-church

3 www.agape.org.uk/Ministries/JesusVideoProject

4 www.mahabbanetwork.com/

5 www.mahabbanetwork.com/the-trio

6 http://southasianconcern.org/

7 https://interserve.org.uk/

8 www.ccj.org.uk/about-us/our-vision/

9 It is worth noting that HMD is an initiative of the UK government, established in 2001 and marked annually on or around 27 January. See www.hmd.org.uk/ for more details. The Jewish Community mark the Holocaust on Yom HaShoah, which is held annually on 27th Nisan, the Jewish month that roughly equates to April or May in the UK calendar. See www.yomhashoah.org.uk/ for more on this.

10 www.holocaust.org.uk/

11 www.ccj.org.uk/branches/

12 www.ccj.org.uk/campus-leadership-scheme/

13 www.ccj.org.uk/our-work/rabbi-clergy-action-network/

14 www.ccj.org.uk/safe-car-wash-resource/

15 www.telegraph.co.uk/news/religion/12108953/David-Cameron-pledges-to-stop-Ofsted-inspectors-raiding-Sunday-schools-and-Scouts-meetings.html

16 www.christianmuslimforum.org/index.php/news/576-mosques-churches-twinning-programme-expands-to-new-cities

17 www.dialoguesociety.org/

18 www.christianmuslimforum.org/downloads/Ethical_Guidelines_for_Witness.pdf

19 www.hinduchristianforum.co.uk/aboutus/who-we-are/code-of-conduct/

20 www.scripturalreasoning.org/. See also www.interfaith.cam.ac.uk/sr

21 See www.scripturalreasoning.org/what-is-scriptural-reasoning.html for more on the process.

22 More details about the charity can be found at www.oneroof.org.uk/

23 www.theguardian.com/society/2016/dec/15/multifaith-homeless-shelter-leicester-churches-synagogue-muslim

24 See www.toilettwinning.org/

6

Not just good, but Christian

In Chapter 1, I began my argument that interfaith engagement is not simply a *good* thing to do but that it can and should be a distinctively *Christian* activity, raising the types of questions that interfaith activity brings to the forefront of one's mind. Chapter 2 introduced the classic three-fold typology of pluralist, inclusivist and exclusivist views, and detailed examples of Christians taking each of these positions. Chapter 3 surveyed ten biblical texts, utilizing the three concepts of hospitality, service and proclamation to form an interpretative grid that helped read the passages with interfaith engagement in mind. Chapter 4 continued using these concepts to discuss when and where interfaith engagement takes place, and Chapter 5 looked into how it might happen. In what follows I recap why I argue that interfaith engagement can be distinctly Christian.

My argument is based on the two fundamental commitments articulated by Matthew Kaemingk and referred to earlier: an uncompromising commitment to the exclusive lordship of Jesus Christ, and an uncompromising commitment to love those who reject that lordship (2018, 16). Many might regard these two as fundamentally incompatible, either from a Christian or from a secularist perspective. A committed Christian might argue that commitment to the lordship of Jesus Christ would necessarily mean condemnation of all other faith and belief systems as false religions and therefore condemnation of all followers of those faith and belief systems. My response is that while there is space for distinguishing clearly between Christian faith and other faith and belief systems, that does not have to be articulated in a judgemental, condemnatory or overtly negative way. A committed secularist might suggest a similar argument, believing that any exclusive faith commitment will necessarily result in the rejection of those who do not share that belief. The logical outworking of this argument is that the secularist should then condemn anyone who does not share her worldview. While some hard-line secularists and atheists do indeed take that approach, many more would rather build positive relationships and engage in robust debate that is nevertheless cordial and aims at building bridges of understanding rather than ditches of disagreement.

My central contention is that if we are to be truly obedient to Jesus' command that as his followers we are to love our neighbours as ourselves, and if we understand 'neighbour' to mean 'fellow human being', including our enemies, as Jesus' teaching suggests (Matthew 5.38–48; Luke 10.25–37), then that means we must be uncompromising in our commitment to seek divine blessing for and the flourishing of all faith and belief communities, regardless of whether we share their convictions or not. This is also the most compelling and powerful form of Christian witness possible as it would be a visible demonstration of the Christian belief that enemies are to be loved rather than attacked. As noted in Chapter 1, Lesslie Newbigin has argued at length that the Church, the gathered body of Christ, is the hermeneutic of the gospel, the visible outworking of Christian faith in how we relate to Jesus and to one another. If our engagement with those of other faiths is primarily motivated either by fear or by a desire to conquer and control, then we are demonstrating only a limited, partial gospel, as Jesus came to free us from fear and to liberate us from our desire to be in control.

There are many other benefits of understanding interfaith engagement as a form of Christian discipleship. First, interfaith engagement forces Christians to think through their approach to active outreach; it reminds us that no one is neutral, everyone has a fundamental worldview, a belief system that Christian faith connects with. Second, if we accept that the Holy Spirit is somehow at work in all faith and belief systems, then it teaches us discernment, enabling us to become better at following his lead and understanding how we are being called to join in with his work of revealing Christ to the world. Third, interfaith engagement forces us out of ourselves. It is very easy for Christian churches to become myopic or navel-gazing, focusing only on their immediate sphere of operation, keeping doing what we've always done because that is the only thing to do. Interfaith engagement can challenge our complacency, force us out of our comfort zones, and enable us to recognize our limitations. A fourth, related point is that the way many people of different faiths live out their beliefs can be a rebuke to sometimes half-hearted Christian attempts at discipleship. To give just a few examples, when I witness Muslim commitment to prayer and fasting I feel an awareness that my own practice is lacking in some respects; when I see Sikh service of others through the provision of hot meals I am challenged as to how much Christian hospitality I actually demonstrate; and when I spend time talking with Buddhists and discuss their desire to focus on meditation and control of the ego, I resolve to develop greater self-discipline myself. Leicester Jain Samaj was the first Jain centre built in Western Europe; all the main branches of

Jainism share the same space, and the priests facilitate the rituals and practices of each. Imagine a Christian church in a major city comfortably celebrating High Catholic Masses, low church Reformed Protestant services of the word, Quaker meditation and middle-of-the-road suburban Christianity, and you begin to get a flavour of the diversity. My question is, would such a church ever exist?

Interfaith engagement is important for the flourishing of society. I am thinking primarily of my own context in an English multicultural city, but the principle applies to many other parts of the world as well. Committed Christians are a small minority of the overall population of the UK, and we must learn how to live with this minority status. We cannot expect society to organize itself according to our wishes, as the majority of the population do not share our fundamental beliefs and convictions. This is a situation that all other faith communities are very used to. I have learnt a lot from them that could be applied in a Christian context. There are important lessons for Christians to learn about how we put time and other resources into raising children and young people to remain faithful to Jesus in a society that does not recognize him as Lord. There are lessons in relation to building alliances across faith communities in order to campaign for the freedom to live out our faith. There are lessons in how to open up places of worship to the public, ensuring that we are a valued part of the local community, and there are lessons in how to explain our faith to those who have no understanding of why we might choose to live according to the principles of a religion that was founded thousands of years ago. As part of our Christian love of our neighbours, through acts of hospitality, service and proclamation, Christians can and ought to engage with people in other faith communities to show them that we care about them, are interested in their well-being and want them to flourish and grow. Interfaith engagement can be difficult, hard work, frustrating, but it can also be exciting, challenging, stimulating, great fun, and the food is usually delicious. Any committed disciple of Jesus should make time for it.

Appendix

Engaging with particular
faith communities

As Amos Yong notes: 'The days when one could pontificate about the religious others without knowing anything about them or without having interacted with them at all are over' (2003, 19). If we want to know what we think about people of other faiths, then we must spend time with them. Depending on your particular geographical context, you may find yourself particularly interested in engaging with one specific faith group. In what follows, I introduce a few key books for deepening your understanding and equipping you to engage at a deeper level. I have focused specifically on books whose subject is bilateral relations. There are many good books that introduce the faiths mentioned here, but that is not my concern. My purpose is to indicate a representative handful of guides for those who wish to take their studies of how to relate to a particular faith community a bit further.

If you want to read just one general book, then the aptly titled *Christian Approaches to Other Faiths* is probably the best choice. *Christian Approaches* is a collection edited by Alan Race and Paul Hedges and is divided into three parts. The first discusses theoretical and methodological approaches, beginning with the three-fold typology discussed in Chapter 2 before exploring 'particularities', feminist approaches and interfaith dialogue. The second part introduces Christian responses to other faiths, with discussions of Judaism, Islam, Hinduism, Buddhism, Sikhism, Chinese traditions, indigenous religions, and new religious movements. The third part consists of discussions of Christianity from other faith perspectives, with contributions from Jewish, Muslim, Hindu and Buddhist authors.

In the sections below, I discuss books that focus on the relationship between Christianity and Judaism, Islam, Hinduism, Sikhism, Buddhism, Confucianism and Modern Paganism. The examples are illustrative rather than exhaustive; they are, I believe, among the better books you can read on these topics, but that is, of course, a subjective view. Although individual Christians do engage with the Baha'i, Jains and other small faith communities, I am not aware of any specific books on relationships with them. General overviews are available, but that is not the focus of the appendix, so I have not included them here.

Judaism

Writing about the relationship between Christianity and Judaism is arguably as old as Christianity itself, not least because the first followers of Jesus did not necessarily identify themselves as members of a new religious group. The precise way in which the two faiths became distinct is the subject of much scholarly controversy. If you wish to build good relationships with Jewish people today, then it is important to have an appreciation of this historical debate, as well as an understanding of how the Christian Church, especially in the West, has treated Jewish people over the past 2,000 years. In this short overview it is not possible even to come close to listing all the books that touch on Christian-Jewish relations. I will limit my remarks to four categories of books: first, some places to begin; second, books related to the history of relationships between Christians and Jewish people; third, twentieth-century anti-Semitism, including the Holocaust; and fourth, the conflict in Israel-Palestine.

First, if you wanted to read just one book, then I would recommend *Deep Calls to Deep*, which is the product of four years of conversations between Christians and Jews. A collection of essays edited by Rabbi Tony Bayfield, it covers eight areas: modern Western culture; how Christians and Jews should live in a modern Western democracy; coping with the past; the legacy of our scriptures; religious absolutism; the nature of respect between people of faith; Christian particularity; and Jewish particularism. Each section includes essays from both Christian and Jewish perspectives; these essays were not simply written and then published, but rather were written, discussed by the group and then modified in the light of that discussion. The theological perspectives of those involved tend more to the progressive than the conservative but nevertheless a range of views is present. *Deep Calls to Deep* is a good introduction to issues in contemporary Jewish-Christian relations.

Sacred Dissonance (LeDonne and Behrendt 2017) records the conversation between two friends, one Jewish, the other Christian, which outline some of the main challenges and fault lines for relationships between the two communities, and demonstrates how to have friendly conversation about complex areas of disagreement. *The Christian and the Pharisee* is a series of letters between R. T. Kendall, a reformed evangelical church leader, and David Rosen, former Chief Rabbi of Ireland, who has spent the past 35 years based in Jerusalem but engaged in national and international interfaith work. The frank and honest interaction between the two authors illuminates many key relational and theological issues between the two faiths.

Two books by Jonathan Magonet (2004a, 2004b), now retired from his role as Principal of Leo Baeck College, a London-based seminary for Liberal Judaism, are useful for Christians who are looking for an introduction to Jewish biblical exegesis. One discusses the psalms in particular and the other the Hebrew Bible as a whole.

Finally for this section, the writings of the former Chief Rabbi Lord Jonathan Sacks are a stimulating introduction to an Orthodox Jewish understanding of coexistence and plurality in a complex world. *Not in God's Name* is Sacks' challenge to religiously motivated violence; *The Dignity of Difference* is his appeal for a plural world order that respects religious difference. In addition, Sacks has written extensively for a Jewish audience, and these writings would also be of interest for a Christian wishing to understand how Jewish people read and interpret the Hebrew Bible.

Second, many books discuss the history of relationships between Christians and Jewish people. The question of exactly when, where, why and how the two faiths became distinct has not yet been agreed by academics, and probably never will be. The current consensus is that the separation took place over time, at different rates in different places and with differing degrees of underlying hostility. Authors who discuss these issues from a Christian perspective include James Dunn, Judith Lieu and N. T. Wright (who writes more accessible books as Tom Wright). Jewish academics who have contributed to the debate include Daniel Boyarin, Paula Fredriksen, Amy-Jill Levine and Adele Reinhartz. While some of their books are quite academic, and so more for the specialist than the general reader, I have found reading these Jewish authors particularly stimulating as they have challenged my understanding of New Testament texts and allowed me to understand how a contemporary Jewish audience hears the Christian message.

Reinhartz's specialism is John's Gospel and her observation that on first reading of the Gospel, 'each Johannine usage of the term *Jew* felt like a slap in the face' (2001, 213) reminds Christians that we are often blind to the polemic inherent in the New Testament. Boyarin's understanding of the origins of Christianity and Judaism as distinct faiths is a controversial one. He argues that leaders within the two faiths gradually created border lines via a negative 'heresiological' route. That is to say, by defining and describing in detail exactly what Christianity was not, men such as Justin Martyr set out the borders of Christianity and so gave definition to the faith. Boyarin is clear that this was a two-way process, and that Jewish leaders were engaged in a similar activity from the opposite direction, in essence defining what emerged as rabbinic Judaism as 'not-Christianity'. Boyarin is wary of the dangers of negative self-definition, arguing that if we always define ourselves in relation to what we are not, then that results in a stunted, aggressively defensive understanding of the self.

Moving on from the first few centuries of Christianity, for those with a specialist interest there is a wealth of mainly academic literature that examines the relationship between Christians and Jews down the centuries. It is a history characterized by polemic and violence against Jewish people, a history that Christians often forget or gloss over, but it has shaped European Jewish identity and must therefore be engaged with as part of the process of establishing good relationships between Christians and Jewish people today. Two figures who are particularly challenging from a Christian perspective are John Chrysostom and Martin Luther. Both are recognized as great figures within church history, but both are also responsible for vitriolic and polemical denunciations of Jewish people. Robert Wilken's *John Chrysostom and the Jews* seeks to explain Chrysostom in his own context, arguing that his polemic against Jewish people was motivated by a fear that his contemporaries were deserting church in favour of the synagogue, and that he was writing in a time when Christians in Antioch felt vulnerable to their Jewish and pagan neighbours. Richard Harvey, a Messianic Jew, has written an accessible introduction to Luther's anti-Judaism, and seeks to explain the context and history behind Luther's polemic as well as setting out his vision for how Messianic Jews can act as a bridge for reconciliation between Christians and Jewish people.

Some may want to understand how Jewish people see Christianity. The honest answer is that most do not really think about it at all, and have little interest in the topic (much as most Christians are not that interested in learning the details of other faiths). But there are some accessible guides. Writing from an American Jewish perspective, in *Opening the Covenant* Michael Kogan develops his Jewish theology of Christianity. It can be summarized as a view that the most positive assessment a Jew can make of Christianity is to see it as the vehicle of God's revelation of himself to the gentiles. Judaism is understood as an obligation for Jews; gentiles are only required to keep the seven Noahide laws, the ethical instructions that were given to Noah and his sons after the Flood. Kogan discusses the history of Jewish views of Christianity, as well as describing his own recent forays into dialogue and mutual learning. He is honest in his assessment of Christian failures in relating positively to Jews, but optimistic about the possibility of future relations and mutual understanding, calling on each faith tradition to retain its positive affirmations, but move on from negative assessments of the other towards theological exchange and learning.

This is only a brief snapshot of a vast and complex area. It is unlikely that many Christians will wish to do much in-depth reading, and I am not suggesting that you have to do so before you build relationships with Jewish neighbours and colleagues. Not every Jew is an expert in the history of their people and they are unlikely to hold the full weight of Christian history against you. Some awareness of issues such as the blood libel is helpful, but the relevant chapters in *Deep Calls to Deep* are a sufficient introduction and guide for further reading. An alternative way of getting a sense of the history of Christian anti-Judaism is through works of fiction, which invoke the world without listing precise historical details. The novels of Isaac Bashevis Singer, of which the Nobel prize-winning *The Slave* is the best known, are one such way in.

Third, moving to more recent times, Christians are, of course, aware of the Holocaust, but perhaps not of the role of the Christian Church both in resisting and in ignoring the reality of this atrocity. Holocaust studies is an active academic field, but my focus here is on accessible and easily obtainable books that would be of interest to a general reader. *The Holocaust and the Christian World*, produced by the Beth Shalom Holocaust Memorial Centre and the Yad Vashem International School for Holocaust Studies, documents the history of anti-Semitism, the role of churches during World War Two and also Christian responses after the war ended. The book makes for uncomfortable reading, but in an age when anti-Semitism is increasing, it is arguably important for Christians to subject themselves to this discomfort in order to avoid repeating the mistakes of the past.

Not all Christians were complicit in the Holocaust, of course, and Philip Hallie's *Lest Innocent Blood be Shed* recounts the story of the French village of Le Chambon whose inhabitants organized themselves to save the lives of thousands of Jewish men, women and children. The Dutch Christian Corrie Ten Boom is well known for her book *The Hiding Place*, which recounts the efforts of her family to save Jewish people in Holland, as well as their capture and time in Ravensbrück concentration camp. Writing from a more theological perspective, in *After the Evil* Richard Harries discusses Christian-Jewish relations in the light of the Holocaust, focusing in particular on issues of forgiveness and reconciliation between people of the two faiths. David Gushee wrote *Righteous Gentiles of the Holocaust* as 'an internal Christian exploration of whether any shred of hope survives for the moral reclamation of Christianity (and, secondarily, of humanity) after the Holocaust' (2003, 13). Gushee surveys the history of the Holocaust, noting Christian responsibility both in carrying out the mass killing of Jews and in failing to resist it. He concludes that only a small number of those who identify as Christian will actually have the combination of compassion and moral courage to act to help those in desperate need, and as such Christianity can reclaim some moral authority, but only to a very limited extent.

Fourth, any engagement between Jewish people and Christians will inevitably turn to Israel-Palestine at some point. *Talking of Conflict*, an edited collection compiled by Jane Clements, is a good place to start. The situation on the ground is constantly changing, so any book is always out of date, but the Christian perspectives presented here provide solid grounding from which to engage with the present reality. *Blood Brothers* recounts Elias Chacour's personal experience as a Palestinian Christian, including how he learnt to love those he had regarded as his enemies. It is a moving account of personal transformation in the middle of a protracted and bloody conflict.

Although not every Christian would agree with their views, the work of Palestinian liberation theologians is highly relevant to any discussion of the situation in Israel-Palestine. The Kairos Palestine movement publishes their views online, and some scholars associated with the movement have written extensively from the perspective of Palestinian liberation theology. One of the most powerful expositions of this case is Mitri Raheb's *Faith in the Face of Empire*, which sets out a Palestinian narrative of biblical interpretation. It is a work of provocative political theology, challenging Western theological assumptions as being rooted in colonialist and imperialist history, failing to recognize the reality of the situation facing Palestinian Christians. Raheb takes in the political situation in the Middle East, what it means for Palestinian Christians to live under occupation, how God is the power that challenges empire, and strategies and spirituality required for change, focusing on non-violent and creative forms of resistance, the pursuit of liberty, freedom, equality for women and abundance of life. Raheb has written extensively on this subject; *The Biblical Text in the Context of Occupation* is a series of academic essays that develop Palestinian liberation theology, offering provocation and challenge to how many Western Christians read the Bible, including in conversation with Jewish people.

Islam

As with Judaism, there are probably hundreds of books about Christian engagement with Islam, and I cannot do justice to them all in this brief introduction. I have limited myself to four categories of book and given a few examples within each, selecting those that would be most accessible to the general reader, in terms of both price and content.

First, many books and courses have been written primarily to equip Christians for evangelistic and missionary engagement with Islam. One organization that is very committed to this area of work is the Christian mission organization Interserve, whose director Steve Bell has written two books explaining what he understands evangelism in a Muslim majority context to be like. *Grace for Muslims?* is useful for those who are unsure whether it is even possible to share Jesus with Muslims, while *Gospel for Muslims* demonstrates how to read the Bible with Islam and Muslims in mind. Interserve has also produced a trio of courses for small groups, of which *Friendship First* is the general introduction to a relationship-based approach to evangelistic outreach. *The Unseen Face of Islam* by Bill Musk is slightly dated but still useful, although the focus is more on the Muslim world than on engagement with Muslims in the UK.

Some who have converted to Christianity from a Muslim background have written evangelistic texts. The best known are probably the writings of Nabeel Qureshi, especially *Seeking Allah, Finding Jesus*, which documents his conversion to Christianity, and *Answering Jihad*, which presents an overview of Muslim teaching on the topic and a Christian response. It is important for readers to be aware that Qureshi, who died in 2017, was by background an Ahmadi Muslim. There is much debate within Islam as to whether this group is genuinely Muslim or not. The majority conservative opinion would be that they are not (much as most Christians would say neither the Jehovah's Witnesses nor the Church of Jesus Christ of Latter Day Saints are Christians), and so it is worth being cautious in quoting Qureshi as an example of a Muslim who became a Christian. The author of *How Shall They Hear?*, E. M. Hicham, also a convert to Christianity from an Islamic background, explains his understanding of Islam in an accessible and straightforward way. The book contains lists of questions often asked by Muslims interested in Christianity, together with Hicham's answers.

Second, Christians have written extensively about theological and biblical engagement with Islam. Ida Glaser and Hannah Kay explain that *Thinking Biblically about Islam* offers 'a framework for taking to the Bible the questions raised by Christian interaction with Islam and with

Muslims' (2016, 2). Glaser and Kay define thinking biblically as thinking that produces the fruit of the Spirit, and discuss four main topics. They first set out a biblical framework for viewing the world, based in particular on Genesis 1—11, arguing that fundamentally we have to see Muslims as human beings. Their second area of discussion, the Gospel accounts of the transfiguration, focuses in particular how Jesus relates to the law and the prophets, as monotheism, prophethood and law are all central to Islam. Third, they examine how the Qur'an relates to this understanding of Jesus, Moses and Elijah, and fourth, they consider Jesus' priorities and what they teach about what God requires of Christians. Glaser and Kay explain that they understand Islam to be reversing the process of transfiguration, removing Jesus' death and divine sonship and putting him back on the same level as Moses and Elijah. One key focus of their book is on how Islam and Christianity think very differently about prophets. Who counts as a prophet – do Christians normally consider Adam or Noah to be prophets, for example? What was the precise nature of their ministry? Did prophets sin? What was their exact message? Are prophets all of one type, or do they vary?

Miroslav Volf's book *Allah* asks a practical question that often comes up in dialogue: do Christians and Muslims worship the same God or different Gods? Volf's answer has ten basic theses: it is the same God who is worshipped within both faiths; what the Qur'an denies about the Trinity is also denied by Christians; both faiths understand God as loving and just; both faiths command us to love our neighbours, albeit understanding that command in different ways; their common moral framework means that Christians and Muslims can work together for the good of all; Christians and Muslims can make common cause against a hedonistic culture; allegiance to the one true God matters more than whether you are Christian or Muslim; all have the right to practise their religion in public; all have the right to witness publicly to their faith; and Christians and Muslims should join together in embracing pluralism as a political project.

There is much academic reflection on the relationship between Christianity and Islam. The distinguished scholar Kenneth Cragg has written extensively on this topic. His *The Call of the Minaret* is the classic text. He is not the most accessible of authors but well worth engaging with if you are looking for depth and academic rigour. *Cross and Crescent* by Colin Chapman is a more recent and easily accessible text. It has five parts: guidance as to how to relate to Muslim neighbours; an overview of Islam; advice before entering into discussion and dialogue; an explanation of the fundamental issues that are at stake in engagement; and suggestions for how to share faith. Finally, I have written a response to the Muslim scholar Tariq Ramadan, entitled *What Kind of Friendship?* This offers Christian responses to Ramadan's vision for social engagement; ethics and medical science; culture and the arts; the role of women; ecology and the economy; society, education and power; and ethics and universals.

A third category of books are those that document personal experiences of living and working with Muslims. Carl Medearis writes of his efforts to talk only about Jesus when engaging in Christian-Muslim dialogue and of his experiences in the Middle East and America in his book *Muslims, Christians and Jesus.* Written primarily for an audience based in the USA, it sets out the basics of Islam from a Christian perspective, but every chapter is full of stories of Medearis' personal encounters and friendships with Muslims. His main point is that we should not talk about Christianity but about Jesus; in doing so we disarm presuppositions and the fault lines that divide us, giving us instead the opportunity to build personal relationships across division.

In *Dangerous Love*, Ray Norman recounts his experiences as Director of World Vision's programmes in Mauritania, including an attempt on his life in the months after 9/11 which resulted in his daughter being seriously wounded. He documents his struggle to forgive those who attacked his family and the impact of his Christian witness on those around him. He relates how his wife read scripture in prison with the man who attacked him, and describes times when people asked him to explain his Christian faith to them on the basis of witnessing his desire to forgive the man who had attempted to kill his family. Stories are often more powerful than theological argument, and I found this book one of the most persuasive expositions of the need to love my Muslim neighbours that I have read.

Closer to home, *Fear and Friendship*, edited by Frances Ward and Sarah Coakley, is the product of reflections among a small group of Anglicans on their experiences of engaging with Islam. The chapters range from an overview of Muslim communities in Britain from Phil Lewis to Nuzhat Ali's reflections on Muslim experiences of anti-Muslim prejudice. Most of the chapters are from Anglican clergy discussing their own learning, which includes the importance and power of public friendships between Christians and Muslims for the cohesion of local community; the fragility of Anglican Christianity in many places where Islam is strong, and the delicate balance of relationships of guest and host that results; and how to navigate identity politics in adult relationships where both affirmation and challenge are possible in the context of a continuing friendship.

Between Naivety and Hostility also collates Christian responses to Islam in Britain. Edited by Steve Bell and Colin Chapman, it is divided into three sections. The first tackles the assumptions and starting points that many make in engaging with Islam. It includes short reflections from Steve Bell and Ida Glaser, which summarize the book-length perspectives discussed above. There are discussions on the different approaches to power taken by Muhammad and Jesus, the range of evangelical Christian responses to Islam in Britain today, and those relations in historical context. The second part discusses critical issues, including conversion from Islam to Christianity; human rights; Islamic radicalism; education; the role of women; and shariah courts. The final section offers models of positive relationships including in a church context, in youth work, in dialogue, and polemics and the place for integrity in relationships. Both *Fear and Friendship* and *Between Naivety and Hostility* are slightly dated, but nevertheless indicate the types of responses that are possible.

A more recent volume, *Encountering Islam*, by Richard Sudworth, focuses specifically on Christian-Muslim relations in the public square. This academic study is blended with Sudworth's experiences as a mission partner with Church Mission Society and as parish priest in a majority Muslim area of Birmingham. It charts both the early and evolving historical relationships between Islam and branches of Christianity (both Roman Catholic and Eastern Christian) to inform a discussion of 'What space within the body politic does the Church of England envisage for Islam?' Of course, this also reflects on how, as the established Church within a political economy, the Church of England accommodates or is accommodated by other Christian denominations and other religions and none.

Fourth, looking at books about Muslim responses to Christianity, the works of Ahmed Deedat are often given to Christians by missionary-minded Muslims. These are polemics against Christianity and are confrontational and condemnatory in their approach. Personally, I am happy to accept the gift as a sign of my friend's interest in me, but am not by temperament given to polemical exchanges as I do not find them especially productive or persuasive. Kamel Hussein's *City of Wrong* was originally written in Arabic and translated into English by Kenneth Cragg. A work of fiction, it explores the life of the resurrected Lazarus and what might have happened to Jesus on that final Friday of his life, all from a Muslim perspective. Cragg argues that the main preoccupation of *City of Wrong* is with

the appeal beyond conscience to the collective in human affairs, the wrong of man's slavishness to communal interest and the inability of religion or law to save man from his tragic rebellion against the truth of conscience unless they themselves, that is, religion and law, are properly related to truth in the capacity of servants not masters. (1994, xiv)

A number of authors have examined Muslim and Qur'anic perspectives on Jesus. These include Oddbjørn Leirvik's *Images of Jesus in Islam* and Tarif Khalidi's *The Muslim Jesus*. Looking more broadly, *The Bible and the Qur'an: Biblical Figures in the Islamic Tradition* (Kaltner and Mirza 2018) is a modern collection of key texts on biblical figures within the Qur'an, which discusses 48 figures including Abraham, angels, Eve, Haman, Jews, Jinn, Korah, Lot, Pharaoh, the Queen of Sheba, Saul, and unbelievers. A much older work, *Stories of the Prophets*, originally compiled by Hafiz Ibn Kathir in the eighth century, does a similar job. It is aimed at Muslims but is very accessible to the general Christian reader, although do not be put off by the inclusion of the Arabic text of the Qur'an!

Finally, as with Judaism, you may find reading a novel a helpful way to begin to understand the Muslim community. For example, you could try *Home Fire* by Kamila Shamsie, an engaging and thought-provoking read; *Brick Lane* by Monica Ali is also justly praised.

Hinduism

Far fewer books have been written on engagement between Christians and Hindus. In what follows I introduce three broad categories of book: those that contrast Hinduism and Christianity, primarily from a Christian perspective; those that discuss relations between Christians and Hindus in the West; and those that approach relations from a more evangelistic and mission-minded perspective. My focus here is primarily on books written in and for a Western audience. There are many books written in and for an Indian context, but these can be harder to get hold of and presume a different social and cultural framework from that of most people in the UK.

Before listing any specific books, it is worth noting that the term 'Hinduism' is a very broad categorization, and the perspectives it includes range from those who deny the existence of a divine being through to those whose whole lives are completely committed to a rigid structure of devotion to a particular deity. All faiths are broad and the range of views that are included within their scope can be considerable. This is especially true of Hinduism, which is commonly described by Hindus as a way of life, *sanatana dharma*, the eternal order.

Looking first at books that compare Hinduism and Christianity, two classics still provide a useful starting point: *Avatar and Incarnation* by Geoffrey Parrinder and *Hindu and Christian in Vrindaban* by Klaus Klostermaier. The former is a useful book for Christians wanting to talk to Hindus because of the way in which it problematizes language. In our eagerness to engage in fruitful dialogue we can quickly fall into the trap of referring to very different concepts with the same English word. Taking the example of the title of Parrinder's work, the Christian conception of incarnation in reference to Jesus Christ is completely different from the Hindu notion of avatar. Once we recognize this and begin to unpack the implications of those differences, as well as points of connection, then a meaningful discussion can start. Parrinder's work is divided into three parts. He first outlines a variety of Hindu perspectives on the concept of avatar; second, he looks at concepts of divine descent in other Indian faiths, specifically Buddhism and Indian expressions of Islam; and third, he contrasts these views with those within Christianity.

Klostermaier's work is a sustained theological reflection on the author's experiences in India. It is useful for the way it brings out how the change in location (and with it climate, food, accommodation, sleeping patterns and so forth) had a significant impact on theological reflection and Christian practice. The chapter 'Theology at 120°F' is a must read for anyone who wants to engage in Hindu-Christian dialogue. I have found it a good place to begin conversation with Hindu friends who are interested in a theological exchange of views.

Christine Mangala Frost compares Orthodox Christian and Hindu beliefs in *The Human Icon*. This is a particularly fruitful area of comparison as iconography of Orthodox Christianity does have crossovers with the *murti* (statue, image of the divine) focused worship of many Hindus. A more academic text, it does require a degree of knowledge to engage with fruitfully.

Second, turning to the relationship between Hindus and Christians in the West, the main text to engage with is a recent publication, Andrew Wingate's *The Meeting of Opposites?* He begins with a discussion of Christian-Hindu relations in India. He then discusses three *bhakti* (devotional movements): the Hare Krishnas, south Indian *bhakti* movements and converts to Christianity from a Hindu background. He then turns to the Swaminarayan movement before evaluating Hindu-Christian relations in the UK, USA and Sweden. The final two chapters look at bilateral engagement and discuss theological questions. The examples he gives of bilateral engagement, the Leicester Hindu-Christian forum and the national Hindu-Christian forum, are both no longer active, but the history of the groups, including the topics discussed and the challenges they faced, are instructive for anyone wishing to revive this area of work. The final chapter has arguably the most practical value for Christians in the UK. Wingate examines issues such as the question of God/gods, of idols, the contrast between grace and karma, the uniqueness of Christ, the nature and ways of salvation and the place of scriptural dialogue.

Third, in the area of books that discuss relationships with Hindus from a primarily missionary or evangelistic perspective, Robin Thomson is the most prolific author. *Engaging with Hindus* is divided into two sections. The first introduces Hinduism through short discussions of Hindus, their beliefs, practices and views on Christianity; the second provides guidance for outreach with Hindus, stressing the importance of love, listening, prayer and working for mutual understanding.

Most other resources are aimed at those from a Hindu background who want to live as a Christian disciple. These include the course *Discovering Jesus through Asian Eyes*, and two books: *Walking the Way of the Cross with our Hindu Friends* (Alexander and Thomson 2011) and *Notes for the Journey: Following Jesus, Staying South Asian* (Rasiah and Thomson 2011). In each case the primary concern is to distinguish between the cultural trappings of Western Christianity and the essence of Jesus' message and how that applies to South Asians today.

Rahil Patel's *Found by Love* is the story of conversion from a Hindu background to Christian faith. Patel documents his upbringing in a typical Hindu family, his decision to become a Hindu priest and then his choice to leave that way of life and become a Christian instead. This book is of particular importance for anyone who wants to engage in evangelistic outreach to Hindus, as it brings home the social and emotional cost of conversion.

Finally, a much more academic text is *Ecclesial Identities in a Multi-Faith Context*, Darren Duerksen's PhD thesis; he conducted ethnographic fieldwork among six *Yeshu Satsangs* or 'Jesus truth-gatherings' held among Sikhs and Hindus in north-west India. A technical work at times, the core insights are nevertheless of value to a wider audience. Duerksen's discussion of how Sikhs and Hindus who have chosen to follow Jesus modify spiritual practices to suit their new faith journey provides much food for thought, as does his examination of boundary markers, especially exactly what is meant by 'insider movements' and 'indigenous church'. Probably only of interest to the specialist reader, this is nevertheless an important work for those who want to consider outreach among Hindu communities in some depth.

Sikhism

Not many books focus specifically on the relationship between Christians and Sikhs in a UK context. One volume that rewards careful reading is John Parry's *The Word of God is Not Bound*, which discusses the interaction between Sikhs and Christians both in the UK and in the Punjab. The first two chapters survey the history of early Christian missionary work among Sikh communities in the Punjab in the mid to late nineteenth centuries. Chapter 3 notes a shift in emphasis among Christians in the mid to late twentieth century, away from blunt efforts at conversion to more nuanced and balanced work in establishing relationships of dialogue. But that observation has a caveat in the fact that Christians in the Punjab were often from marginalized and poor communities, and so struggled to bring the appropriate intellectual and material resources to the enterprise of dialogue. Chapter 4 outlines the positive assessment of Sikhi made by a range of Christian authors writing primarily in an Indian context.

Parry's discussion of interaction between Sikhs and Christians in the UK begins by recounting the work of the United Reformed Church to encourage bilateral engagement. Beginning in 1984, the first meetings focused on reading texts from the New Testament and the Guru Granth Sahib in parallel. One fascinating insight that Parry recounts concerns different understandings of grace in the two faiths. Sikhs, he explains, have a 'monkey-hold' doctrine of grace. When a tribe of monkeys comes under attack, a baby monkey will run and hold onto its mother for protection. So, Sikhs argue, it is when human beings first experience difficulties that they run to God. Christians, by contrast, are argued to have a 'cat-hold' doctrine of grace. A mother cat will take the initiative, searching out a kitten, and grabbing it by the scruff of the neck. Christians argue that God searches out the recipients of his grace in a proactive way (2009, 96). Parry also examines Sikh reasons for rejecting the doctrine of the incarnation, while upholding a concept of divine presence among God's people (2009, 101) and the histories of martyrdom in the two faiths (2009, 102).

In the second half of the book Parry examines Christianity from a Sikh perspective. He outlines eight challenges for Christianity. First is the nature of atonement and its relation to vicarious suffering. Second is the nature of humanity, seen more in terms of ignorance to be overcome than sin to be atoned for. The third concerns the precise meaning of incarnation, since Sikhs accept the presence of God among God's people without subscribing to the idea of the divinity of Christ. Fourth, related to this are explorations of what Christians mean by 'the Word' of God. Fifth is how discipleship is practised as a constant search to determine the will of God and live it out; and the sixth concerns living a spiritual life that is still engaged with the harsh reality of the world. Seventh is a discussion of the nature of grace, in particular whether the initiative lies with God or with humanity; and eighth, the nature of witness and identity, concerns how easily should a person of faith be visible in their dress and in their lifestyle (2009, 111–12).

Parry also discusses the reasons why Sikhs are concerned about Christianity; association with Western colonialism and disagreement with evangelical exclusivism are probably the two main points of contention. Theologically, Sikhs struggle with the idea of God being addressed as 'Father', regarding God as much more than this: Mother, Friend, Companion and so forth. Parry quotes Wazir Singh's suggestions of possible starting points for dialogue, which include discussion of God's gifts to humanity, understanding how God is part of the sufferings of his people, the ecstasy of divine love, the love of God as shown in one's love for humanity, and the suffering of Jesus in contrast with the sufferings of the two martyred gurus, Arjan and Tegh Bahadur (2009, 145). Finally, Parry discusses Gopal Singh's book *The Man Who Never Died*, a poem about the life of Jesus Christ written in a *bhakti* (devotional) style.

Gopal Singh's poem is a spiritual and challenging read as he interprets the life of Christ through the lens of his own Sikh faith. Doubtless Christians will find elements to quibble with, but I found much to meditate upon. One interesting extract comes in the retelling of John 4, which has Jesus say to the Samaritan woman, 'Nay, Nay, you've had five husbands – Ego, Wrath, Envy, Infatuation and Greed. But now what you live with – Time – is not your husband. So pray that you are released out of this illicit union, and then you draw water of Timelessness from your own well' (1990, 24–5). Another is the comment Gopal puts on Jesus' lips that 'the food of the inner man is not the boredom of the breadful, but the freedom of the graceful' (1990, 38).

A third book worth reading is *Sikhism and Christianity: A Comparative Study*. In this co-authored volume, Cole and Sambhi engage in a detailed comparison of the similarities and differences between their respective faiths. They note at the outset that both are derived religions, from Judaism and Hinduism respectively. Both have a high regard for history, but a very different relationship with the land in which their faith originated, as Christianity is more diasporic than Sikhi in its present form. Cole and Sambhi discuss ten points of contact between the two faiths. First, the discussion on God notes that both faiths are monotheistic but understand that term differently, as is seen in the names and nature each faith ascribes to the divine. A simple illustration would be the ease with which a Sikh might describe God as Father, Mother, Brother, Kin. Second, Jesus is contrasted with the ten Sikh gurus, noting disagreement on the doctrine of Jesus as the incarnate Son of God who performed miracles. Gurus are seen, by contrast, as wise teachers who have attained enlightenment. Third, spiritual liberation and salvation are conceived very differently. Sikhs have a more positive view of the basic human condition than Christians, but both believe in the importance of divine grace. Where they differ is in how grace is accessed. Fourth, both traditions are scriptural, although with different attitudes towards the scriptures of the tradition from which they came; Christians are more positive about the Jewish sacred texts than Sikhs are about Hindu ones. This is seen particularly in the extensive quotation of the Hebrew scriptures in the New Testament in a way that has no parallel in the Guru Granth Sahib. A second difference is in the status of the sacred text; the Guru Granth Sahib is seen as a living guru, not simply a written text, and is accorded the same care and respect owed to any guru. Fifth, both Sikhi and Christianity engage in gathered, corporate worship. Sikhs gather for *kirtan* and *katha*, that is, singing hymns and hearing sermons based on the Guru Granth Sahib. They follow a pattern that is in essence unchanged from the time of the tenth guru, which stands in marked contrast to the variety and range of Christian expressions of gathered corporate worship. A particular point of contact and discussion concerns the distinction between *karah parshad*, a sweet pudding given out to all present at the end of Sikh worship, and the Christian institution of Holy Communion.

Sixth, personal devotion is common to both faiths. Sikhs may well have a special room in their home where the family copy of the Guru Granth Sahib is kept with appropriate reverence, while it is rare for Christians to designate a room in this way. Followers of either faith might use aids to prayer, such as prayer beads or recorded sermons or singing. Seventh, both faiths have an initiation ceremony and both have ways of celebrating marriage and marking the death of loved ones. Eighth is the issue of authority. This is contested in both traditions. There are those who have authority over significant numbers within the community, such as the Pope for Catholics and archbishops for Protestant denominations. Similarly, the Akal Takht has authority for some but not all Sikhs. At a more local level, there are behavioural and doctrinal definitions of Sikh identity and local authority figures, known as *sant*, who have a reputation as a teacher and spiritual guide. Ninth is ethics. The greatest Sikh virtue, *seva*, normally translated as 'service', is offered to every human being regardless of background. Cole and Sambhi note two particular ethical concerns of the early Sikh community: to stand against *sati*, the practice of wives immolating themselves on their husband's funeral pyre, and female infanticide. They argue that Sikhi has demonstrated a more consistently positive regard for women than Christianity, although they recognize that modern Sikh communities do not have as many women on their management committees or in positions of overall leadership as might be expected. Tenth, Sikhs and Christians have different positions in relation to other religions. Christians have a range of perspectives on other faiths, but Sikhs tend to be more accepting of the authenticity of faith traditions that are not their own.

Gurnam Singh Sanghera's *Interfaith Relations: A Sikh Perspective* presents a typically Sikh view, arguing against exclusivism or inclusivism and in favour of pluralism. It is worth reading as it challenges much of Christian history, starting with the simple observation that 'history stands witness that during the past couple of centuries, Christianity became an associate of Western colonialism in the exploitation of the so-called Third World' (2008, 29). Sanghera is critical not just of Christianity (although he does engage in a lengthy critique of the actions of Western Christians in India), but of any exclusivist understanding of religion, especially that which results in discrimination or violence against those who hold differing views. He argues in favour of pluralism as the only possible solution to harmonious coexistence in our diverse and varied modern society, building on the arguments of John Hick. Sanghera's critique of British Christianity includes questioning why Christians did not stand up in opposition to the racism experienced by Sikhs (2008, 119) and why churches are not prepared to sell their redundant buildings to Sikhs (2008, 126). His exposition of the Sikh scriptures is also thoroughly pluralist in outlook. Christians who want to engage further with Sikhs would benefit from Sanghera's book as a formal exposition of a view that is held by a significant proportion of Sikhs.

Finally, for those wanting to read an account of life as a Sikh in the UK, then Sathnam Sanghera's *The Boy with the Topknot* is an easy and engaging read and Sunjeev Sahota's *The Year of the Runaways* is an engaging novel themed around Sikh migration to the UK.

Buddhism

Probably the most prolific writer on Buddhism from a Christian perspective is Paul Knitter. In his 2009 book Knitter argues that *Without Buddha I Could Not Be a Christian*. This book does pretty much what you would expect, given the title. Knitter wrestles with the question of whether following the teachings of both Jesus and the Buddha is a form of spiritual promiscuity or a valid form of hybrid spirituality, which is often termed 'dual-belonging'. Knitter argues that he remains Christian, and his loyalty to Jesus is primary, but this loyalty has been greatly shaped and influenced by the teachings of the Buddha. Much of the book concerns the questions and difficulties Knitter has with his Christian faith. First, he discusses transcendence and the problem of dualism, whereby God has been so separate, he is unreachably distant from creation, including from humanity. Knitter argues that Buddhism can help address this issue through its focus on experience rather than discussion of whether God exists or not. This points Knitter towards Christian mystics, such as John of the Cross or Julian of Norwich, and an argument for the non-duality, that God and creation are neither two nor one. Second, Knitter discusses anthropomorphism of God, and in particular the disconnect between God as all-powerful Other and the reality of human experience of failure and disappointment, which results in struggles in his relationship with God. Here Knitter draws on Buddhist teaching of relationship between self and all creation, arguing that Buddhist reluctance to speak clearly of God or of evil allows for a non-dual approach, a two-partner dance between spirit and Spirit, divine grace and human freedom. Third, Knitter discusses what he regards as the verbosity of Christian theology in the face of the mystery of God, arguing that Buddhist teaching helped him restore the balance between knowledge and incomprehensibility.

Having discussed his understanding of the nature of God in the first three chapters, Knitter turns to comparison. Chapter 4 discusses nirvana and heaven, and Knitter explains his discomfort with Christian doctrines of eternal suffering in hell and personal immortality in heaven, preferring the Buddhist emphasis on the immediate and the possibility of rebirth shaped by who we are in the present. Chapter 5 contrasts Jesus the Christ and Gautama the Buddha. Knitter explains how he moved from a literalist to a metaphorical understanding of Jesus as born of a virgin, dying for the sins of humanity and raised from the dead. By contrast, he finds in Gautama an attractive figure that he could identify as a saviour as well as a teacher of spiritual truth. This allows Knitter to argue that he understands Jesus as an 'awakened one' and that salvation is primarily about the revelation of God to the world. Chapter 6 focuses on prayer and meditation as spiritual practices. For Knitter, Christian prayer can be too wordy and too shaped by a parent-child relationship; even Christian meditation was unsatisfactory. He understands Buddhist meditation to be a process of moving beyond words or concepts, under the guidance of a teacher, to comprehend reality as it actually is. And this is what he finds spiritually nourishing: a wisdom-seeking silence, a Buddhist-influenced bucket from which to draw on the Christian well. The final main chapter discusses action in the world, where Knitter outlines how Buddhist spirituality has helped him in his efforts to help bring in the kingdom of God, in particular the challenge that one must be (at) peace in order to bring peace.

Knitter develops the theme of dual belonging further in *Jesus and Buddha*, co-authored with Roger Haight. This volume is a record of conversation between the two theologians, with Knitter providing a Buddhist-Christian viewpoint and Haight a Christian perspective. They discuss questions such as the nature of spirituality and interreligious dialogue, the identity and teachings of Buddha and Jesus, the problem and potential of human nature, the interface between peace and justice and the possibility of religious dual belonging.

Turning to a more academic focus, *Buddhist-Christian Dual Belonging* (D'Costa and Thompson 2016) is an essay collection that describes itself as 'a kind of "feasibility study" of whether it makes religious sense' to claim affiliation to both Buddhism and Christianity. It is the product of a symposium that was participated in by Buddhists and Christians both supportive of and negative about the idea of dual belonging, and by individuals who describe themselves as dual belonging. The symposium asked three questions. First, can Christian and Buddhist understandings of the human situation and journey be reconciled without loss? Or should the Buddhist-Christian be regarded as a confused follower of two pathways leading in different directions? Second, is dual belonging possible when one faith is centred on a creator God while the other rejects creation and regards belief in God as irrelevant and inimical? Third, does dual belonging necessarily subordinate one religious framework to another, or possibly to a third, liberal framework, or does it liberate both faiths from their past cultural frameworks? The essays are academic but nevertheless accessible, although some presume a degree of specialist knowledge. They are written from a range of perspectives, from Daniel Strange's rejection of the possibility of dual belonging to Paul Knitter's defence of his own experience of dual belonging. Essays from a Buddhist perspective also cover this range of views.

Buddhism and Christianity in Dialogue (Schmidt-Leukel 2005) is another essay collection that brings the two perspectives into conversation. The book records four series of lectures, on life and death, the ultimate, the mediators, and the quest for peace. In each case a Christian and a Buddhist presented their perspective on the topic under discussion and then wrote a short response to the lecture that set out the other view.

The approach taken is largely dialogical but does presume some academic knowledge; it is a text for deepening rather than starting a conversation between Buddhism and Christianity.

Confucianism

In *Confucius for Christians*, Gregg Elshof reflects on how his engagement with the teachings of Confucius led him to a deeper appreciation of what it means to be a follower of Jesus Christ. He argues that Western Christians are 'Platonic Christians', by which he means that all Western philosophy is, to oversimplify, 'a series of footnotes to Plato' and hence all Western Christianity is, consciously or not, shaped by Platonic categories. By recognizing and exploring the radical alternative of Confucian philosophy we can come to a deeper understanding of what it means to be a disciple of Christ. Elshof argues that Confucian thought is 'a wisdom tradition', and in this book he 'seeks to experiment with reflection on the perennial questions of human interest with the teachings of Jesus and Confucius in mind' (2015, 6). Following an introduction, four main chapters tackle family, learning, ethics and ritual. On family, Elshof argues that Western individualistic Christianity needs to hear the 'Confucian call' to recover the importance of family relationships for self-development as a rounded, complete human being. On learning, he builds on the Confucian love of learning and warns against the twin dangers of 'wild' scholars, who were only interested in the new, and 'fastidious' scholars, who focus solely on the learning of the past, to argue that Christians must be both open to the new and rooted in the past. For ethics, Elshof's main point is that the Confucian teaching of the importance of contextual ethical responses can guard against Christian legalism. His discussion of ritual emphasizes the need for both spontaneity and also training and obedience to ritual. Many of the points Elshof makes can, and have, been made from other perspectives, but his argument is nevertheless a stimulating one that enables Christians to reflect on their own beliefs and practices.

K. K. Yeo takes this experiment further in *Musing with Confucius and Paul*, through a detailed intertextual exposition of Confucius' *Analects* and Paul's letter to the Galatians. Yeo explains his book as an attempt to 'articulate how it is possible to maintain a Chinese identity and a Christian identity *concomitantly* without capitulating to some western or other cultural model of Christian identity' (2008, xxi–xxii). The result is a mix of autobiographical and theological reflection with detailed scholarly analysis and exposition of two very different texts which nevertheless display some surprising connections and points of intersection. Yeo explores the concept of hybridity, of what his traditional Chinese upbringing, including his rigorous study of Confucian thought, brings to his life-transforming experience of encountering Christ. One clear result is the confidence and vocabulary with which to challenge standard Western understandings of Pauline texts. These include Yeo's argument that Paul does not see human flesh as sinful or evil; that Paul argues for freedom, not for individuals alone but for individuals in harmonious and plural-istic community which display the fruit of the Spirit; and for the role of music and the concept of beauty and harmony in Paul's social ethic of unity and self-giving for the sake of others. What is particularly striking in Yeo's work is his self-awareness of the interpretative lenses he brings to his Christian faith. As well as enabling the reader to develop a clearer understanding of a Confucian worldview, Yeo challenges us to be as self-aware in our own explanations of how we understand the Christian life.

Paganism

Paul Cudby is an Anglican priest in Birmingham Diocese who utilized a three-month sabbatical in 2012 to travel throughout the UK increasing his knowledge of and engagement with the Pagan community. He has written up his reflections in *The Shaken Path*. The first two chapters introduce the basics of paganism and discuss why people choose to follow a Pagan path. Christians may find this second chapter particularly uncomfortable reading as Cudby discusses the different reasons Pagan practitioners have given him for their decision to leave Christianity and become Pagans instead. The next five chapters discuss different aspects of Paganism: Wicca and Witchcraft, Druidry, Animism and Panpsychism, Shamanism and Heathenism. The final chapter discusses the Forest Church movement. Each chapter is accessible and gives basic information about the practices and beliefs of those who follow that particular path. The chapter on Wicca and Witchcraft includes a thought-provoking discussion on the practice of cursing, explaining the limited circumstances in which a few Pagans would choose to curse someone. The chapter on Druidry contains an explanation of the three orders of Bards, Obviates and Druids, and how these contrast with roles within Christian ministry. The chapter on Animism and Panpsychism focuses particularly on questions of conscious-ness: what do we mean by 'mind', 'soul', 'spirit' and 'self'? It also asks how Christians can engage with the understanding of panentheism. The chapter on Shamanism begins with a detailed explanation of the variety of

Shamanic rituals and spiritual journeys before bringing out the points of connection and difference with Christian belief and practice. The chapter on Heathenism outlines the core Heathen beliefs, concerning the spiritual realm and the identity of gods and goddesses. In his final chapter, Cudby explains his involvement in Forest Church, a Christian group that meets for worship outdoors rather than in a building. He argues that while some of their rituals and practices may have similarities to those utilized by some Christians, that is where the similarity ends. *The Shaken Path* directs the reader to discover the reality of Paganism as lived out in Britain today, and as such is a useful resource.

Celebrating Planet Earth: A Pagan/Christian Conversation (Cush 2015) is a record of a discussion that took place between groups of Christians and Pagans who met at the Ammerdown Centre near Bath in early 2014. It is organized over three broad themes. In the first, 'addressing our fears and prejudices', two authors offer a Christian and a Pagan perspective on the relationship between the two faith communities. In the second, 'possibilities for cooperation', four chapters explore how Christians and Pagans have managed to work well together. The third section discusses the role of ritual practice, myth, music and poetry in Pagan and in Christian tradition, as well as in interfaith encounter. This book is particularly useful in that it enables Christians to hear authentic Pagan voices that are interested in relationship and dialogue. What particularly strikes the reader are the potential areas for cooperation; while Christians may have different motivations from Pagans, the authors from both perspectives share a concern for the environment and a desire to look after the less fortunate and under-served of society. The range of viewpoints is clear in that some chapters discuss the possibility of 'walking a path' that combines elements of both Paganism and Christianity, while for others (in both traditions) that is not possible. It is also noticeable that while several authors mention leaving Christianity to become Pagan, no reference is made by any author of a journey in the opposite direction, although several authors explain how their encounters with Paganism led to a deepening of their Christian faith and practice. *Celebrating Planet Earth* both helps Christians understand Paganism and is a resource that could be used in entering into conversation with Pagans.

What about the rest?

There are many other faith traditions for which I have not suggested any resources, because I am not aware of any good books aimed at Christians in the West that make engagement with those faith traditions their central theme. In particular, the lack of theological engagement with Sikhi, Jainism and the Baha'i is a gap that deserves to be filled. There are, of course, books written from an Indian cultural context that reference the first two of these, but I have not listed them here because the presuppositions of the authors are generally quite different from those of most Western Christians (the primary audience of this book).

Bibliography

Alexander, E. and Thomson, R. (eds), 2011, *Walking the Way of the Cross with our Hindu Friends*, Grassroots Mission Publications.

Ali, M., 2004, *Brick Lane*, London: Black Swan.

Allen, L. C., 1976, *The Books of Joel, Obadiah, Jonah and Micah*, New International Commentary on the Old Testament, Grand Rapids, MI: Eerdmans.

Amaladoss, M., 2008, *Beyond Dialogue: Pilgrims to the Absolute*, Bangalore: Asian Trading Corporation.

Amaladoss, M., 2017, *Interreligious Encounters: Opportunities and Challenges*, New York: Orbis.

Babb, L. A., 2015, *Understanding Jainism*, Edinburgh: Dunedin.

Baker, D. L., 2009, *Tight Fists or Open Hands? Wealth and Poverty in Old Testament Law*, Grand Rapids, MI: Eerdmans.

Barnes, M., 2002, *Theology and the Dialogue of Religions*, Cambridge: Cambridge University Press.

Barnes, M., 2012, *Interreligious Learning: Dialogue, Spirituality and the Christian Imagination*, Cambridge: Cambridge University Press.

Barnett, P., 2000, *1 Corinthians: Holiness and Hope of a Rescued People*, Focus on the Bible, Fearn: Christian Focus.

Barrick, W. D., 2000, 'Living a new life: Old Testament teaching about conversion', *The Master's Seminary Journal* 11(1): 19–38.

Bayfield, T., 2017, *Deep Calls to Deep: Transforming Conversations between Jews and Christians*, London: SCM Press.

Beaman, L., 2017, *Deep Equality in an Era of Religious Diversity*, Oxford: Oxford University Press.

Beasley-Murray, G. R., 1999, *John*, Word Biblical Commentary Vol. 36, Nashville, TN: Thomas Nelson.

Bell, S., 2006, *Grace for Muslims? The Journey from Fear to Faith*, Milton Keynes: Authentic.

Bell, S., 2012, *Gospel for Muslims: Learning to Read the Bible Through Eastern Eyes*, Milton Keynes: Authentic.

Bell, S. and Chapman, C. (eds), 2011, *Between Naivety and Hostility: Uncovering the Best Christian Responses to Islam in Britain*, Milton Keynes: Authentic.

Bevans, S., 2015, 'Contextual Theology and Prophetic Dialogue', in C. Ross and S. Bevans (eds), *Mission on the Road to Emmaus: Constants, Context and Prophetic Dialogue*, London: SCM Press, 227–37.

Bevans, S. and Schroeder, R., 2005, *Constants in Context: A Theology of Mission for Today*, New York: Orbis.

Bevans, S. and Schroeder, R., 2011, *Prophetic Dialogue: Reflections on Christian Ministry Today*, New York: Orbis.

Boom, C. T., 2004, *The Hiding Place*, London: Hodder and Stoughton.

Boyarin, D., 2004, *Border Lines: The Partition of Judaeo-Christianity*, Philadelphia: University of Pennsylvania Press.

Boyarin, D., 2012, *The Jewish Gospels: The Story of the Jewish Christ*, New York: The New Press.

Briggs, R. S., 2010, *The Virtuous Reader: Old Testament Narrative and Interpretive Virtue*, Grand Rapids, MI: Baker Academic.

Brueggemann, W., 2007, '2 Kings 5: Two Evangelists and a Saved Subject', *Missiology: An International Review* 35(3): 263–72.

Bush, F. W., 1996, *Ruth, Esther*, Word Biblical Commentary Vol. 9, Nashville, TN: Thomas Nelson.

Carson, D. A., 1991, *The Gospel According to John*, Pillar New Testament Commentary, Leicester: Apollos.

Casey, L., 2016, *The Casey Review: A Review into Opportunity and Integration*, London: Department for Communities and Local Government. Available to download at https://assets.publishing.service.gov.uk/government/uploads/system/uploads/attachment_data/file/575973/The_Casey_Review_Report.pdf

Chacour, E., 2013, *Blood Brothers: The Dramatic Story of a Palestinian Christian Working for Peace in Israel*, 3rd edn, Grand Rapids, MI: Baker Books.

Chalmer, A., 2012, *Exploring the Religion of Ancient Israel: Prophet, Priest, Sage and People*, London: SPCK.

Chapman, C., 2003, *Cross and Crescent: Responding to the Challenge of Islam*, Downers Grove, IL: InterVarsity Press.

Charlesworth, J. H., 2001, 'The Gospel of John: Exclusivism caused by a social setting different from that of Jesus (John 11:54 and 14:6)', in R. Bieringer, D. Pollefeyt and F. Vandecasteele-Vanneuville (eds), *Anti-Judaism and the Fourth Gospel*, Louisville, KY: WJK Press, 247–78.

Chester, T. and Timmis, S., 2011, *The World We All Want*, Epsom: Good Book Company.

Clements, J. (ed.), 2012, *Talking of Conflict: Christian Reflections in the Context of Israel and Palestine*, Kibworth: Matador.

CMF, 2017a, *Religious Supplementary Schools*, London: Christian Muslim Forum.

CMF, 2017b, *Casey Review: Integration and Opportunity*, London: Christian Muslim Forum.

Cohn, R. L., 1983, 'Form and Perspective in 2 Kings V', *Vetus Testamentum* 33(2): 171–84.

Cole, O. W. and Sambhi, P. S., 1993, *Sikhism and Christianity: A Comparative Study*, London: Macmillan Press.

Cooling, T. and Cooling, M., 2013, *Distinctively Christian Learning?* Cambridge: Grove Books.

Cox, B., 2017, *Jo Cox: More in Common*, London: Two Roads.

Cox, J., 2011, *More than Caring and Sharing: Making a Church School Distinctive*, Stowmarket: Kevin Mayhew.

Cracknell, K., 2005, *In Good and Generous Faith: Christian Responses to Religious Pluralism*, London: Epworth Press.

Cragg, K., 1985, *The Call of the Minaret*, New York: Orbis.

Cragg, K., 1999, *Jesus and the Muslim: An Exploration*, 2nd edn, Oxford: Oneworld.

Cudby, P., 2017, *The Shaken Path: A Christian Priest's Exploration of Modern Pagan Belief and Practice*, Winchester: Christian Alternative.

Cush, D. (ed.), 2015, *Celebrating Planet Earth: A Pagan/Christian Conversation*, Winchester: Moon Books.

D'Costa, G., Knitter, P. and Strange, D., 2011, *Only One Way?* London: SCM Press.

D'Costa, G. and Thompson, R. (eds), 2016, *Buddhist-Christian Dual Belonging: Affirmations, Objections, Explorations*, Farnham: Ashgate.

Davie, G., 2007, 'Vicarious Religion: A Methodological Challenge', in N. T. Ammerman (ed.), *Everyday Religion: Observing Religious Lives*, Oxford: Oxford University Press, 21–35.

Davis, D. R., 2003, *The Wisdom and the Folly: An Exposition of the Book of First Kings*, Fearn: Christian Focus.

Deedat, A., 1993, *The Choice: Islam and Christianity*, Verulam: IPC.

Droge, A. J., 2013, *The Qur'an: A New Annotated Translation*, Sheffield: Equinox.

Duerksen, D. T., 2015, *Ecclesial Identities in a Multi-Faith Context: Jesus Truth-Gatherings (Yeshu Satsangs) among Hindus and Sikhs in Northwest India*, Cambridge: Lutterworth Press.

Dundas, P., 2002, *The Jains*, 2nd edn, London: Routledge.

Dunn, J. D. G., 2006, *The Partings of the Ways: Between Christianity and Judaism and their Significance for the Character of Christianity*, 2nd edn, London: SCM Press.

Dunn, J. D. G., 2016, *Neither Jew nor Greek: A Contested Identity*, Christianity in the Making Volume 3, Grand Rapids, MI: Eerdmans.

Effa, A. L., 2007, 'Prophets, Kings, Servants, and Lepers: A Missiological Reading of an Ancient Drama', *Missiology: An International Review* 35(3): 305–13.

Elshof, G., 2015, *Confucius for Christians*, Grand Rapids, MI: Eerdmans.

Fee, G., 1987, *The First Epistle to the Corinthians*, New International Commentary on the New Testament, Grand Rapids, MI: Eerdmans.

Fernando, A., 1998, *Acts: The NIV Application Commentary*, Grand Rapids, MI: Zondervan.

France, R. T., 2007, *The Gospel of Matthew*, New International Commentary on the New Testament, Grand Rapids, MI: Eerdmans.

Frazier, J., 2011, *Bridges and Barriers to Hindu-Christian Relations*, Oxford: Oxford Centre for Hindu Studies.

Fredriksen, P. and Reinhartz, A. (eds), 2002, *Jesus, Judaism and Christian Anti-Judaism: Reading the New Testament after the Holocaust*, Louisville, KY: WJK Press.

Frost, C. M., 2017, *The Human Icon: A Comparative Study of Hindu and Orthodox Christian Beliefs*, Cambridge: James Clarke.

Gaston, R., 2017, *Faith, Hope and Love: Interfaith Engagement as Practical Theology*, London: SCM Press.

Glaser, I. and Kay, H., 2016, *Thinking Biblically about Islam: Genesis, Transfiguration, Transformation*, Carlisle: Langham Publishing.

Green, J., 1997, *The Gospel of Luke*, New International Commentary on the New Testament, Grand Rapids, MI: Eerdmans.

Greenlee, D., 2013, *Longing for Community: Church*, Ummah, *or Somewhere in Between?* Pasadena, CA: William Carey Library.

Gushee, D., 2003, *The Righteous Gentiles of the Holocaust: A Christian Interpretation*, 2nd edn, St Paul, MN: Paragon House.

Hallie, P., 1994, *Lest Innocent Blood be Shed: The Story of the Village of Le Chambon and How Goodness Happened There*, New York: HarperCollins.

Harries, R., 2003, *After the Evil: Christianity and Judaism in the Shadow of the Holocaust*, Oxford: Oxford University Press.

Harvey, R., 2017, *Luther and the Jews: Putting Right the Lies*, Eugene, OR: Cascade Books.

Hicham, E. M., 2009, *How Shall They Hear? Sharing your Christian Faith with Muslims*, Belfast: Ambassador.

Hick, J., 1977, 'Jesus and the World Religions', in J. Hick (ed.), *The Myth of God Incarnate*, London: SCM Press, 167–85.

Hick, J., 1980, *God has Many Names*, London: Macmillan.

Hick, J., 2004, *The Fifth Dimension: An Exploration of the Spiritual Realm*, Oxford: Oneworld.

Hick, J., 2010, *Between Faith and Doubt: Dialogues on Religion and Reason*, Basingstoke: Palgrave Macmillan.

HM Government, 2018, *Out-of-school Education Settings: Report on the Call for Evidence November 2015 to January 2016*, London. Available to download at https://assets.publishing.service.gov.uk/government/uploads/system/uploads/attachment_data/file/698250/Out-of-school_education_settings-Report_on_the_call_for-evidence.pdf

Hughes, D., 2016, *The World on Our Doorstep: Evangelical Mission and Other Faiths*, London: Evangelical Alliance.

Hussein, K., 1994, *City of Wrong: A Friday in Jerusalem*, Oxford: Oneworld.

Kaemingk, M., 2018, *Christian Hospitality and Muslim Immigration in an Age of Fear*, Grand Rapids, MI: Eerdmans.

Kaltner, J. and Mirza, Y., 2018, *The Bible and the Qur'an: Biblical Figures in the Islamic Tradition*, London: Continuum.

Keener, C. S., 1999, *A Commentary on the Gospel of Matthew*, Grand Rapids, MI: Eerdmans.

Keener, C. S., 2003a, *The Gospel of John: A Commentary, Vol. 1*, Peabody, MA: Hendrickson.

Keener, C. S., 2003b, *The Gospel of John: A Commentary, Vol. 2*, Peabody, MA: Hendrickson.

Kendall, R. T. and Rosen, D., 2006, *The Christian and the Pharisee: Two Outspoken Religious Leaders Debate the Road to Heaven*, London: Hodder and Stoughton.

Khalidi, T., 2001, *The Muslim Jesus: Sayings and Stories in Islamic Literature*, Cambridge, MA: Harvard University Press.

Klink, E. W., 2007, *The Sheep of the Fold: The Audience and Origin of the Gospel of John*, Society for New Testament Studies Monograph Series 141, Cambridge: Cambridge University Press.

Klostermaier, K., 1969, *Hindu and Christian in Vrindaban*, London: SCM Press.

Knitter, P., 2009, *Without Buddha I Could Not Be a Christian*, Oxford: Oneworld.

Knitter, P. and Haight, R., 2015, *Jesus and Buddha: Friends in Conversation*, New York: Orbis.

Kogan, M., 2012, *Opening the Covenant: A Jewish Theology of Christianity*, Oxford: Oxford University Press.

Kruse, C., 2012, *Paul's Letter to the Romans*, Pillar New Testament Commentary, Nottingham: Apollos.

LeDonne, A. and Behrendt, L., 2017, *Sacred Dissonance: The Blessing of Difference in Jewish-Christian Dialogue*, Peabody, MA: Hendrickson.

Leirvik, O., 2010, *Images of Jesus Christ in Islam*, London: Continuum.

Levine, A.-J., 2006, *The Misunderstood Jew: The Church and the Scandal of the Jewish Jesus*, New York: HarperOne.

Lieu, J., 2015, *Neither Jew nor Greek?* London: Continuum.

Ling, T. J. M., 2006, *The Judaean Poor and the Fourth Gospel*, Society for New Testament Studies Monograph Series 136, Cambridge: Cambridge University Press.

Magonet, J., 2004a, *A Rabbi Reads the Bible*, 2nd edn, London: SCM Press.

Magonet, J., 2004b, *A Rabbi Reads the Psalms*, 2nd edn, London: SCM Press.

Marshall, I. H., 1978, *The Gospel of Luke: A Commentary on the Greek Text*, New International Greek Testament Commentary, Grand Rapids, MI: Eerdmans.

Martin, D., 1995, *The Corinthian Body*, New Haven, CT: Yale University Press.

McLaughlin, R. P., 2013, 'Jonah and the Religious Other: An exploration of biblical inclusivism', *Journal of Ecumenical Studies* 48(1): 71–84.

Medearis, C., 2008, *Muslims, Christians and Jesus: Gaining Understanding and Building Relationships*, Minneapolis, MN: Bethany Books.

Michaels, J. R., 2010, *The Gospel of John*, New International Commentary on the New Testament, Grand Rapids, MI: Eerdmans.

Mogra, I., 2018, 'Religious Education at Crossroads in the United Kingdom: Muslim Responses to Registration, Regulation and Inspection', *Journal of Muslim Minority Affairs* 38(2): 198–217.

Moo, D., 1996, *The Epistle to the Romans*, New International Commentary on the New Testament, Grand Rapids, MI: Eerdmans.

Musk, B., 1989, *The Unseen Face of Islam*, Crowborough: Monarch.

Netland, H., 1991, *Dissonant Voices: Religious Pluralism and the Question of Truth*, Vancouver: Regent College.

Netland, H., 2015, *Christianity and Religious Diversity: Clarifying Christian Commitments in a Globalizing Age*, Grand Rapids, MI: Baker Academic.

Newbigin, L., 1986, *Foolishness to the Greeks: The Gospel and Western Culture*, London: SPCK.

Newbigin, L., 1989, *The Gospel in a Pluralist Society*, London: SPCK.

Newbigin, L., 1991, *Truth to Tell: The Gospel as Public Truth*, London: SPCK.

Newbigin, L., 1995a, *Proper Confidence: Faith, Doubt and Certainty in Christian Discipleship*, Grand Rapids, MI: Eerdmans.

Newbigin, L., 1995b, *The Open Secret: An Introduction to the Theology of Mission*, 2nd edn, Grand Rapids, MI: Eerdmans.

Ngan, L. L. E., 1997, '2 Kings 5', *Review and Expositor* 94: 589–97.

Nolland, J., 2005, *The Gospel of Matthew: A Commentary on the Greek Text*, The New International Greek Testament Commentary, Grand Rapids, MI: Eerdmans.

Norman, R., 2015, *Dangerous Love: A True Story of Tragedy, Faith and Forgiveness in the Muslim World*, Nashville, TN: Nelson Books.

Nwaoru, E. O., 2008, 'The Story of Naaman (2 Kings 5:1–19): Implications for Mission Today', *Swedish Missiological Themes* 96(1): 27–41.

Okoye, J. C., 2010, 'The God of Love in the Old Testament: Jonah', *New Theology Review* 23(3): 62–8.

Panikkar, R., 1964, *The Unknown Christ of Hinduism*, London: Darton, Longman and Todd.

Parrinder, G., 1997, *Avatar and Incarnation: The Divine in Human Form in the World's Religions*, 2nd edn, Oxford: Oneworld.

Parry, J., 2009, *The Word of God is Not Bound*, Bangalore: Centre for Contemporary Christianity.

Patel, R., 2016, *Found by Love: A Hindu Priest Encounters Jesus Christ*, Watford: Instant Apostle.

Paul, R., 2009, *Jesus in the Lotus: The Mystical Doorway between Christianity and Yogic Spirituality*, Novato: New World Library.

Pike, J. and Jardim, G., 2018, *Storying Christian and Muslim Faith Together: Building Relationships Through the Stories of the Bible and Qur'an*, Grove Mission and Evangelism MEv121, Cambridge: Grove Books.

Pineda, A. M., 2010, *Practicing our Faith: A Way of Life for a Searching People*, 2nd edn, San Francisco, CA: Jossey-Bass.

Qureshi, N., 2014, *Seeking Allah, Finding Jesus*, Grand Rapids, MI: Zondervan.

Qureshi, N., 2016, *Answering Jihad: A Better Way Forward*, Grand Rapids, MI: Zondervan.

Race, A., 1983, *Christians and Religious Pluralism: Patterns in the Christian Theology of Religions*, London: SCM Press.

Race, A. and Hedges, P. (eds), 2008, *Christian Approaches to Other Faiths*, London: SCM Press.

Raheb, M. (ed.), 2012, *The Biblical Text in the Context of Occupation: Towards a New Hermeneutics of Liberation*, CreateSpace Independent Publishing.

Raheb, M., 2014, *Faith in the Face of Empire: The Bible Through Palestinian Eyes*, New York: Orbis.

Rahner, K., 1966, *Theological Investigations 5*, London: Darton, Longman and Todd.

Rasiah, C. and Thomson, R. (eds), 2011, *Notes for the Journey: Following Jesus, Staying South Asian*, Sutton: South Asian Concern.

Reinhartz, A., 2001, '"Jews" and Jews in the Fourth Gospel', in R. Bieringer, D. Pollefeyt and F. Vandecasteele-Vanneuville (eds), *Anti-Judaism and the Fourth Gospel*, Louisville, KY: WJK Press, 213–27.

Rittner, C., Smith, S. D. and Steinfeldt, I., 2000, *The Holocaust and the Christian World*, London: Kuperard.

Robinson, B., 2012, *Jesus and the Religions: Retrieving a Neglected Example for a Multi-cultural world*, Eugene, OR: Wipf and Stock.

Sacks, J., 2003, *The Dignity of Difference: How to Avoid the Clash of Civilizations*, 2nd edn, London: Continuum.

Sacks, J., 2015, *Not in God's Name: Confronting Religious Violence*, London: Hodder and Stoughton.

Sahota, S., 2016, *The Year of the Runaways*, London: Picador.

Sanghera, G. S., 2008, *Interfaith Relations: A Sikh Perspective*, Amritsar: Singh Brothers.

Sanghera, S., 2009, *The Boy with the Topknot: A Memoir of Love, Secrets and Lies in Wolverhampton*, London: Penguin.

Schmidt-Leukel, P. (ed.), 2005, *Buddhism and Christianity in Dialogue: The Gerald Weisfeld Lectures 2004*, London: SCM Press.

Schmidt-Leukel, P., 2017, *Religious Pluralism and Interreligious Theology*, New York: Orbis.

Shamsie, K., 2017, *Home Fire*, London: Bloomsbury.

Singer, I. B., 1996, *The Slave*, London: Penguin.

Singh, G., 1990, *The Man Who Never Died*, Honesdale: Himalayan International Institute of Yoga Science and Philosophy of the USA.

Simply Eat: Everyday Stories of Friendship, Food and Faith, Watford: Instant Apostle.

Smith, A., 2018, *Vibrant Christianity in Multifaith Britain*, Oxford: BRF.

Smith, J. K. A., 2017, *Awaiting the King: Reforming Public Theology*, Grand Rapids, MI: Baker Academic.

Strange, D., 2014, *'For Their Rock is Not as Our Rock': An Evangelical Theology of Religions*, Nottingham: Apollos.

Strhan, A., 2015, *Aliens and Strangers? The Struggle for Coherence in the Everyday Lives of Evangelicals*, Oxford: Oxford University Press.

Stuart, D., 1987, *Hosea-Jonah*, Word Biblical Commentary Vol. 31, Nashville, TN: Thomas Nelson.

Sudworth, R., 2007, *Distinctly Welcoming: Christian Presence in a Multifaith Society*, Bletchley: Scripture Union.

Sudworth, R., 2017, *Encountering Islam: Christian-Muslim Relations in the Public Square*, London: SCM Press.

Swamy, M., 2016, *The Problem with Interreligious Dialogue: Plurality, Conflict and Elitism in Hindu-Christian-Muslim Relations*, London: Bloomsbury.

Thiessen, E., 2011, *The Ethics of Evangelism: A Philosophical Defence of Ethical Proselytizing and Persuasion*, Milton Keynes: Paternoster.

Thiselton, A., 2000, *The First Epistle to the Corinthians: A Commentary on the Greek Text*, New International Greek Testament Commentary, Grand Rapids, MI: Eerdmans.

Thomson, R., 2014, *Engaging with Hindus: Understanding their World, Sharing the Good News*, Epsom: The Good Book Company.

Volf, M., 2011, *Allah: A Christian Response*, New York: HarperOne.

Walton, J. H., 2001, *The NIV Application Commentary: Genesis*, Grand Rapids, MI: Zondervan.

Ward, F. and Coakley, S. (eds), 2012, *Fear and Friendship: Anglicans Engaging with Islam*, London: Continuum.

Wenham, G., 1987, *Genesis*, Word Biblical Commentary Vol. 1, Waco, TX: Word.

Wilken, R. L., 2004, *John Chrysostom and the Jews: Rhetoric and Reality in the Late 4th Century*, Eugene, OR: Wipf and Stock.

Wilson, T., 2013, *All United Together: Christian Ministry in Multicultural Schools*, Gloucester: Wide Margin.

Wilson, T., 2014, *A Theology of Hospitality for Anglican Schools*, Grove Education eD20, Cambridge: Grove.

Wilson, T., 2015a, *What Kind of Friendship? Christian Responses to Tariq Ramadan's Call for Reform within Islam*, Eugene, OR: Wipf and Stock.

Wilson, T., 2015b, *Hospitality and Translation: An Exploration of How Muslim Pupils Translate their Faith in the Context of an Anglican Primary School*, Newcastle-upon-Tyne: Cambridge Scholars Publishing.

Wilson, T. and Ravat, R., 2017, *Learning to Live Well Together: Case Studies in Interfaith Diversity*, London: Jessica Kingsley.

Wingate, A., 2005, *Celebrating Difference, Staying Faithful: How to Live in a Multi-Faith World*, London: Darton, Longman and Todd.

Wingate, A., 2014, *The Meeting of Opposites? Hindus and Christians in the West*, London: SPCK.

Witherington, B., 1995, *Conflict and Community in Corinth: A Socio-Rhetorical Commentary on 1 and 2 Corinthians*, Grand Rapids, MI: Eerdmans.

Witherington, B., 1998, *The Acts of the Apostles: A Socio-Rhetorical Commentary*, Grand Rapids, MI: Eerdmans.

Wright, N. T., 2013, *Paul and the Faithfulness of God*, Parts III and IV, London: SPCK.

Yeo, K. K., 2008, *Musing with Confucius and Paul: Toward a Chinese Christian Theology*, Eugene, OR: Cascade.

Yong, A., 2003, *Beyond the Impasse: Toward a Pneumatological Theology of Religions*, Eugene, OR: Wipf and Stock.

Yong, A., 2008, *Hospitality and the Other: Pentecost, Christian Practices, and the Neighbor*, New York: Orbis.

Yong, A., 2014, *The Missiological Spirit: Christian Mission Theology in the Third Millennium Global Context*, Cambridge: James Clarke.

Yong, A., 2015, 'Christological Constants in Shifting Contexts: Jesus Christ, Prophetic Dialogue and the *Missio Spiritus* in a Pluralistic World', in C. Ross and S. Bevans (eds), *Mission on the Road to Emmaus: Constants, Context and Prophetic Dialogue*, London: SCM Press, 19–33.

Index

Abraham 55–9, 105, 131
Amaladoss, M. 29–31

Baha'i 15, 17, 105, 132
Barnes, M. 37–9
Bevans, S. 39–41
Buddhism 28, 35, 48, 79, 95,
  160–3
Buddhist 12, 13, 14, 17, 35, 48,
  96, 105, 108, 132, 142

Council of Christians and Jews
  122–5
Centurion's Servant 71–3
Christmas 6–7, 86, 92, 117
Christian-Muslim Forum 125–9
Confucianism 36, 163–4
Conversion 11, 47, 50, 68, 90–3,
  120–1, 128, 150, 156,157
Cracknell, K. 31–3, 78–80

D'Costa, G. 24–5

Elijah 62–7, 151
Elisha 67–9
Enemies 12, 14, 44, 71, 73–4, 142
Eucharist 30, 39, 92–3, 95, 118

Fear of interfaith relations 3–5,
  13, 15, 57, 100, 142
Festivals of other faith
  communities 87–8, 95, 104–6

Friendship 14, 32, 50, 61, 93, 97,
  98, 105, 107–9, 115–18, 119,
  135–6

Good Samaritan 73–5, 129
Growth 15–17

Hindu-Christian Forum 129–30
Hick, J. 29, 33–4, 48–9, 160
Hindu 7–8, 11, 16, 27, 46, 51,
  78–9, 87–8, 99, 105, 108, 115,
  121, 137
Hinduism 28, 35, 80, 92, 133–5,
  154–6
Holy Book Club 131
Home 107–9
Hospitality 1–2, 9, 13, 30, 39,
  42, 43–4, 47, 58–9, 59–61, 64,
  67–9, 72, 73, 76–7, 86, 90, 91,
  93, 94, 97, 98–9, 104, 105, 107,
  109, 117, 121, 131, 138
Hughes, D. 45–7

Islam 14, 16, 27, 35, 87, 89, 92,
  102, 108, 131, 150–4

Jew, Jewish 3, 10–11, 16, 28, 35,
  80, 82–4, 87, 94, 95, 104, 108,
  118, 132
John 14.6 77–81
Jonah 69–70
Judaism 74, 80, 87, 104, 107–8,
  145–9

Kaemingk, M. 13–14, 26, 28, 53, 103, 141
Knitter, P. 25, 160–2

Muslim 6–7, 12–14, 16, 26, 27, 47, 51, 68, 72, 76, 79, 87, 99–100, 102, 104–5, 106, 110–11, 120–21, 130–1, 132, 142

Neighbour 2, 3, 12, 14, 21, 40, 42, 49–50, 57, 73–5, 102, 106, 115–17, 129, 142–3
Netland, H. 47–9
Newbigin, L. 17–22, 53, 142

Pagan, Paganism 13, 14, 17, 27, 105, 164–5
Paul, Apostle 20, 21, 81–5, 109
Presence and Engagement 90–3
Proclamation 1, 2, 39–41, 47, 49, 52, 63, 67, 69, 72, 74, 76, 80, 81, 84, 87, 90, 92–3, 94, 97, 98, 100, 105, 117, 121, 136, 138, 143
Prophets' Stories 131
Public Square 110–13

Religious Supplementary Schools 126

Ruth 59–61

Schmidt-Leukel, P. 34–6, 162
Schools 42, 88, 98–101
Schroeder, R. 39–41
Scriptural Reasoning 131
Service 1, 2, 56, 59, 61, 67, 72, 73–4, 84, 85, 90, 91, 96, 99, 103, 109, 117, 121, 138, 141, 142, 143
Sikh 1, 2, 9, 12, 17, 30, 35, 50, 87–8, 92, 93–4, 99, 105, 108, 121, 132, 142
Sikhism 80, 92, 157–60
Smith, A. 14, 49–51, 107, 139
Social Action 40, 42, 90, 96–98, 124, 137–8
Strange, D. 25, 27, 51–2, 54
Sudworth, R. 41–3, 85, 110, 153

Vaishnav-Anglican Dialogue 133–5
Vigils 90, 94, 106, 110–13

Woman at the Well 75–7

Yong, A. 26, 43–5, 54, 144